Inclusion Practices with Special Needs Students: Theory, Research, and Application

Steven I. Pfeiffer
Linda A. Reddy
Editors

Inclusion Practices with Special Needs Students: Theory, Research, and Application has been co-published simultaneously as *Special Services in the Schools,* Volume 15, Numbers 1/2 1999.

The Haworth Press, Inc.
New York • London • Oxford

Inclusion Practices with Special Needs Students: Theory, Research, and Application has been co-published simultaneously as *Special Services in the Schools* ™ ,Volume 15, Numbers 1/2 1999.

The Haworth Press, Inc., 10 Alice Street, Binghamton, NY 13904-1580 USA

Cover design by Thomas J. Mayshock Jr.

Library of Congress Cataloging-in-Publication Data

Inclusion practices with special needs students: theory, research, and application / Steven I. Pfeiffer, Linda A. Reddy, editors.
     p. cm.
    "Co-published simultaneously as Special services in the schools, volume 15, numbers 1/2 1999."
    Includes bibliographical references and index.
    ISBN 0-7890-0843-2 (alk. paper) -- ISBN 0-7890-0954-4 (alk. paper)
    1. Inclusive education--United States. 2. Mainstreaming in education--United States. I. Pfeiffer, Steven I. II. Reddy, Linda A.

LC 1201 .I538 2000
371.9'046--dc21

99-058741

428 6236

INDEXING & ABSTRACTING

Contributions to this publication are selectively indexed or abstracted in print, electronic, online, or CD-ROM version(s) of the reference tools and information services listed below. This list is current as of the copyright date of this publication. See the end of this section for additional notes.

- *AURSI African Urban & Regional Science Index*

- *BUBL Information Service: An Internet-based Information Service for the UK higher education community <URL: http://bubl.ac.uk>*

- *Cabell's Directory of Publishing Opportunities in Education (comprehensive & descriptive bibliographic listing with editorial criteria and publication production data for selected education and education-related journals)*

- *Child Development Abstracts & Bibliography*

- *CNPIEC Reference Guide: Chinese National Directory of Foreign Periodicals*

- *Contents Pages in Education*

- *Education Digest*

- *Educational Administration Abstracts (EAA)*

- *ERIC Clearinghouse on Counseling and Student Services (ERIC/CASS)*

- *ERIC Clearinghouse on Rural Education & Small Schools*

- *Exceptional Child Education Resources (ECER), (CD/ROM from SilverPlatter and hard copy)*

- *Family Studies Database (online and CD/ROM)*

- *International Bulletin of Bibliography on Education*

- *Linguistics and Language Behavior Abstracts (LLBA)*

- *Mental Health Abstracts (online through DIALOG)*

- *National Clearinghouse for Bilingual Education*

(continued)

- *OT BibSys*
- *Social Services Abstracts*
- *Social Work Abstracts*
- *Sociological Abstracts (SA)*
- *Sociology of Education Abstracts*
- *Special Educational Needs Abstracts*

Special Bibliographic Notes related to special journal issues (separates) and indexing/abstracting:

- indexing/abstracting services in this list will also cover material in any "separate" that is co-published simultaneously with Haworth's special thematic journal issue or DocuSerial. Indexing/abstracting usually covers material at the article/chapter level.
- monographic co-editions are intended for either non-subscribers or libraries which intend to purchase a second copy for their circulating collections.
- monographic co-editions are reported to all jobbers/wholesalers/approval plans. The source journal is listed as the "series" to assist the prevention of duplicate purchasing in the same manner utilized for books-in-series.
- to facilitate user/access services all indexing/abstracting services are encouraged to utilize the co-indexing entry note indicated at the bottom of the first page of each article/chapter/contribution.
- this is intended to assist a library user of any reference tool (whether print, electronic, online, or CD-ROM) to locate the monographic version if the library has purchased this version but not a subscription to the source journal.
- individual articles/chapters in any Haworth publication are also available through the Haworth Document Delivery Service (HDDS).

Inclusion Practices with Special Needs Students: Theory, Research, and Application

CONTENTS

ABOUT THE EDITORS

Steven I. Pfeiffer, PhD, ABPP, is Executive Director of the Talent Identification Program at Duke University (Durham, NC) and Research Professor of Psychology. Previously, Dr. Pfeiffer served as Executive Director of the Devereux Foundation's Institute of Clincial Training & Research in Villanova, PA. He received his Ph.D. in 1977 from the University of North Carolina, Chapel Hill, and is a Fellow of the American Psychological Association and Diplomate and Vice President of the American Board of Professional Psychology–School Psychology Section. Dr. Pfeiffer served as a Clinical Psychologist in the Navy, as a Pediatric Psychologist at the Ochsner Clinic & Alton Ochsner Foundation Hospital, and on the faculty of the University of Pennsylvania, Fordham University, Kent State University and Fairleigh Dickinson University. He serves on the Editorial Review Board of six professional journals, and is author of almost 100 articles and four books, and two highly acclaimed tests recently published by the Psychological Corporation/Harcourt Brace Co. Dr. Pfeiffer received a three year grant from the Department of Education investigating the efficacy of interagency collaboration in transitioning seriously emotionally disturbed students to less restrictive settings. Dr. Pfeiffer was invited in 1994 to testify before the federal Child Mental Health Committee of the Clinton Health Care Initiative.

Linda A. Reddy, PhD, is Assistant Professor and Director of the Child and Adolescent ADHD Clinic at Fairleigh Dickinson University in Teaneck, NJ. Dr. Reddy is also Research Associate at the Devereux Foundation Institute of Clinical Training and Research. She received her doctorate from the University of Arizona in 1994, and completed a two-year Postdoctoral Fellowship at the Devereux Institute of Clinical Training and Research. Dr. Reddy's research interests include family and school interventions, child behavior disorders, consultation, and test validation. She has presented at numerous national professional conferences and published several articles and book chapters. Dr. Reddy is currently co-editing a book entitled *Innovative Mental Health Prevention Programs for Children.*

Introduction

Steven I. Pfeiffer

Duke University

This edited volume addresses a timely and critically important topic in American education: The overall mission, scope, and responsibility of general education and the future role of special education as we enter the 21st century. The inclusion movement speaks to the heart of what education in America stands for.

Some of the contributors argue–from ethical, philosophical and even empirical bases–that there is abundant justification for full inclusion in a democratic society (Thousand and Villa). Other contributors represent a more conservative interpretation of inclusion that puts at the forefront the best interests of the student and encourages a "least restrictive environment" (Cook and Semmel; Coleman, Webber and Algozzine). Two articles discuss the major historical, sociopolitical, legal, professional and familial forces that have served as the impetus for educational reform initiatives such as inclusion schooling (Reddy; Lombardi and Woodrum). We hope that these articles, inlcuding the commentary by Fagan, provide a useful backdrop for understanding some of the acrimony and heated controversy fueling the debate over inclusion schooling.

Finally, a group of authors discuss how the best practices of instructional consultation (Gravois, Rosenfield and Vale), systematic ethical

[Haworth co-indexing entry note]: "Introduction." Pfeiffer, Steven I. Co-published simultaneously in *Special Services in the Schools* (The Haworth Press, Inc.) Vol. 15, No. 1/2, 1999, pp. 1-2; and: *Inclusion Practices with Special Needs Students: Theory, Research, and Application* (ed: Steven I. Pfeiffer, and Linda A. Reddy) The Haworth Press, Inc., 1999, pp. 1-2. Single or multiple copies of this article are available for a fee from The Haworth Document Delivery Service [1-800-342-9678, 9:00 a.m. - 5:00 p.m. (EST). E-mail address: getinfo@haworthpressinc.com].

1

decision-making (Little and Little), and interagency collaboration (Pfeiffer and Cundari) all increase the likelihood of successful inclusion education. These interventions are certainly not unique to special needs students, however, and the reader may find them equally applicable to work with all students in the schools.

We at the Duke University Talent Identification Program serve the academically gifted student and have encountered a unique tension in terms of the inclusion movement. Society has vacillated between the issues of equity and excellence–oftentimes treating them as antagonistic and mutually exclusive polarities.

Special programs for the gifted receive priority and special attention when excellence is a predominant societal issue. This is perhaps best represented by the Soviet Union's launching of the Sputnik in 1957, winning the initial race into space and creating a tremendous infusion of U.S. dollars into gifted programs. On the other hand, when equity becomes the predominant societal concern, as in the 1960s and 1970s, special programs for the gifted are quickly eliminated. Critics argue that the gifted will "make it on their own, anyway," and that scarce resources would better go to students "who really need them."

My coeditor, Dr. Linda Reddy, and I hope that you find this volume informative, thought-provoking, and useful in your work in the schools. We want to express our heartfelt appreciation to all of the contributors, who were fully committed to ensuring that this volume presented a timely, well-balanced and scholarly discussion of the major issues facing inclusion schooling.

Inclusion of Disabled Children and School Reform: A Historical Perspective

Linda A. Reddy

Fairleigh Dickinson University

SUMMARY. Over the past three decades, special and general education have undergone dramatic philosophical and structural changes. The mission of special and general education and the roles and responsibilities of school personnel have become increasingly blurred. The inclusion movement has captivated the interest of scholars, educators, politicians and the public alike. This paper reviews the major historical and current socio-political, legal, and professional forces that have led to the inclusion movement and national educational reform initiatives (e.g., Goals 2000, IASA, IDEA) in America. Psychologists assume significant leadership roles in the refinement and implementation of inclusion models and national reform initiatives. The expertise and contributions of psychologists to this movement are outlined. Critical issues and unanswered questions are presented to stimulate future research and debate. *[Article copies available for a fee from The Haworth Document Delivery Service: 1-800-342-9678. E-mail address: getinfo@haworthpressinc.com <Website: http://www.haworthpressinc.com>]*

KEYWORDS. Inclusion movement, trends, history of inclusion, least restrictive environment, legal and political factors

---

Address correspondence to: Linda A. Reddy, Fairleigh Dickinson University, Department of Psychology, 1000 River Road, T110A, Teaneck, NJ 07666 (e-mail: reddy@alpha.fdu.edu).

[Haworth co-indexing entry note]: "Inclusion of Disabled Children and School Reform: A Historical Perspective." Reddy, Linda A. Co-published simultaneously in *Special Services in the Schools* (The Haworth Press, Inc.) Vol. 15, No. 1/2, 1999, pp. 3-24; and: *Inclusion Practices with Special Needs Students: Theory, Research, and Application* (ed: Steven I. Pfeiffer, and Linda A. Reddy) The Haworth Press, Inc., 1999, pp. 3-24. Single or multiple copies of this article are available for a fee from The Haworth Document Delivery Service [1-800-342-9678, 9:00 a.m. - 5:00 p.m. (EST). E-mail address: getinfo@haworthpressinc.com].

As an outgrowth of educational reform and mental health initiatives (e.g., Goals 2000: Educate American Act, 1994; Health Security Act, 1994; IDEA, 1997), special education is experiencing increased pressures to change. The face of special education and the relationships among professionals are evolving as school systems move toward integrative full service delivery models (e.g., Pfeiffer & Reddy, 1998; Reddy & Barboza-Whitehead, 1998). Within this change, inclusion schooling has emerged as among the most widely and hotly debated topics in special education today.

Consensus on what constitutes inclusive schools is lacking (e.g., Townsend & Paul, 1997). For example, definitions of inclusive schools vary from selective placement of disabled students in one or more general education classes to full-time placement of all disabled students in general education. In general, inclusion refers to educating students with mild to severe disabilities in the general education classroom.

Advocates of full inclusion believe that restricting students with disabilities from full participation in general education fails to serve their needs, is stigmatizing, and deprives them from the rich and diverse academic and social opportunities found in general education (e.g., Gartner & Lipsky, 1987; Stainback & Stainback, 1992; 1996). It is asserted that the separateness of special and general education and the continuum of special education placement options result in a fragmented, inefficient, and costly service delivery system for children with special needs. Opponents have argued that the inclusion movement is based on vague and loosely defined models and driven by philosophical rhetoric rather than empirical research (e.g., Fuch & Fuch, 1994; Kauffman, 1993; MacMillan, Gresham, & Forness, 1996). Those in support of the continuum of placement options assert that full inclusion into the general education classroom may not represent the most appropriate and least restrictive environment for all students with disabilities (e.g., MacMillan, Gresham, & Forness, 1996). Rather, opponents of inclusion affirm that the cascade of services offer disabled students options for fulfilling their diverse academic and social/emotional needs.

The momentum of the inclusion movement continues to grow despite strong opposition and the lack of unequivocally strong efficacy data (e.g., Cook & Semmel in this volume; Coleman, Webber, & Algozzine in this volume; Forness, Kavale, Blum, and Lloyd, 1997).

Consideration of the historical and current socio-political, professional, legal, and legislative influences are needed to fully appreciate the status of America's education and need for reform.

The present paper has three objectives. First, it provides a comprehensive historical perspective of the evolution of special education and inclusion over the past century. Special attention is given to the forces that have influenced current debate, ideology, and national educational reform efforts. Second, it outlines the leadership roles and contributions of psychologists to the inclusion movement and special education reform. Third, it offers a synthesis of critical questions to guide future research and debate.

SPECIAL EDUCATION IN AMERICA

Early American Public Schooling

During early colonial America, schooling was not compulsory and focused on the socialization of the wealthy homogenous Anglo-Saxon culture. Children were primarily taught in the home (Fagan & Wise, 1994). Schooling was not viewed as essential in preparing children for the workforce.

With the advent of compulsory education in 1852 and influx of large numbers of immigrant children, America was faced for the first time with educating an increasingly heterogenous group of students. These children had diverse social and cultural backgrounds and exhibited many learning, developmental, physical, and emotional/behavioral problems. During the 1920s, separate schools were established for the blind, deaf, and more severely retarded. However, mildly disabled students were educated in regular schools. As the number of students increased in the regular schools, educators began developing separate classes for disabled students (Wallin, 1924; 1955). The reasons behind the segregation of disabled students resemble contemporary views of today. For example, it was believed that students with special needs required separate classes where individualized instruction could be provided from specially trained teachers. In addition, it was believed that children with disabilities would reduce the level of academic demands presented to their nondisabled peers in the regular classroom (Wallin, 1955).

The optimism to successfully identify and train disabled children faded during the 1930s and 1940s. Special education classes were held in the least desirable rooms with few resources, teachers were inadequately trained, and curriculum was watered-down (Semmel, Gottlieb, & Robinson, 1979). Although many parents and educators expressed outrage about these deplorable conditions, school systems offered little action. During the 1950s, parents became increasingly intolerant toward the educational status of America's schools and began forming coalitions. As a result of the parent movement, Brown v. The Board of Education in 1952 was passed. This landmark case clarified the rights of minority children with disabilities and the responsibilities of school systems for educating them. This law cleared the way for future policy and legislation for children with disabilities.

During the Civil Rights movement of the 1960s, many began questioning the homogeneity of minority students in special education classes. The disproportionate number of minority students from low socioeconomic backgrounds in special education became the impetus of several court cases (e.g., Larry P. v. Riles, 1972) and legislative initiatives (i.e., Elementary and Secondary Education Act of 1965; Head Start programs).

The Mainstreaming Movement

As a result of the Civil Rights movement and early national health and mental health initiatives (e.g., The Community Mental Health Centers Act, P.L. 88-164), American schools exhibited a philosophical shift from segregating students with special needs to *mainstreaming* students into the least restrictive environment (LRE) (Fagan & Wise, 1994). Although the term mainstreaming has been widely defined and debated, it generally refers to educating children with disabilities in settings with their nondisabled peers. This movement initially focused on children with mental retardation and later included children with emotional/behavioral disorders and learning disabilities (Townsend & Paul, 1997).

The mainstreaming movement was spawned by litigation led by parents of children with disabilities and special interest groups (e.g., Larry P. v. Riles, 1972; Pennsylvania Association for Retarded Children (PARC) v. Commonwealth of Pennsylvania, 1971). These landmark court cases provided the legal and socio-political momentum for The Education for All Handicapped Children Act of 1975 (P.L. 94-142), reauthorized as The Individuals with Disabilities Education

Act (IDEA) in 1997. This act helped to secure the continued role of the psychologist as diagnostician and gatekeeper for special education. P.L. 94-142 guaranteed all students with disabilities the right to a free and appropriate education in the LRE. However, what constitutes an appropriate education for children with disabilities within the LRE has been debated. The premise of the LRE is that children with disabilities can and should be educated with their nondisabled peers. It is believed that students with disabilities will benefit from the instruction in a mainstreamed classroom. However, efficacy data is inconclusive (e.g., Reynolds, Wang, & Walberg, 1987; Semmel, Gottlieb, & Robinson, 1979). For example, early meta-analytic studies (e.g., Carlberg & Kavale, 1980) have found that separate placements (e.g., full-time classes, resource rooms) for mildly disabled students did not substantially improve social and/or academic functioning.

Some argued that the general education setting as the LRE is not least restrictive for all children. Vergason and Anderegg (1992) point out that P.L. 94-142 emphasizes the importance of the instructional environment rather than the physical environment. For example, under P.L. 94-142, removal from general education classes is to occur "only when the nature or severity of handicap is such that education in regular classes with the use of supplementary aids and services cannot be achieved satisfactorily" (20 U.S.C. § 1412[5][b]).

The original intent and spirit of the Education for All Handicapped Children Act (1975) was ambitious and commendable. However, results on the quality of special education and impact of the mainstreaming movement have been less than encouraging. The National Longitudinal Transition Study (Wagner, D'Amico, Mardre, Newman & Blackorby, 1993) on mildly and moderately disabled students mainstreamed (i.e., part-time or full-time) into general education reported that: (1) only 57% of students in special education graduate with either a diploma or certificate of graduation; and (2) 12% of youth with disabilities have been arrested at some point in their lives, compared to 8% of the general population. Almost one in five students classified as emotionally disturbed are arrested while in secondary school; (3) only 13.4% of all youth with disabilities (aged 15-20) live independently up to two years after leaving secondary school, as opposed to 33.2% of the general post-secondary school population; and (4) only 49% of out-of-school youth with disabilities (aged 15-20) are employed between one and two years after high school. It has been hypothesized that these findings are partly due to the unnecessary segregation and labeling of children for special services and ineffective practice of mainstreaming (National Association of State Boards of Education, 1992). In addition, these findings may also be related to the dramatic health, mental health, and economic problems faced by American families and communities over the past two decades (Pfeiffer & Reddy, 1998).

The Regular Educational Initiative (REI): Bridging Regular and Special Education

Following the mainstreaming movement, social, political, and fiscal pressures gave birth to yet another school reform movement, The Regular Education Initiative (REI). Several national reports on the status of general education offered evidence for the need for reform. For example, *A Nation at Risk: The Imperatives for Educational Reform* (National Commission on Excellence in Education, 1983), *A Place Called School: Prospects for the Future* (Goodlad, 1984), *Tomorrow's Teachers* (The Holmer Group Publication, 1986), and *A Nation Prepared: Teachers for the Twenty-First Century* (Carnegie Forum on Education and the Economy, 1986) served as catalysts for the REI. The report, *A Nation at Risk* (1983) conducted by a government task force, educators, business leaders, and parents fueled public outcry about the low performance of American schools and students relative to other nations. This report emphasized that American schools were inferior and at best average to those in other nations. Although strongly challenged by scholars in education (e.g., Berliner & Biddle, 1995; Bracey, 1996), this report as well as other published reports (e.g., *A Nation Prepared, 1986; A Place Called School, 1984*) remains the focus of many Americans even today.

In 1986, Madeline Will, the then Assistant Secretary of Education, questioned the segregation of students with learning disabilities and the separateness of special and general education. Will's timely paper, *Educating Children with Learning Problems: A Shared Responsibility* (1986) spearheaded the REI movement. This paper proposed an integrated system of education for all children with mild to moderate disabilities. Will (1986) and others (e.g., Gartner & Lipsky, 1987; Stainback & Stainback, 1985) contended that separating general and special education was costly, ineffective, promoted capricious classification, and fostered derogatory labeling.

REI leaders had three general goals. The first goal was to merge special and general education into one integrative system. It was believed that all learners would profit from a unified system in which special and general educators shared responsibility for providing instruction in the classroom. The second goal was to use full-scale mainstreaming, as opposed to a case-by-case approach, to increase the number of students with disabilities in the mainstream classroom. The third goal was to enhance the academic performance of students with mild and moderate disabilities and those at-risk for school failure.

Although REI was intended as a movement to revolutionize both general and special education practices, general education went virtually untouched. The REI movement has been considered a special education initiative. Advocates for REI primarily questioned the efficacy of special education policies and practices. Some have even associated special education to practices that led to the civil rights movement such as slavery (Stainback & Stainback, 1985), segregation (Gartner & Lipsky, 1989), and apartheid (Lipsky & Gartner, 1987). At the core of most REI proposals is the claim that the general education classroom is a place where all learners, without labels, could be optimally educated (Kauffman, 1993). However, *who* would profit from general education varied between proposals (Fuch & Fuch, 1994). For example, some REI proposals identified students with high-incidence disabilities such as mild to moderate mental retardation, learning disabilities, and behavior disorders, while other proposals identified students with low-incidence disabilities such as pervasive developmental disorders, profound mental retardation, and psychotic disorders. Lack of clarity on what constitutes REI and who would ultimately benefit from this initiative has been questioned (Fuch & Fuch, 1994).

Kauffman (1990) stated that REI is "a loosely connected set of propositions and proposals for reform of the relationship between special and general education" (p. 57). Those against REI argued that both special and general education practices are ineffective for students with disabilities and that reform is needed for both systems. REI opponents also charged that research on instructional models for integrating students with and without disabilities lacked sound methodological controls and offered inconclusive evidence for or against the effectiveness of special education services (Lloyd & Gambatese, 1990).

National associations have also questioned the efficacy of REI. For example, The Council for Children with Behavior Disorders (CCBD) and The Association for Children and Adults with Learning Disabilities (ACLD) (1986) cautioned that the general education classroom may not be the least restrictive environment for children with behavior disorders and learning disabilities. The CCBD argued that regular educators do not have the knowledge and training in behavioral management and crisis intervention. In addition, removing the label of "behavior disordered" from students will not change the way others view and interact with them. The ACLD also expressed concerns that restricting the continuum of placement options for those with learning disabilities would limit learning opportunities for some children.

As debates continue many recognize that reform needs to be made in both special *and* general education. Reform initiatives which emphasize outcomes for students with disabilities and educational processes that achieve these outcomes are warranted.

THE INCLUSION MOVEMENT: A CONTINUATION OF THE DEBATE OVER PLACE

During the late 1980s, debates escalated on *who, where,* and *how* disabled students would be successfully integrated into the general education classroom. As a result of these heated debates, a new and radical ideology of educating students with disabilities emerged. This new philosophical initiative became known as the inclusion movement. Although the concept of inclusion holds different meanings and assumptions for many people, in general inclusion refers to educating *all* students with disabilities including those with severe disabilities in the general education setting. Stainback and Stainback (1990) have defined inclusion schooling as "the inclusion of all students in the mainstream of regular education classes and school activities with their age peers from the same community" (p. 225). Inclusion schools embrace the values of diversity and learning communities. Student needs (i.e., academic and/or social) are accomplished through the implementation of combined resources and supports within one setting.

Those who advocate for the inclusion movement can be conceptualized into three groups. The first group, and probably the most radical, includes those who advocate for the full dismantling of special education, eliminating special education placements and labels of special education teachers and students (e.g., Stainback & Stainback, 1992; 1996). The second group represents those who support that special education teachers should provide instructional services to disabled students and their nondisabled peers in the regular education classroom (e.g., Giangreco, Dennis, Cloninger, Edelman, & Schattman, 1993). Finally, the third group includes politicians, policy makers, and administrators who view inclusion as a means to reduce special education expenditures (e.g., Leo, 1994). Regardless which group or groups one ascribes to, all three believe that students with disabilities should be educated in the regular education setting full time.

Shifts in Ideology

In comparison to REI, the inclusion movement represents several philosophical shifts. First, leaders of inclusion advocate for reconstructing the entire special education system (Lipsky & Gartner 1987; Stainback & Stainback, 1992; Thousand & Villa in this volume). As mentioned, some full inclusionists propose to eliminate not just the top or near top of the continuum of special education placement options, as argued by REI supporters, but the entire cascade of services. "An inclusive school or classroom educates all students in the mainstream. No students, including those with disabilities, are relegated to the fringes of the school by placement in segregated wings, trailers, or special classes" (Stainback & Stainback, 1992, p. 34). The shift from restricting to eliminating the cascade of services may be, in part, due to a number of firmly held beliefs about special education. One explanation is that special education has been historically viewed as general education's dumping ground for those students viewed as unteachable or undesirable. The continuation of separate placements for disabled students enables regular education teachers to avoid dealing with these students and creating a more humanistic learning environment. Another possible explanation is that some view special education as the cause of general education's shortcomings to accommodate the needs of many students (e.g., Stainback & Stainback, 1992).

The second philosophical shift is in the stated mission and objectives. One of the primary objectives of REI was to strengthen the academic performance of students with mild and moderate disabilities and those at risk for school failure. In contrast, full inclusionists emphasize the need to improve social competence in students with mild to severe disabilities and to change attitudes toward persons with disabilities.

The rationale for educating students with severe disabilities in integrated settings is to ensure their normalized community participation by providing them with systematic instruction in the skills that are essential to their success in the social and environmental contexts in which they ultimately use these skills. (Gartner & Lipsky, 1987, p. 386)

Snell (1991) outlined three benefits of integration: "(1) the development of social skills. . . . across all school age groups, (2) the improvement in the attitudes that nondisabled peers have for their peers with disabilities, and (3) the development of positive relationships and friendships between peers as a result of integration" (pp. 137-138). Relatedly, as mission statements change so will efforts to define and evaluate successful outcome. Evaluating the success of inclusion initiatives will likely focus on the improvement of social competence and social acceptance rather than academic success.

A third philosophical shift rests in the acceptability of the general education curriculum. Standard curricula has been increasingly deemphasized and in some cases outright rejected by full inclusionists. For example, Stainback and Stainback (1992) stated that the standard curricula represented in textbooks is antiquated: "there is no longer a single, discreet, stagnant body of information" (p. 69). They also pointed out that standard curriculum "does not accommodate the inherent diversity in background experiences, learning needs, styles, and interests of all students" and is "boring, uninteresting, and lacking in meaning or purposefulness for many students" (p. 69). Full inclusionists advocate for a process approach to education in that "there is little or no focus on remediating deficits and weaknesses–these are addressed or compensated for as children become excited about learning and engage in real-life, purposeful projects and activities" (Stainback & Stainback, 1992, p. 70).

Influence of National Professional Organizations

The inclusion movement was spawned by several national professional organizations. One organization that has profoundly influenced the inclusion movement is The Association for Persons with Severe

Handicaps (TASH). While other organizations gradually developed and remained on the periphery of the policy arena, TASH leaders quickly and aggressively helped to shape state and national initiatives. For example, TASH influenced the special education policy in several states (e.g., New Mexico State Department of Education, Michigan Department of Education) and local school districts across the country. It provided direction for educational funding initiatives for the Office of Special Education Programs. In addition, the vision of TASH can be seen in the report, *Winners All: A Call for Inclusive Schools* (1992) published by the National Association of State Boards of Education. This report outlined the mission and strategic plan for implementing and financing inclusive schools for America. The accomplishments of TASH have also attracted national media attention. For example, *Educating Peter,* an Academy Award winning documentary shown in 1993 depicted the challenges and rewards of including a 10 year old boy with Downs Syndrome in the general education classroom. This documentary has been televised five times on HBO and earned front page coverage in the *New York Times.*

The Association for Retarded Citizens (ARC) a small, but influential organization has also impacted the inclusion movement. Leaders of ARC have rejected the notion of the least restrictive environment, claiming that schools have two critical and related goals for students with disabilities. These goals are: (1) to improve the social competence of disabled students and (2) to change the attitudes of school administrators, teachers, and nondisabled students about those with disabilities. ARC leaders advocate that these goals are accomplished in a mainstreamed or integrated education setting (Gartner & Lipsky, 1987). In addition, these two goals are not viewed as independent, but rather as one of the same. For example, ARC leaders state that providing disabled students the opportunity to socially interact with their nondisabled peers is the appropriate education for students with disabilities.

The *National Study of Inclusive Education* (1994; 1995) conducted by the Center on Educational Restructuring and Inclusion has also sparked interest in inclusion schooling. The *National Study* (1994, 1995) surveyed over 1,000 school districts on inclusive education efforts and identified several general factors of success for integrating inclusion practices. These factors include: visionary leadership, collaboration, refocused use of assessment, support for staff and students, effective parental involvement, the implementation of effective program models, effective classroom practices, and funding. Although the results of the *National Study* are commendable, approaches to achieve these factors were not identified. For example, the factors of collaboration and effective parental involvement are loosely defined and discussed from a philosophical viewpoint. (For a detailed review of these factors and approaches to achieve them, see Thousand and Villa in this volume.)

National professional organizations, such as The American Council of the Blind (1994), The Commission on the Education of the Deaf (1988), The Learning Disabilities Association (1993), The Council for Exceptional Children (1993), and The National Joint Committee on Learning Disabilities (1993), strongly endorse special education placement options and, implicitly or explicitly, reject full inclusion. According to the American Federation of Teachers (1993), 77% of surveyed teachers opposed inclusion practices and reported that their schools were either currently practicing inclusive schooling or moving towards that direction. Limited time and the management of behavioral problems in the classroom were among the primary complaints most reported. Of this group, only 22% received special inservice training for inclusion practices and only 11% felt that it was sufficient or adequate. (For a discussion on staff development see Gravois, Rosenfield, and Vail in this volume.)

Organizational leaders and scholars have also asserted that TASH's slogan for advocating for *all* children with disabilities is misleading and inconsistent. Fuchs and Fuchs (1994) eloquently point out that the TASH leadership has been unresponsive to advocates of deaf, blind, and/or emotional and behavioral disordered students. In addition, TASH has been accused of not acknowledging others' views and research findings (e.g., Kauffman, 1993; MacMillan, Gresham, & Forness, 1996).

Despite opposition to inclusion, this movement continues to gain momentum. The inclusion movement has been supported, directly and indirectly, by a number of federal educational reform initiatives. The following section briefly outlines four recent national initiatives.

Recent National Educational Initiatives

Earlier educational initiatives have provided valuable insight for shaping current national reform efforts. The first wave of educational reform was sparked by the report *A Nation at Risk: The Imperative for Educational Reform* (1983) and has been described "as being top-down and driven by state government actions" (Tharinger et al., 1996 p. 25). This report attributed America's educational problems to low academic standards and poor instruction. Although unsuccessful in its implementation, reform efforts focused on increasing the number of math and science classes, raising graduation requirements, adding teaching credentials, raising teaching salaries, and increasing the use of assessment of students. Similar findings were reported by the Commission on the Skills of the American Workforce (CSAW, 1990) and the Secretary's Commission on Achieving Necessary Skills (SCANS, 1991). These reports indicated that higher academic achievement was needed for young persons to successfully compete in the workforce. In addition, international studies have reported that U.S. students rank near last in mathematics and in the middle to bottom range in science (Stedman, 1994).

The second wave of reform was led by the report, *A Nation Prepared: Teachers for the 21st Century* (1986), by the Carnegie Foundation on Education and the Economy. *A Nation Prepared* advocated a bottom-up approach to reform initiatives by focusing on local needs, enhancing the professional status of teachers, and decentralizing decision making. Because of results from early reform efforts and fear that U.S. students would continue to be inadequately prepared for the increasingly competitive world, the federal government adopted a broader systemic approach to reform.

Goals 2000: Educate America Act. A national response to the educational needs of American students was addressed in the 1989 Charlottesville Education Summit by President Bush and the nation's governors. This meeting resulted in six national educational goals which provided a broad framework for states and communities to begin reform. In 1994, President Clinton signed into law Goals 2000: Educate America Act which established eight goals, six of which were adopted from the 1989 National Summit. This Act included two additional educational goals (i.e., Goal 4: Teacher education and professional development and Goal 8: Parental participation) which emphasize the importance of ongoing professional development and parental involvement in school reform efforts. Goals 2000: Educate America Act (1994) states that by the year 2000:

- all children in America will start school ready to learn;
- the high school graduation rate will increase to at least 90%;
- all students will leave Grades 4, 8, and 12 having demonstrated competency in challenging subject matter, including English, mathematics, science, foreign languages, civics and government, economics, arts, history, and geography, and every school in America will ensure that all students learn to use their minds well, so they will be prepared for responsible citizenship, further learning, and productive employment in the nation's modern economy;
- the nation's teaching force will have access to programs for the continued improvement of their professional skills and the opportunity to acquire the knowledge and skills needed to instruct and prepare all American students for the next century;
- U.S. students will be first in the world in science and mathematics achievement;
- every American adult will be literate and will possess the knowledge and skills necessary to compete in a global economy and exercise the rights and responsibilities of citizenship;
- every school in the United States will be free of drugs, violence, and the unauthorized presence of firearms and alcohol and will offer a disciplined environment conducive to learning; and
- every school will promote partnerships that will increase parental involvement and participation in promoting the social, emotional, and academic growth of children.

Goals 2000 established high academic standards for all students by allowing state and local educational agencies flexibility in identifying effective strategies to accomplish these goals. This Act reflects a shift in educational reform policy from mandating changes in education to monitoring the educational process with increased accountability. As Resnick, Nolan, and Resnick (1995) state: "the new education-reform movement is aiming for governance by outputs–that is, requiring education institutions to meet outcome criteria by leaving them free to devise their own procedures" (p. 438).

Goals 2000 has appropriated over $471 million dollars, reaching 12,000 schools and approximately 6.7 million students (U.S. Department of Education, 1996). This Act provides the financial support for reshaping service delivery and evaluating educational outcomes of students with disabilities and those at risk for school failure (Tirozzi & Uro, 1997). However, Goals 2000 does not explicitly support the vision of full inclusionists (e.g., TASH, Stainback & Stainback, 1996). *Improving America's Schools Act (IASA).* The Elementary and Secondary Education Act (ESEA, 1965), reauthorized as the Improving America's Schools Act (IASA, 1994) has dramatically increased federal funding for elementary and secondary education programs across the nation. IASA reaffirms the commitment of Goals 2000 by supporting the inclusion of students with disabilities in educational reform. IASA has allocated tremendous financial support to devise rigorous content and performance standards for all students at the school, community, and state level. In alignment with Goals 2000, IASA emphasizes accountability, requiring states to evaluate student progress against the performance standards of Goals 2000 or standards which reflect similar rigor. Local educational agencies and states are required to include students with disabilities in state assessments and to examine the educational progress of disabled students separately from results of nondisabled students. Those educational agencies which do not demonstrate progress, as defined by the state plan, may be subject to corrective actions (e.g., withholding funding, alternative governance) by their district or state. Thus, IASA offers states and local educational agencies financial incentives to participate in Goals 2000, establish high standards, and include students with disabilities in program planning and evaluation efforts.

School-to-Work Opportunity Act. The School-to-Work Opportunity Act (1994) established a national framework for creating educational programs to improve the postsecondary outcomes of disabled and nondisabled students. In keeping with Goals 2000 and IASA, the School-to-Work Opportunity Act supports performance-based education and training programs such as school training and counseling, career awareness, and community-based mentorship and employment. This Act forges partnerships between schools, community agencies, and local employers. Programs (e.g., individualized transition programs) funded by this law complement those services required for students with disabilities under Part B of the Individuals with Disabilities Education Act (IDEA, 1997) (Norman & Bourexis, 1995).

IDEA (P.L.105-17). President Clinton's reauthorization of IDEA in June of 1997, also referred to as P.L. 105-17, reflects a greater commitment and accountability for the educational progress of disabled

students. As previously mentioned, students with disabilities historically have not been the focus of educational reform. Under the reauthorization of IDEA, however, states must establish performance standards which are more closely aligned with goals for nondisabled
students. States are also required to include students with disabilities
in state assessments with appropriate accommodations or the use of
alternative assessment methods. New individualized educational plan
provisions require: (1) information on how the student's disability
influences his or her involvement in general education, (2) measurable
goals which relate to the general education curriculum, and (3) evaluation of progress towards annual goals.

Historically, this law has required schools to provide a free, appropriate public education (FAPE) for all students with disabilities. It
has also required that to the maximum extent appropriate, students
with disabilities be educated with students who are not disabled (i.e.,
LRE). In contrast to the inclusion movement, IDEA supports the continuum of special education placement options and does not use the
terms inclusion and/or mainstreaming. Nevertheless, this law has resulted in the increased classification of students with disabilities (i.e.,
73% increase since 1979) and full-time and/or part-time placement of
students in general education (U.S. Department of Commerce, 1997).

How the new provisions of IDEA (1997) will impact the inclusion
movement is not yet known. What is known is that the controversy
surrounding what constitutes the LRE and whether or not general
education can best serve the needs of disabled students will continue
(Little & Little in this volume; Yell, 1995).

Goals 2000, IASE, the School-to-Work Opportunities Act, and the
reauthorization of IDEA have dramatically transformed the educational process for all students at the federal, state, and local level. The
zeitgeist of the inclusion movement and establishment of national
educational initiatives afford psychologists several leadership opportunities.

CONTRIBUTIONS OF THE PSYCHOLOGIST
IN THE INCLUSION MOVEMENT

As local educational agencies, communities, and states undergo
philosophical and structural changes so will the roles and functions of
psychologists. Goals 2000, IASA, School-to-Work Opportunities Act,

and IDEA offer a comprehensive framework for psychologists to design and evaluate innovative ways to educate and socialize students with disabilities. The training and expertise of contemporary psychologists offer many important contributions to the inclusion movement and national reform initiatives. Areas of expertise include:

- interpretation and use of federal and state special education laws in the implementation of school reform initiatives (e.g., Goals 2000, IASA, IDEA) (Jacob-Timm & Hartshorne, 1998).
- decision making skills about the inclusion of students in the general education classroom and accommodations needed to optimize learning (Little & Little in this volume).
- securing various stakeholders' (e.g., parents, educators, administrators) interest and commitment in program development and system-wide assessment of disabled and nondisabled students (Lombardi & Woodrum in this volume).
- knowledge of alternative evaluation approaches for measuring educational progress and accommodations for testing disabled students.
- documentation and presentation of program results (intended and unintended outcomes) designed to accomplish state and national educational goals.
- familiarity with empirically-based instructional interventions (e.g., curriculum-based measurement, direct instruction, authentic learning environments) for disabled students (Forness, Kavale, Blum, & Lloyd, 1997).
- inservice training and consultation with families, school personnel, and agencies in instructional remediation, behavioral management, crisis intervention, and socialization skills (e.g., Gravois, Rosenfield, & Vail, 1999; Reddy, Barboza-Whitehead, Files & Rubel, 1999).
- fostering parental involvement/empowerment through the implementation of home and school interventions (Pfeiffer & Reddy, 1998).
- advice and expertise for teacher preparation training in course content such as behavioral management and instructional strategies. (Gravois, Rosenfield, & Vail, 1999)
- development of learning environments that embody social and cultural awareness/sensitivity.

- interagency collaboration skills to access resources, design transition plans, and develop partnerships with agencies (Pfeiffer & Cundari in this volume).

SOME CRITICAL ISSUES AND QUESTIONS

Whether inclusive schools will meet some or all of the needs of disabled students is yet unknown. At present, a substantial body of research on the efficacy of inclusion models is missing. This movement will profit from further research and the continuation of scholarly debate. Some key questions that should be addressed are: (1) What are the essential elements of inclusion? Before fully adopting and/or endorsing a policy reform approach at the local, state, and national level, it is critical to delineate the key components of such a model. (2) How are inclusion models best evaluated? What aspects of an individual's functioning, background, and environment lead to intentional (and unintentional) outcomes? (3) What are the effects of inclusion on students with different disabilities and age groups (e.g., preschoolers versus adolescents)? Which populations benefit the most or least from this model? What are the effects of inclusion on students without special needs? (4) What are the long-term cost effectiveness and cost benefits of inclusion versus traditional special education? (5) What instructional approaches are most effective for students with disabilities and those at risk for school failure? (6) What systemic factors and/or processes increase the frequency and extent of successful integration of students with special needs into the general education classroom?

As we look to the 21st century, there are many unanswered questions regarding the efficacy and long-term benefits of inclusive schooling. New lines of investigation need to include rigorous research methodology and a core set of values and principles that embrace the unique needs, rights, and social/cultural contexts of families with disabled children.

CONCLUSION

This article provides a review of the major historical and current socio-political, professional, and legal influences on the inclusion movement. Historically, policy and educational reform has preceded without substantial empirical support for such initiatives. This recurring theme of our American educational history can be daunting and disenchanting to many scholars, educators, and parents of children with disabilities.

As this movement continues to grow, it will increasingly rely on the conceptual and empirical bases developed by psychologists. Psychologists possess unique skills and areas of expertise as highlighted in this paper. Psychologists will continue to assume important leadership roles in national policy reform.

REFERENCES

American Council on the Blind. (1994). *Full inclusion of students who are blind and visually impaired: A position statement.* Washington, DC: Author.

American Federation of Teachers. (1993). *Draft AFT position on inclusion.* (Available from American Federation of Teachers, 555 New Jersey Avenue, N.W., Washington, DC 20001).

Association for Children and Adults with Learning Disabilities. (1986). Position statement on a regular education/special education initiative. *Academic Therapy, 22,* 99-103.

Berliner, D. C., & Biddle, B. J. (1995). The manufactured crisis: Myths, fraud, and the attack on America's public schools. Reading, MA: Addison Wesley.

Board of Education, Sacramento Unified School District v. Holland, 786 F.Supp 874, 73 Ed. Law Rep. 969 (E.D. Cal. 1992); *aff'd sub nom. Board of Education, Sacramento Unified School District v. Rachel H.,* 14F. 3d 1398, 89 Ed. Law Rep. 57 (9th Cir. 1994).

Bracey, G. W. (1996). International comparisons and the condition of American education. *Educational Researcher, 25* (1), 5-11.

Brown v. Board of Education, 347 U.S. 483 (1954).

Carlberg, C., & Kavale, K. (1980). The efficacy of special versus regular class placement for exceptional children: A meta-analysis. *Journal of Special Education, 14,* 295-309.

Carnegie Forum on Education and the Economy. (1986). A nation prepared: Teachers for the 21st century. Washington, DC: Author (ERIC Document Reproduction Service No. ED 12 322).

Community Mental Health Centers Act, P.L. 88-164 U.S.C. §§ 2681 et seq.

Commission on the Education of the Deaf. (1988). Toward equality: Education of the deaf. Washington, DC: U.S. Government Printing Office (ERIC Document Reproduction Service No. ED 303 932).

The Council for Exceptional Children (1993). *Statement on inclusive schools and communities.* Reston, VA: Author.

CSAW. (1990). America's choice: High skills or low wages! (Executive Summary). Rochester, NY: National Center on Education and the Economy and the Commission on the Skills of the American Workforce.

Education of All Handicapped Children Act of 1975, Pub. L. No. 94-142. amended by 20 U.S.C. 1400 et seq. (West).

Elementary and Secondary Education Act of 1965, 20 U.S.C. §§ 2701 et seq.

Fagan, T. K., & Wise, P. S. (1994). *School psychology: Past, present, and future.* NY: Longman.

Forness, S. R., Kavale, K. A., Blum, I. M., & Lloyd, J. W. (1997). Mega-analysis of meta-analyses: What works in special education. *Teaching Exceptional Children, 29* (6), 4-9.

Fuchs, D., & Fuchs, L. S. (1994). Inclusive schools movement and the radicalization of special education reform. *Exceptional Children, 60,* 294-309.

Gartner, A., & Lipsky, D. K. (1987). Beyond special education. *Harvard Educational Review, 57,* 367-395.

Gartner, A., & Lipsky, D. K. (1989). *The yoke of special education: How to break it.* Rochester, NY: National Center on Education and the Economy.

Giangreco, M. F., Dennis, R., Cloninger, C., Edelman, S., & Schattman, R. (1993). I've counted Jon": Transformational experiences of teachers educating students with disabilities. *Exceptional Children, 59,* 359-372.

Goals 2000: Educate America Act, Pub. L. No. 103-227, 103rd Cong., 2nd sess. (1994).

Goodland, J. I. (1984). A place called school: Prospects for the future. New York: McGraw-Hill.

Health Security Act of 1994, H.R. 3600, 103rd Cong. (1994).

Holmes Group. (1986, April). *Tomorrow's teachers.* East Lansing, MI: Author.

Improving America's Schools Act of 1994, Pub. L. No. 103-382, 108 Stat. 3518 (1994).

Individuals With Disabilities Education Act of 1997 20 U.S.C. §§ 1400-1485 (1997).

Jacob-Timm, S., & Hartshorne, T. (1998). *Ethics and law for school psychologists* (3rd ed.). NY: John Wiley & Sons, Inc.

Kauffman, J. M. (1990). Restructuring in sociopolitical context: Reservations about the effects of current reform proposals on students with disabilities. In J. W. Lloyd, A. C. Repp, & N. N. Singh (Eds.), The regular education initiative: Alternative perspectives on concepts, issues, and models (pp. 57-66). Sycamore, IL: Sycamore Publishing Co.

Kauffman, J. M. (1993). How we might achieve the radical reform of special education. *Exceptional Children, 60,* 6-16.

Larry P. v. Riles, 343 F. Supp. 1306 (N.D. Cal. 1972).

Learning Disabilities Association (1993). *Position paper on full inclusion of all students with learning disabilities in the regular education classroom.* Pittsburgh, PA: Author.

Leo, J. (1994). Mainstreaming's Jimmy problem. *U.S. News and World Report, 116,* 25: 22.

Lipsky, D. K., & Gartner, A. (1987). Capable of achievement and worthy of respect: Education for handicapped students as if they were full-fledged human beings. *Exceptional Children, 54,* 69-74.

Lloyd, J. W., & Gambatese, C. (1990). Reforming the relationship between regular and special education. In J. W. Lloyd, A. C. Repp, & N. N. Singh (Eds.), *The* regular education initiative: Alternative perspectives on concepts, issues, and models (pp. 3-13). Sycamore, IL: Sycamore Publishing Co.

MacMillan, D. L., Gresham, F. M., & Forness, S. R. (1996). Full inclusion: An empirical perspective. *Behavior Disorders, 21,* 145-159.

National Commission on Excellence in Education. (1983). *A nation at risk: The imperatives for educational reform.* Washington, DC: U.S. Government Printing Office.

National Association of State Boards of Education. (1992). *Winners all: A call for inclusive schools.* Washington, DC: Author.

National Joint Committee on Learning Disabilities. (1993). *A reaction to "full inclusion": A reaffirmation of the right of students with learning disabilities to a continuum of services.* Author.

National Study of Inclusive Education (1994, 1995). New York: The City University of New York, National Center on Educational Restructuring and Inclusion.

National Transition Network. (Summer, 1994). *Youth with disabilities and the school-to-work opportunities.* Washington, DC: CCSSO.

Norman, M. E., & Bourexis, P. S. (1995). *Including students with disabilities in school-to-work opportunities.* Washington, DC: CCSSO.

Pennsylvania Association for Retarded Citizens (P.A.R.C) v. Commonwealth of Pennsylvania, 334 F.Supp. 1257 (D.C.E.D. Pa 1971), 343 F.Supp. 279 (D.C.E.E. Pa 1972).

Pfeiffer, S. I., & Reddy, L. A. (1998). School-based mental health programs in the United States: Present status and a blueprint for the future. *School Psychology Review, 27,* 84-96.

U.S. Congress. (1994, March). *Goals 2000: Educate America Act. Public Law 103-227.* 103d Congress.

Reddy, L. A., & Barboza-Whitehead, S. (1998). Educating the Disabled Student: Old and New Challenges and Future Opportunities. [Review of the book *Issues in Educating Students with Disabilities*]. Contemporary Psychology.

Reddy, L. A., Barboza-Whitehead, S., Files, T., & Rubel, R. (1998). *Clinical and empirical focus of consultation outcome research with children and adolescents.* Poster presented at the American Psychological Association Conference, San Francisco, CA.

Resnick, L. B., Nolan, K. J., & Resnick, D. P. (1995). Benchmarking education standards. *Educational Evaluation and Policy Analysis, 17,* 438-461.

Reynolds, M. C., Wang, M. C., & Walberg, H. J. (1987). The necessary restructuring of special and regular education. *Exceptional Children, 53,* 391-398.

SCANS. (1991). *What work requires of schools: A SCANS report for America 2000.* Washington, DC: U.S. Department of Labor.

Semmel, M. I., Gottlieb, J. & Robinson, N. M. (1979). Mainstreaming: Perspectives on educating handicapped children in the public school. In D. Berliner (Ed.), *Review of research in education.* (Vol. 7, pp. 223-279). Chicago: Peacock Publishers.

Snell, M. E. (1991). Schools are for all kids: The importance of integration for students with severe disabilities and their peers. In J. W. Lloyd, A. C. Repp, & N.

N. Singh (Eds.), *The Regular Education initiative: Alternative perspectives on concepts, issues, and models* (pp. 133-148). Sycamore, IL: Sycamore.

Stainback, W., & Stainback, S. (1985). *Integration of students with severe handicaps into regular schools.* Reston, VA: Council for Exceptional Children (ERIC Document Reproduction Service No. ED 255 009).

Stainback, W., & Stainback, S. (1990). A rationale for integration and restructuring: A synopsis. In J. W. Lloyd, A. C. Repp, & N. N. Singh (Eds.), *The regular education initiative: Alternative perspectives on concepts, issues, and models* (pp. 226-239). Sycamore, IL: Sycamore Publishing Co.

Stainback, S., & Stainback, W. (1992). *Curriculum considerations in inclusive classrooms: Facilitating learning for all students.* Baltimore: Paul Brookes.

Stainback, S., Stainback, W., & Ayres, B. (1996). Schools as inclusive communities. In W. Stainback & S. Stainback (Eds.), *Controversial issues confronting special education* (2nd ed., pp. 31-43). Boston: Allyn and Bacon.

Stedman, L. C. (1994). Incomplete explanations: The case of U.S. performance in the international assessment of education. *Educational Researcher, 23* (7), 24-32.

Tharinger, D. J., Lambert, N. M., Bricklin, P. M., Feshbach. N., Johnson, N. F., Oakland, T. D., Paster, V. S., & Sanchez, W. (1996). Education reform: Challenges for Psychology and Psychologists. *Professional Psychology: Research and Practice, 27,* 24-33.

Tirozzi, G. N., & Uro, G. (1997). Education reform in the United States: National policy in support of local efforts for school improvement. *American Psychologists, 52,* 241-249.

Townsend, B. L., & Paul, J. L. (1997). School reform and inclusion of children with disabilities. In J. L. Paul, N. H. Berger, P. G. Osnes, Y. G. Martinez, & W. C. Morse (Eds.), *Ethics and decision making in local schools: Inclusion, policy, and reform.* (pp. 49-69). Baltimore, MD: Paul H. Brookes Publishing Co.

U.S. Department of Commerce (1997). *Statistical abstract of the United States, 1997* (117th ed.). Washington, DC: Author.

U.S. Department of Education. (1996). Justifications of appropriation estimates to the Congress, fiscal year 1997 (Vol. 1). Washington, DC: Author.

Vergason, G. A., & Anderegg, M. L. (1992). Preserving the least restrictive environment. In W. Stainback & S. Stainback (Eds.), *Controversial issues confronting special education: Divergent perspectives* (pp. 45-54). Boston: Allyn & Bacon.

Wagner, M., D'Amico, R., Mardre, C., Newman, L., & Blackorby, J. (1993). What happens next? Trends in postschool outcomes of youths with disabilities. *The Second Comprehensive Report from the National Longitudinal and Transition Study of Special Education Students.* CA: SRI International.

Wallin, J. E .W. (1924). *The education of the handicapped children.* Boston: Houghton Mifflin.

Wallin, J. E. W. (1955). *Education of mentally handicapped children.* NY: Harper & Brothers.

Will, M. C. (1986). Educating children with learning problems: A shared responsibility. *Exceptional Children, 52,* 411-415.

Yell, M. L. (1995). Least restrictive environment, inclusion, and students with disabilities: A legal analysis. *The Journal of Special Education. 28* (4), 389-404.

Inclusion and Students with Emotional/Behavioral Disorders

Maggie Coleman

University of Texas at Austin

Jo Webber

Southwest Texas State Univeristy

Bob Algozzine

University of North Carolina at Charlotte

SUMMARY. This article presents a point/counterpoint approach to the issue of full inclusion of all students with emotional/behavioral disorders. To set the stage for the discussion that follows, the academic, social, and behavioral characteristics of these students pertinent to classroom performance are reviewed. The pros and cons of these four issues are then presented: (a) appropriateness of the general education curriculum for students with EBD; (b) social acceptance and other social competence issues; (c) mental health interventions and supports in general education settings; and (d) legality of full inclusion. Under the legality issue, case law on full inclusion pertaining to students with EBD is briefly reviewed. The basic premise of the authors who are full inclusion opponents is that a continuum of placements, including full-time placement in general education classrooms, should be preserved so that

Address correspondence to: Dr. Margaret C. Coleman, Texas Center for Reading and Language Arts, College of Education, The University of Texas at Austin, Austin, TX 78712-1299.

[Haworth co-indexing entry note]: "Inclusion and Students with Emotional/Behavioral Disorders." Coleman, Maggie, Jo Webber, and Bob Algozzine. Co-published simultaneously in *Special Services in the Schools* (The Haworth Press, Inc.) Vol. 15, No. 1/2, 1999, pp. 25-47; and: *Inclusion Practices with Special Needs Students: Theory, Research, and Application* (ed: Steven I. Pfeiffer, and Linda A. Reddy) The Haworth Press, Inc., 1999, pp. 25-47. Single or multiple copies of this article are available for a fee from The Haworth Document Delivery Service [1-800-342-9678, 9:00 a.m. - 5:00 p.m. (EST). E-mail address: getinfo@haworthpressinc.com].

decisions about appropriate settings can be made on an individual basis. The basic premise of the author who is a full inclusion proponent is that, rather than maintaining two separate systems, we should direct our energies toward correcting the inadequacies of the general education classroom for the benefit of all students, including those with EBD. *[Article copies available for a fee from The Haworth Document Delivery Service: 1-800-342-9678. E-mail address: getinfo@haworthpressinc.com <Website: http:// www.haworthpressinc.com>]*

KEYWORDS. Full inclusion, emotional disorders, behavioral disorders, EBD

Debate about the appropriateness of a full inclusion policy for students with disabilities has simmered for more than a decade (see Reddy in this series). This movement to integrate special and general education students has polarized not only the education community in general, but also the special education community. Whereas some leaders within the field have supported the idea of full inclusion (Thousand & Villa in this series), others have argued that the current concepts of least restrictive environment and a continuum of placements should be preserved. Meanwhile, the adoption of full inclusion practices across the country continues.

For students with emotional and behavioral disorders (EBD), the inclusion debate has been particularly polarized (e.g., Braaten, Kauffman, Braaten, Polsgrove, and Nelson, 1988; Kauffman, Braaten, Nelson, Polsgrove, & Braaten, 1990; Algozzine, Maheady, Sacca, O'Shea, & O'Shea, 1990). These students, who typically display disturbing behaviors and interpersonal relationship difficulties, have not historically found refuge in general education classrooms. In fact, many educators believe that under-trained teachers who must teach large numbers of students and who are coercive and authoritarian, using punishment as a primary discipline tool, have contributed to students' behavioral and emotional problems (e.g., Walker, Colvin, & Ramsey, 1995). On the other hand, others believe that segregated special education placement has not only failed to help these challenging students but has actually contributed to a 55% dropout rate, the high rate of law enforcement involvement (22% while in school), and several negative post high-school outcomes (e.g., Basset, Jackson, Ferrell, Luckner, Hagerty, Bunsen, & MacIsaac, 1996).

POINT/COUNTERPOINT

We offer two positions in the debate: (a) full inclusion is not appropriate for all students and (b) full inclusion is appropriate for all students. Our intent in the remainder of this article is to provide a "point-counterpoint" perspective on the pros and cons of full inclusion for students with EBD.

THE POSITION AGAINST FULL INCLUSION

For the purposes of this article, full inclusion is defined as the full-time placement of all students with disabilities in general education settings. Such a definition presumes elimination of a continuum of placements that is currently required by law and an integral part of the special education service delivery model. Accordingly, the concept of least restrictive environment (LRE) also becomes a moot point. This definition of full inclusion is not to be confused with the inclusive schools movement, which aims to overhaul both general and special education in an effort to provide better instruction and more comprehensive services to all students without eliminating a continuum of placements.

The placement of students with EBD into general education classrooms generates strong debate because the students themselves typically generate strong reactions. The academic, social, and behavioral characteristics of students who have been labeled EBD typify students who are often disturbing to those who try to educate them. We would like to review these characteristics because they relate directly to our concerns about full inclusion practices.

Few would argue that students with EBD fail to achieve in school. Research over the past 25 years has indicated that the intellectual functioning of these youngsters as measured by IQ tests is consistently below average (Coleman, 1996). A review of 25 studies documenting achievement of students with EBD by Mastropieri, Jenkins, and Scruggs (1985) showed that they are typically deficient in all areas of academic functioning, with some studies reporting more serious deficits in math. Further complicating the picture is the fact that many students with EBD also have a learning disability (Fessler, Rosenberg, & Rosenberg, 1991). Given these difficulties, it is not surprising to find a dropout rate that is over 50 percent, which is twice the dropout rate of the general population. Thus, one of our major concerns about full inclusion with all students with EBD is the appropriateness of the general education curriculum, especially at the secondary level, for teaching these students basic literacy skills and preparing them for the workforce.

Social and behavioral characteristics of students with EBD are often described within an internalizing/externalizing framework (Achenbach & Edelbrock, 1983). The externalizing factor represents extroversive behaviors such as aggression, acting out, overactivity, disobedience, delinquency, and impulsivity. The internalizing factor represents problems of a different nature (e.g., worries, fears, somatic complaints, anxiety, and depression). These factors sometimes overlap and are not mutually exclusive (i.e., persons may be both conduct disordered and depressed). Social skills deficits certainly are implied in both factors.

Students with either externalizing or internalizing disorders may be at particular risk in general class placements, albeit for different reasons. Students characterized as externalizers have historically been perceived negatively by teachers and peers, and continue to be so despite our best attempts at social skills training aimed at successful integration into general class settings. They continue to be rejected by both teachers and peers in general education settings. Students characterized by internalizing disorders (particularly those who are depressed and /or anxious) are at risk of being placed in general education classrooms with teachers who are unequipped and therefore unable to offer the support the students may need to function in that setting. Thus, in addition to possible academic failure, we have concerns about social competence and acceptance of students with EBD, and the ability of educators in a general education setting to provide needed support via affective or therapeutic interventions. A further concern is grounded in the legality of full inclusion policies and that which MacMillan, Gresham, and Forness (1996) termed, the "assault on the continuum of placements" (p. 150).

Four areas associated with the unilateral placement of all students with EBD full-time in general education classrooms are problematic: (1) The inappropriateness of the general education curriculum for many of these students; (2) The lack of social acceptance and other social competence issues in general education settings; (3) The lack of mental health interventions and supports in general education settings; and (4) The fact that wholesale placement decisions for special education students is illegal.

Each is discussed in further detail in support of the position against inclusion.

Curriculum

Curricular decisions may be the single most important issue pertaining to the inclusion of students with EBD. By law (IDEA), a professional/parent team is charged with the task of delineating exactly what an individual student needs to learn. It is imperative, once the individualized education plan is established, to assure that teachers are teaching what the student needs to learn. Herein lies the difficulty for special education students.

Standardized vs. individualized curriculum. General education curriculum is standardized–not based on presenting symptoms or individualized assessment–but rather on national and state goals (e.g., National Education Goals Panel, 1994). Therefore, unless it is determined that a student with emotional and behavioral problems needs to learn only a college-bound curricula, then placement exclusively with teachers who teach only that content makes little sense.

The National Education Goals, established in 1990 by the nation's governors (Buzbee, 1995) challenged general education to produce responsible, informed citizens ready for productive employment. That same group, along with myriad state education agencies and local school boards, has decided that the best way to reach this goal is through a standardized curricula emphasizing English, math, science, foreign languages, civics, economics, art, history and geography (National Education Goals Panel, 1994). For students with EBD who usually display severe social/behavioral problems, psychological pathology, lower than average intelligence, possible neurological deficits, high rates of drug abuse, low motivation, and high rates of contact with law enforcement agencies (Knitzer et al., 1990; Bassett et al., 1996), the pathway to responsible citizenship may not be through mastery of science and math content. Instead of, or in addition to, academics these students may need to learn self-control skills, coping strategies, social skills, learning strategies, functional life skills, vocational skills, and social problem-solving (Knitzer, 1990; Brooks & Sabatino, 1996).

However, if these skills are to be taught in general education classrooms, then first, general education teachers would have to give up academic instructional time to do it; second, they would need to be trained to teach these skills; and third, they must be willing to teach alternate curricula to only a few of their large numbers of students. This scenario seems unlikely (Beals, 1983; Scanlon, Deshler, & Schumaker, 1996; MacMillan, Gresham, & Forness, 1996) since the general education charge is to teach more academic content with higher mastery standards, and since general educators apparently were unable to teach these things to the students with EBD prior to special education referral. Thus, placement in general education classrooms may actually preclude the mastery of critical curriculum objectives.

Mixed results from general education placement. Even if it is determined that a student with EBD should master a predominantly academic curriculum, the assumption that the general education classroom is the best place for all students to learn academic content has not been substantiated. Although most research on academic achievement of students with disabilities in general education classes has not specifically focused on students with EBD (MacMillan et al., 1996), research with students with mild disabilities may be used to draw some conclusions; to date, this research is mixed (e.g., Fisher, Schumaker, & Deshler, 1995).

Some studies of included students with mild disabilities have found that special education students in general education classrooms improved academically (Lipsky & Gartner, 1996; Wolak, York, and Corbin, 1992; Maheady, Sacca, & Harper, 1988; Slavin, Madden, & Leavey, 1984b; Higgens & Boone, 1992; Kelly, Gersten, & Carnine, 1990). Most of these studies inspected specific "inclusive practices" utilized in general education classrooms (e.g., cooperative learning, peer tutoring, strategy instruction) rather than placement alone, and some found improvement only when class sizes were smaller and some pullout resource room instruction was utilized (e.g., Maheady et al., 1988; Pomerantz, Windell, & Smith, 1994; Marston, 1996). Since placement was not the dependent variable, conclusions about its effectiveness are not warranted.

Even with the presence of "inclusive practices," some studies found non-significant effects on the academic achievement of many included students (Slavin, Madden, & Leavey, 1984a; Jenkins et al., 1991; Bulgren, Schumaker, & Deshler, 1988; 1994). In one study, almost half of the special education students placed in general education classrooms did not improve their academic performance (Zigmond et al., 1995). Fuchs, Deshler, and Zigmond (1994) reported that many special education students with mild disabilities achieved better academically in special education classrooms than in general education classrooms. Given the mixed review regarding the effectiveness of general education classroom placement on academic achievement and the fact that few researchers have targeted students with EBD, recommending wholesale placement of these students in general education classes for the purpose of achieving academic curricula seems imprudent and, perhaps, unfair.

Another factor is that most of these students lag behind academically and lack the necessary prerequisites to succeed in the standardized curricula at their grade level (Knitzer et al., 1990; MacMillan et al., 1996). If these students are given tasks that are too difficult or that are different from those given other students in the class, then the effect may be inappropriate behavior on the part of the included student (Fox & Conroy, 1995). In this case, exposure to curricula that is frustrating and possibly irrelevant sets the stage for the very behaviors that resulted in the student's being labeled EBD in the first place.

Social Acceptance and Competence Issues

Sometimes placement into general education classrooms is recommended for the purpose of facilitating interpersonal relationships (Glassberg, 1994; Meadows, Neel, Scott, & Parker, 1994). Although studies assessing the social improvement of students with EBD in general education are mixed, results generally do not support the assumption of acceptance and improved peer relations. In addition, ample data suggests that students with EBD continue to be a concern for general education teachers because of the obvious implications for teaching and managing difficult behavior. Teachers and peers are the primary socialization agents in general education settings, and it appears that little progress has been made in combating their negative perceptions. Such perceptions may also have been embraced by many administrators in the system, as indicated during the negotiations on reauthorization of IDEA.

Social acceptance by teachers. Students labeled as emotionally or behaviorally disordered have, over the decades, been the least accepted of students in any disability category (Badt, 1957; Haring, Stern, & Cruickshank, 1958; Parish, Dyck, & Kappes, 1979; Johnson, 1987). Aggressive kids, even when compared to children with other behavior problems, evoke the most negative attitudes from teachers (Coleman, 1982; Walker, 1979, 1996; Mooney & Algozzine, 1978). As Walker and his colleagues explain, "They can put extreme pressures on the management and instructional skills of classroom teachers and often disrupt the instructional process for other children" (Walker et al., 1995, p. 13).

Some studies have assessed teacher attitudes relative to disability and have found, unsurprisingly, that general education teachers are more willing to deal with students they perceive to have mild disabilities over those that they perceive to have more serious learning and/or behavior problems (Berryman & Berryman, 1981; Center & Ward, 1987). Scruggs and Mastropieri (1996) addressed stability of teacher attitudes over time in their literature review of 28 studies of teacher self-reported perceptions of mainstreaming/inclusion conducted from 1958 to 1995. The sample included 10,560 teachers, the majority of whom reported acceptance of the concept of mainstreaming or inclusion in general. Fewer, although still a majority, reported that they were willing to include students with disabilities in their own classes; responses varied according to disability label and the perceived commensurate responsibilities. However, two-thirds to three-fourths of the teachers believed that they did not have sufficient time, skills, training, nor resources needed for mainstreaming/inclusion.

One of the most salient findings was that responses were consistent across time and geography, leading the authors to ponder that ". . . teachers regard students with disabilities in the context of procedural classroom concerns (which have improved little, if any, in recent decades) rather than in the context of social prejudice and attitudes toward social integration (which appear to have improved somewhat in recent decades)" (p. 71). It seems clear that while the majority of teachers are philosophically unopposed to such concepts as mainstreaming and full inclusion, they remain concerned about how students with disabilities will affect their own responsibilities in the classroom. Students with EBD, particularly aggressive ones, remain at the top of the list of teacher concerns.

Social acceptance by peers. One of the basic premises of full inclusion is that students with disabilities, once they are placed in general education classrooms, will become less stigmatized and more accepted by their peers without disabilities. This premise has yet to be borne out by research on full inclusion practices, especially with students with EBD.

Sale and Carey (1995) assessed perceptions of students with disabilities and their peers in a full inclusion elementary school. The school had instituted a policy whereby students were no longer referred and labeled with the traditional disability categories. Based upon both positive and negative peer nomination methods, the researchers found that the institution of full inclusion policies did not eliminate negative social perceptions about students with disabilities. The practice of not identifying students with special education labels did not improve sociometric status of these students. And although the researchers offered cautions with their interpretations, they further indicated that students with emotional/behavioral disorders were the lowest on social preference scores, even among students with disabilities. Findings such as these indicate that school-related behaviors of these students–with or without special education labels–continue to set them apart from their peers.

Sabornie and Kauffman (1985) studied the sociometric status of secondary students with EBD. Forty-three students with EBD in six schools were matched with controls and rated by peers in 33 physical education classrooms. In keeping with previously reported literature, students with EBD were ranked lower in status than matched controls without disabilities. Sabornie (1987) found similar results with an elementary sample of students with EBD and matched controls.

Social rejection is apparently established early and resistant to change (Coie & Dodge, 1983; Hollinger, 1987). Once negative perceptions have been established, peers are unforgiving and unwilling to change. In their work with aggressive and antisocial children, Walker and his colleagues have concluded that these children continue to be socially rejected even after extensive social skills training, and that social skills training is a necessary but not sufficient condition for changing the social status of these students (Walker, Colvin, & Ramsey, 1995).

These studies are consistent with the failure of Gresham (1982) to find that students with disabilities who were mainstreamed increased in either social competence or in acceptance by their peers. In one study, Farmer and Hollowell (1994) found that students with EBD did form friendships with their peers without disabilities in general education classrooms; however, the students in this study chose to associate with classmates who tended toward aggressive and disruptive behavior while supporting the problem behavior of students with EBD.

In their literature review, MacMillan, Gresham, and Forness (1996) make two additional points about acceptance and competence issues: (1) that students with disabilities who are placed in general education settings do not necessarily learn from the supposed better models of behavior provided therein; and (2) that the contact hypothesis may actually work in reverse, i.e., students with EBD may be viewed less favorably by peers when placed in general education classrooms. Again, the aggressive, externalizing behavior of many of these students causes them to be set apart from their peers.

Social acceptance by the system. Our concerns about lack of social acceptance are supported by the recent discipline debate over special education students who are aggressive and violent in the reauthorization process for IDEA (Individuals with Disabilities Act). This debate stemmed from the public's continuing concern about discipline in the public schools and the general attitude of vengeance toward aggressive youth (Elam, Rose, & Gallup, 1996; Rose, Gallup, & Elam, 1997). The debate also grew from dissatisfaction with the dual discipline system now separating special and general education students. The preferential treatment afforded to students with disabilities has often been the focus of local hearings and judicial reviews (Katsiyannis, 1995). For the first time since its inception, the right to a free appropriate public education (FAPE) was threatened for those special education students who displayed disruptive behavior (predominantly those with EBD).

Certain legislators sought to allow schools to expel disruptive students with no provision of educational services and with no regard to the relationship of the behavior and the disorder nor to the cause of the disruptive behavior. Only through extended negotiations with advocates did the reauthorization finally protect FAPE rights for all students with disabilities and provide safeguards for any change of placement for disciplinary reasons (Smith, 1997). Some educators believe that the unilateral inclusion of students with EBD in general education classrooms often acts as a setting event for disciplinary action, whereby school administrators rush to exclusion in order to maintain their legitimacy under public pressure (Katsiyannis & Maag, 1998) thus precipitating this attack on FAPE for disruptive special education students. The need for exclusion and further segregation (i.e., alternative school placement) may be reduced by the preservation of a full continuum of services, particularly self-contained classrooms.

Mental Health Support in General Education Classrooms

Most experts in the field of emotional and behavioral disorders agree that "short-term interventions with narrow foci are not likely to be successful with this population" (Greenbaum et al., 1996, p. 145). Given the complexity of their problems, the persistence over time, and the large numbers of negative outcomes in relation to school, adaptive behavior, and criminal activity, it is generally recommended that comprehensive and integrated services be provided (e.g., Knitzer, 1990; Greenbaum et al., 1996; Brooks & Sabatino, 1996; Pfeiffer & Reddy, 1998; Stroul & Friedman, 1986). These services might include case management, crisis intervention, group discussions and meetings, effective behavior management programs, self-control and social skills training, mental health services including individual and family counseling, family support, substance abuse intervention, prevocational and vocational training, a therapeutic and psychologically safe environment, interagency collaboration and funding, and a good teacher.

Providing these services does not necessarily preclude full-time placement in general education classes, but full-time placement in general education classes may preclude provision of some of these services and curricula (e.g., Knitzer, Steinberg, & Fleisch, 1990; MacMillan et al., 1996). Few, if any, general education teachers provide therapeutic group meetings on a regular basis or teach self-control and social skills, and few have the skills to structure appropriate peer relationships and assure psychological protection for emotionally fragile students (i.e., a therapeutic milieu). Only a few general education teachers, usually at the secondary level, address functional life skills, prevocational and/or vocational skills. The provision of crisis management, substance abuse intervention, and counseling may require students to be pulled from the general education classroom, resulting in their spending less time in academic instruction, possibly causing them to fall behind with subsequent behavioral ramifications. By definition, the full inclusion movement discourages any type of pull-out services, assuming that all necessary services can be provided in the general education classroom. Thus, many of the mental health interventions needed by this group of students may be rendered unavailable by full inclusion.

Full integration for students with EBD will work only when general educators reform their curricula to include goals for obtaining psychological resilience, mastering social competence, and developing lifelong learning strategies. Until this massive reform occurs, the inappropriate placement of students with EBD in general education classrooms might continue to result in students' failure to master what their peers can achieve, to learn important "life skills" material, and to receive appropriate treatment for their psychological disorders. Furthermore, it may actually precipitate inappropriate behavior, subsequently relegating these students to non-therapeutic segregated campuses such as alternative schools (Webber & Scheuermann, 1997).

Placement relies on decisions about curriculum and treatment for individual students. Placement is simply a means to an end, not the end itself. As Staples (1997) wrote in his short, clear description of special education, ". . . the central goal (of special education) was always to educate children who had traditionally been viewed as ineducable. Integration was an important but distinctly secondary objective. . . . Society needs to worry a good deal more about what these children are taught and a good deal less about who sits next to them in class" (p. 4B).

Legal Considerations

Whatever the philosophical and empirical bases for–or against–full inclusion may be, educators still must comply with laws governing special and general education. Case law stemming from lawsuits filed in the 1980s and 1990s has established recommendations regarding placement decisions for special education students and students with EBD specifically.

Much of what is advocated by full inclusion advocates has not been supported by the courts (see Little & Little, in this series). Although one of the litigants filed a petition to be heard before the Supreme Court, the Court refused to hear the case. To date, the Supreme Court has not reviewed a case related to inclusion of students with disabilities, leaving the highest authority with the various district and circuit courts.

It is important to note that in none of these cases did courts want to usurp the authority of educators in issues of curriculum or what constitutes appropriate instruction; rather, courts have sought to determine to what extent school districts have complied with the law by upholding the mandates of least restrictive environment, i.e., that children with disabilities be educated with children without disabilities to the maximum extent possible. Some rulings have been interpreted as favoring the continuum of placements, while other more recent ones have been interpreted as favoring inclusion. However, all of these cases involved students with mild to moderate mental disabilities who did not present serious management or behavior problems in their classrooms. *Clyde K. and Sheila K. v. Puyallup School District* (1994) brought these issues to the attention of the court.

Ryan K. was a fifteen-year-old diagnosed with attention deficit hyperactivity disorder and Tourette's syndrome who became increasingly disruptive. He had been placed in the general education classroom with supplementary resource room help. However, Ryan was eventually suspended after evidencing noncompliance, obscene language, and two serious assaults. School personnel recommended a change in placement to a special education program outside the school. Although parents initially agreed to the placement, they subsequently changed their minds and asked that Ryan be placed back in the general education classroom with an aide. The case was eventually heard by the Ninth Circuit Court of Appeals. According to Yell (1995), the court reasoned thus: (1) Academic benefits of general class placement: Ryan's testing indicated academic regression in spite of a number of aids and services. (2) Nonacademic benefits of general class placement: these were judged minimal, as Ryan did not benefit from modeling his peers without disabilities, and was described as a social isolate. (3) Effects of student's presence on others in the classroom: the most serious consideration by the court, as Ryan's aggressive behavior clearly had a highly negative effect on teachers and peers. The court also determined that the school has an obligation to provide all students a safe environment, and further, that school officials may take action when a student's behavior interferes with the learning of others. In this case, the court upheld that the special education program was the least restrictive environment for Ryan K.

Yell (1995), in his analysis of case law and IDEA relative to inclusion, summarizes thus: the legal preference is to educate students with disabilities, including those with EBD, in integrated settings, and schools must make good faith efforts to comply. With students with EBD who evidence behavior problems, supplementary aids and services may include behavior management plans, training the general education teacher in the management strategies, and use of a behavioral specialist as an aide. When an education in the general education classroom cannot be achieved with such aids, courts have supported placement in a more restrictive setting. More restrictive settings have been upheld in two instances: (1) when the student is not benefiting either academically or nonacademically from the general education classroom, and (2) when the student significantly disrupts the learning environment of other students.

Some students with EBD will meet both of these criteria, thus satisfying the legal requirements for placements outside the general education classroom. However, perhaps the most important point about case law and inclusion is that courts have made it clear that they will refuse to mandate full inclusion in all cases, but instead will consider each case on its individual merit (Yell, 1995). By preserving a continuum of placements for students with EBD, we will have the same opportunity: to decide each case on the basis of its individual merit. To do less is to shortchange students of their right to a free, appropriate public education in the least restrictive environment.

THE POSITION IN SUPPORT OF FULL INCLUSION

In Akira Kurosawa's Japanese film classic, *Rashomon,* an investigation yields four very different versions of a brutal attack and viewers are left with at least one conclusion when considering the truth: It's all in how you look at it. Clearly, some questions cannot be answered completely with data because interpretations are "in the eye of the beholder" and there are often too many variables (reporter, setting, intervention, type of students, research method) influencing outcomes. Consider the following:

> After extensively reviewing 19 research investigations of inclusive educational programs, Hunt and Goetz (1997) reached several favorable conclusions. The benefits of inclusion for students with severe disabilities included: (a) positive academic and learning outcomes, (b) acceptance, interactions, and friendships; and

(c) positive outcomes for peers as well. Alternatively, an extensive review of 11 articles representing eight models of inclusion, Manset and Semmel (1997) concluded, "[t]he answer to the question of whether inclusive programs are effective for students with mild disabilities is at best inconclusive." (p. 177)

Different authors, different methods, different settings, different students, different perspectives, different conclusions; it is all in how you look at it.

The position against full inclusion is grounded in four perceived problem areas: the inappropriateness of general education curriculum, the lack of social acceptance of special education students by their general education peers, the lack of mental health interventions in general education settings, and the legal mandates directing placement in least restrictive environments. Clearly, there are opinions and evidence to support the importance of considering these factors in making decisions about the appropriateness of blending the borders between general and special education placements. Interestingly, data to support full- or part-time placement of students with disabilities in special education classes are less prevalent and less well-regarded than opinions against inclusion. Put another way, eliminating inclusion in no way guarantees that curriculum decisions for students with disabilities will be appropriate, that they will be accepted, or that mental health interventions will be part of their educational programs. More importantly, providing education in special settings does not ensure that the intent of legislation designed to support individuals with disabilities will be realized.

To support full inclusion a slight change is included in its definition: continuous placement of all students with disabilities in general education settings, as long as this arrangement ensures a free, appropriate education. Such a definition presumes control of the need for a continuum of placements that is currently accepted as an integral part of the special education service delivery model. Similarly, the concept of least restrictive environment (LRE) also becomes a central point of controversy. According to the U. S. Department of Education (U. S. D. E., 1998), "[t]o the maximum extent appropriate, children with disabilities, including children in public or private institutions or other care facilities, are educated with children who are not disabled, and special classes, separate schooling, or other removal of children with disabilities from the regular educational environment occurs only when the nature or severity of the disability of a child is such that education in regular classes with the use of supplementary aids and services cannot be achieved satisfactorily" (p. 30).

Issues focused on *curriculum* limitations and unsatisfactory *social acceptance* are easiest to dismiss. There is no argument with the observation that much of what goes on in general education is inappropriate and unrewarding for students with disabilities. In fact, it is irrelevant and unprofitable for many students without disabilities. There is no argument that a college-bound curriculum emphasizing basic skills such as English, math, science, foreign languages, civics, economics, art, history, and geography is not appropriate for all students. Clearly, alternative content such as self-control skills, coping strategies, social skills, learning strategies, functional life skills, vocational skills, and social problem-solving should be a part of the curriculum for many students. The problems are not with the limitations of curriculum but more with the extent to which professionals can decide who shall receive what and where it will be taught. The risk in not making any curriculum accessible to all students is obvious and separate but unequal education is fundamentally wrong (*Brown v. Board of Education,* 1954).

Evidence that basic skills and alternative content are taught better by special education personnel are seldom provided in arguments against inclusion. More often, the implication is that since they are not taught or taught so poorly in general education, they will be taught to students with disabilities in special education. Similarly, if students with disabilities are not accepted in general education, where are the data showing that they are better accepted in special education? Lack of social acceptance is a long-standing problem that is not remedied by separation and exclusion.

None of the problems related to *inadequate curricula* or *insufficient social acceptance* are corrected by removing students with disabilities from general education classrooms. If the problem is appropriateness of curriculum or lack of social acceptance, then resources should be brought to bear to change the curriculum and foster social acceptance. There is no reason to believe that this cannot be done in general education settings with the support of special education personnel. If a successful alternative curriculum exists in special education and if methods for improving social acceptance are part of special education methods, making them part of general education is the challenge of full inclusion.

There is no argument with the need for *mental health support* in general education classrooms. Clearly, case management and crisis intervention services, therapeutic group discussions and meetings, effective behavior management programs, self-control and social skills training, individual and family counseling, family support programs, substance abuse interventions, prevocational and vocational training, safe environments, interagency collaboration, and good teachers should be available to students with disabilities. Again, the need for such support is universal, not particular (Pfeiffer & Reddy, 1998). If full-time placement in general education classes precludes provision of some of these services and supports, then changing general education is the remedy since there is little evidence that they will be available simply by moving to a special education classroom. And, if they can be provided within special education, then the challenge of full inclusion is to provide them for students receiving special education in general education classrooms as well. Besides, ". . . [s]ociety needs to worry a good deal more about what these children are taught and a good deal less about who sits next to them in class" (Staples, 1997, p. 4B). Mental health support is not beyond general education nor is it guaranteed by full- or part-time placement in special education.

The Individuals with Disabilities Education Act does not include reference to guaranteeing a continuum of services or defining "least restrictive environment" in fostering efforts to provide a free, appropriate education for students with disabilities. *Legal arguments* require judicial interpretations and courts have made it clear that they will not refuse to mandate full inclusion in all cases, but instead will consider each case on its individual merit (Yell, 1995). And, that is how legal concerns should be handled.

Before women were entitled to the right to vote, many thought it was a good idea to keep it from them. After all, a hundred years of history was tough to argue with, especially when the logic of the day went something like this: The forefathers have done just fine without them and think of the catastrophes they might cause.

Before people with disabilities were entitled to free, appropriate education, many thought it was a good idea to keep it from them. After all, a hundred years of institutional care, treatment, and education was tough to argue with, especially when the logic of the day went something like this: People with disabilities need protection from a society where they will not be treated well.

As they say, "We've come a long way baby." Today, women are important contributors in every area of American life. And, though some might argue that full equality has not been achieved, discrimination on the basis of gender is increasingly unacceptable. Equally great changes have been made in the lives of people with disabilities. Again, though some might argue that full inclusion has not been achieved, inferior treatment on the basis of disability is increasingly unacceptable. For example, during recent school years, approximately 12 percent of elementary and secondary students received special education services (a 44 percent increase since the beginning of the program in 1975) and 95 percent of those students were served in regular school buildings (U.S.D.E., 1996). Time in regular education and vocational classes for secondary education students was associated with positive results; secondary education students who succeeded in regular education had higher employment, independent living, and community participation rates. Of course, arguments about the value of practices like full inclusion are not made more or less acceptable with data.

CLOSING COMMENTS

Alex Mont stood in the middle of the Candlewood Elementary School cafeteria, his face flushed, his voice strained, almost frantic. The table where he always sat, alone and apart from everyone else, had been moved for afternoon band practice, and the rising din of children talking and lunch boxes clattering was like a sensory assault.

"It's too loud," he complained, hands over his ears. Suddenly, he flung off his glasses and collapsed to the floor, mumbling a string of numbers: "One million, 999,999 . . ."

Thirteen days later, the same 9-year-old boy, slightly buck-toothed and beaming with innocent delight, stood center stage in the Rockville school's gymnasium as his fourth-grade teacher presented him with a gold trophy as several hundred students applauded wildly. Many already knew the award was for his perfect score on a national mathematics test–the first such performance in Candlewood history, it was announced proudly. What they didn't know was that more than 85,000 students had taken the exam. Only 268 of them–including just seven fourth-graders–got every question right. (Levine, 1997, p. A1)

Alex is a boy with autism, an obviously complex disability. Autism is not part of the constellation of conditions and symptoms associated with serious emotional disturbance. Unlike Alex, most students with emotional and behavioral disabilities do not have competencies to overcome their problems and, too often, they are not tolerated as well by the general public or their peers. Regardless the anecdote nicely illustrates two sides of inclusion for students with disabilities. One is positive, the other negative. Clearly, behavior sometimes creates conditions that are difficult to manage, even for the most experienced teachers. This is a challenge that is part of teaching, and for some, it is overshadowed by the potential for positive learning and socialization experiences within a natural environment that can only be achieved when people with disabilities are fully included in America's schools and communities. And, if the natural environment fails to provide for them, then the natural environment and the people in it may need the intervention, not the people with disabilities and their educational placement. If the curriculum is not appropriate for students with behavior disorders, professionals should be worried that it is not appropriate for any students. The preferred approach is correcting the ills, inadequacies, and insufficiencies of general education for students with emotional and behavioral disorders by cooperation, collaboration, and connection, not by making a separate system for them especially when there is no guarantee that disunion will correct the problems.

REFERENCES

Achenbach, T. M., & Edelbrock, C. S. (1983). *Manual for the child behavior checklist.* Burlington, VT: University of Vermont Department of Psychiatry.

Algozzine, B., Maheady, L., Sacca, K. C., O'Shea, L., & O'Shea, D. (1990). Sometimes patent medicine works: A reply to Braaten, Kauffman, Braaten, Polsgrove, & Nelson. *Exceptional Children, 56*, 552-557.

Badt, M. (1957). Attitudes of university students toward exceptional children and special education. *Exceptional Children, 23*, 286-290.

Banerji, M., & Dailey, R. (1995). A study of the effects of an inclusion model on students with specific learning disabilities. *Journal of Learning Disabilities, 28*, 511-522.

Bassett, D. S., Jackson, L., Ferrell, K. A., Luckner, J., Hagerty, P. J., Bunsen, T. D., &

MacIsaac, D. (1996). Multiple perspectives on inclusive education: Reflections of a university faculty. *Teacher Education and Special Education, 19(4),* 355-386.

Beals, V. L. (1983). The effects of large group instruction on the acquisition of specific learning strategies by learning disabled adolescents. *Unpublished doctoral dissertation,* University of Kansas, Lawrence.

Berryman, J. D., & Berryman, C. R. (1981, April). *Use of the "Attitudes Toward Mainstreaming Scale" with rural Georgia teachers.* Paper presented at American Education Research Association, Los Angeles (ERIC Document Service No. ED 201 420).

Braaten, S., Kauffman, J. M., Braaten, B., Polsgrove, L., & Nelson, C. M. (1988). The regular education initiative: Patent medicine for behavioral disorders. *Exceptional Children, 54,* 21-27.

Brooks, B. L., & Sabatino, D. A. (1996). *Personal perspectives on emotional disturbance/behavioral disorders.* Austin, TX: Pro Ed.

Bulgren, J. A., Schumaker, J. B., & Deshler, D. D. (1988). Effectiveness of a concept teaching routine in enhancing the performance of LD students in secondary-level mainstream classes. *Learning Disability Quarterly, 11,* 3-17.

Bulgren, J. A., Schumaker, J. B., & Deshler, D. D. (1994). The effects of a recall enhancement routine on the test performance of secondary students with and without learning disabilities. *Learning Disabilities Research & Practice, 9(1),* 2-11.

Buzbee, S. (1995, November 19). *School goals effort gets middling report card.* Austin American Statesman, p. A27.

Center, Y., & Ward, J. (1987). Teachers' attitudes towards the integration of disabled children in regular schools. *The Exceptional Child, 31(1),* 41-56.

Clement, B., Laughlin, K., Lynch, P., Merryman, S. L., & Lamb, D. (1995, April). *Restructuring for inclusion through shared decision making and programmatic blending.* Presentation at the annual meeting of the Council for Exceptional Children, Indianapolis, IN.

Clyde K. & Sheila K. v. Puyallup School District, 21 IDELR 664, (9th Cir. 1994).

Coie, J. D., & Dodge, K. A. (1983). Continuities and changes in children's social status: A longitudinal five-year study. *Merrill-Palmer Quarterly, 29,* 261-262.

Coleman, M. C. (1996). *Emotional and behavioral disorders: Theory and practice* (3rd edition). Boston: Allyn & Bacon.

Coleman, M. C., & Gilliam, J. E. (1983). Disturbing behaviors in the classroom: A survey of teacher attitudes. *Journal of Special Education, 17(2),* 121-129.

Elam, S. M., Rose, L. C., & Gallup, A. M. (1996). The 28th annual Phi Delta Kappa/Gallup poll of the public's attitude toward the public schools. *Phi Delta Kappan, 78,* 41-59.

Farmer, T. W. (1994). *The social affiliations of students with emotional and behavioral disorders: Implications for intervention in a system of care.* Paper presented at the seventh annual conference on a system of care for children's mental health, Tampa, FL.

Farmer, T. W., & Hollowell, J. H. (1994). Social networks in mainstream classrooms: Social affiliations and behavioral characteristics of students with EBD, *Journal of Emotional and Behavioral Disorders, 2(3),* 143-155, 163.

Fessler, M. A., Rosenberg, M. S., & Rosenberg, L.A. (1991). Concomitant learning disabilities and learning problems among students with emotional/behavioral disorders. *Behavioral Disorders, 16,* 97-106.

Fisher, J. B., Schumaker, J. B., & Deshler, D. D. (1995). Searching for validated inclusive practices: A review of the literature. *Focus on Exceptional Children, 28(4),* 1-19.

Fuchs, D., Deshler, D., & Zigmond, N. (1994, March). *How expendable is general education ? How expendable is special education?* Paper presented at the meeting of the Learning Disabilities Association of America, Washington, DC.

Gersten, R., Walker, H. M., & Darch, C. (1988). Relationships between teachers' effectiveness and their tolerance for handicapped students: An exploratory study. *Exceptional Children, 54,* 433-438.

Gresham, F. (1982). Misguided mainstreaming: The case for social skills training with handicapped children. *Exceptional Children, 48,* 422-433.

Greenbaum, P. E., Derrick, R. F., Friedman, R. M., Kutash, K., Brown, E. C., Lardieri, S. P., & Pugh, A. M. (1996). National adolescent and child treatment study (NACTS): Outcomes for children with serious emotional and behavioral disturbance, *Journal of Emotional and Behavioral Disorders, 4(3),* 130-146.

Haring, N., Stern, G., & Cruickshank, W. (1958). *Attitudes of educators toward exceptional children.* Syracuse: Syracuse University Press.

Higgins, K., & Boone, R. (1992). Hypermedia computer study guides for social studies: Adapting a Canadian history text. *Social Education, 56(3),* 154-159.

Hollinger, J. D. (1987). Social skills for behaviorally disordered children as preparation for mainstreaming: Theory, practice, and new directions. *Remedial and Special Education, 8,* 17-27.

Hunt, P., & Goetz, L. (1997). Research on inclusive educational programs, practices, and outcomes for students with severe disabilities. *The Journal of Special Education, 31,* 3-29.

Jenkins, J. R., Jewell, M., Leicester, N., Jenkins, L., & Troutner, N.M. (1991). Development of a school building model for educating students with handicaps and at-risk students in general education classrooms. *Journal of Learning Disabilities, 24,* 311-320.

Johnson, A. (1987). Attitudes toward mainstreaming: Implications for inservice training and teaching the handicapped. *Education, 107,* 229-233.

Katsiyannis, A. (1995). Disciplining students with disabilities: What principals should know. *NASSP Bulletin, 79(575),* 92-96.

Katsiyannis, A., & Maag, J. W. (submitted for publication). *Disciplining students with disabilities: Practice considerations for implementing IDEA '97.*

Kauffman, J. M., Braaten, S., Nelson, C. M., Polsgrove, L., & Braaten, B. (1990). The regular education initiative and patent medicine: A rejoinder to Algozzine, Maheady, Sacca, O'Shea, & O'Shea. *Exceptional Children, 56,* 558-560.

Kelly, B., Gersten, R., & Carnine, D. (1990). Student error patterns as a function of curriculum design: Teaching fractions to remedial high school students and high school students with learning disabilities. *Journal of Learning Disabilities, 23(1),* 23-29.

Knitzer, J., Steinberg, Z., & Fleisch, B. (1990). *At the schoolhouse door.* New York: Bank Street College of Education.

Levine, S. (1997). A life not yet figured out. *The Washington Post,* pp. A1, A8.

Lipsky, D. K., & Gartner, A. (1996). Questions most often asked: What research says about inclusion. *Impact on Instructional Improvement, 25(1),* 77-82.

MacMillan, D. L., Gresham, F. M., & Forness, S. R. (1996). Full inclusion: An empirical perspective. *Behavioral Disorders, 21(2),* 145-159.

Maheady, L., Sacca, M. K., & Harper, G. F. (1988). Classwide peer tutoring with mildly handicapped high school students. *Exceptional Children, 55(1),* 52-59.

Manset, G., & Semmel, M. I. (1997). Are inclusive programs for students with mild disabilities effective? A comparative review of model programs. *The Journal of Special Education, 31,* 155-180.

Marston, D. (1996). A comparison of inclusion only, pull-out only, and combined service model for students with mild disabilities. *Journal of Special Education 30,* 121-132.

Mastropieri, M., Jenkins, V., & Scruggs, T. (1985). Academic and intellectual characteristics of behavior disordered children and youth. In R.B.Rutherford, Jr. (Ed.), *Severe behavior disorders of children and youth.* (Vol. 8, pp. 86-104). Reston, VA: Council for Children with Behavioral Disorders.

Mooney, C. & Algozzine, R. (1978). A comparison of the disturbingness of behaviors related to learning disability and emotional disturbance. *Journal of Abnormal Child Psychology, 6,* 401-406.

National Education Goals Panel (1994). *The national education goals report: Building a nation of learners.* Washington DC: U.S. Government Printing Office.

Parish, T., Dyck, N., & Kappes, B. (1979). Stereotypes concerning normal and handicapped children. *The Journal of Psychology, 102,* 63-70.

Pfeiffer, S. I., & Reddy, L. A. (1998). School-based mental health programs in the United States: Present status and a blueprint for the future. *School Psychology Review, 27(1),* 84-96.

Pomerantz, D. J., Windell, I. J., & Smith, M. A. (1994). The effects of classwide peer tutoring and accommodations on the acquisition of content area knowledge by elementary students with learning disabilities. *LD Forum, 19(2),* 28-32.

Rose, L. C., Gallup, A. M., & Elam, S. M. (1997). The 29th annual Phi Delta Kappa/Gallup poll of the public's attitude toward the public schools. *Phi Delta Kappan, 79,* 41-56.

Sabornie, E. J. (1987). Bi-directional social status of behaviorally disordered and non-handicapped elementary school pupils. *Behavioral Disorders, 12,* 45-57.

Sabornie, E. J., & Kauffman, J. M. (1985). Regular classroom sociometric status of behaviorally disordered students. *Behavioral Disorders, 10,* 268-274.

Sale, P., & Carey, S. M. (1995). The sociometric status of students with disabilities in a full inclusion school. *Exceptional Children, 62(1),* 6-19.

Scanlon, D., Deshler, D. D., & Schumaker, J. B. (1996). A strategy for students in inclusive classrooms to organize and represent content. *Learning Disabilities Research & Practice, 11,* 41-57.

Scruggs, T. E., & Mastropieri, M. A. (1996). Teacher perceptions of mainstreaming/inclusion, 1958-1995: A research synthesis. *Exceptional Children, 63,* 47-57.

Slavin, R. E., Madden, N. A., & Leavey, M. (1984a). Effects of cooperative learning and individualized instruction on mainstreamed students. *Exceptional Children, 50(5)*, 434-443.

Slavin, R. E., Madden, N. A., & Leavey, M. (1984b). Effects of team assisted individualization on the mathematics achievement of academically handicapped and nonhandicapped students. *Journal of Educational Psychology, 76(5)*, 813-819.

Smith, C. R. (1997). Advocacy for students with emotional and behavioral disorders: One call for redirected efforts. *Behavioral Disorders, 22*, 96-105.

Staples, B. (1997, September 28). *Mainstreaming not answer for disabled kids.* The Eugene Register-Guard, pp. 1B, 4B.

Stroul, B. A., & Friedman, R. M. (1986). *A system of care for severely emotionally disturbed children and youth.* Washington, DC: Georgetown University Child Development Center CASSP Technical Assistance Center.

U. S. Department of Education. (1996). *Eighteenth annual report to Congress on the implementation of the Individuals with Disabilities Education Act: To assure the free appropriate public education of all children with disabilities.* Washington, DC: Author.

U. S. Department of Education, Office of Special Education and Rehabilitative Services. (1998). *Individuals with Disabilities Education Act.* Washington, DC: Author.

Walker, H. M. (1979). *The acting-out child: Coping with classroom disruption.* Boston: Allyn & Bacon.

Walker, H. M., Colvin, G., & Ramsey, E. (1995). *Antisocial behavior in schools: Strategies and best practices.* Pacific Grove, CA.: Brooks/Cole.

Webber, J., & Scheuermann, B. (1997). A challenging future: Current barriers and recommended action for our field. *Behavioral Disorders, 22(3)*, 141-151.

Wolak, M., York, J., & Corbin, N. (1992). Building new capacities to overcome tradition-bound practices. *The School Administrator, 49(2)*, 26-28.

Vacc, N. A. (1968). A study of behavior disordered children in regular and special classes. *Exceptional Children, 35*, 197-204.

Yell, M. L. (1995). *Clyde K .and Sheila K. v. Puyallup School District:* The courts, inclusion, and students with behavioral disorders. *Behavioral Disorders, 20(3)*, 179-189.

Zigmond, N., Jenkins, J., Fuchs, L. S., Deno, S., Fuchs, D., Baker, J. N., Jenkins, L., & Couthino, M. (1995). Special education in restructured schools. Findings from three multi-year studies. *Phi Delta Kappan, 76*, 531-540.

Inclusion and Students with Mental Retardation: Theoretical Perspectives and Implications

Bryan G. Cook

Kent State University

Melvyn I. Semmel

University of California at Santa Barbara

SUMMARY. The present article examines the implications of inclusion for students with mental retardation. An overview of inclusion terminology and recent changes in the definition and classification of individuals with mental retardation are presented. The academic and social outcomes of students with mental retardation in inclusive settings are examined by employing tolerance theory, a joint model of outcome production, and a model of differentiated expectations. The analyses examine how inclusion interacts with the unique learning needs and characteristics of students with mild and severe mental retardation. The authors recommend implementing partial, not full, inclusion for most students with mental retardation; to consider the interaction of severity of disability and student variance in making inclusive placements to maximize social outcomes; and to continue to conduct theory-based research in an effort to provide the most appropriate education to students with mental retardation. *[Article copies available for a fee from The Haworth Document Delivery Service: 1-800-342-9678. E-mail address: getinfo@haworthpressinc.com <Website: http://www.haworthpressinc.com>]*

Address correspondence to: Bryan G. Cook, Kent State University, 405 White Hall, Kent, OH 44224 (e-mail: bcook@educ.kent.edu).

[Haworth co-indexing entry note]: "Inclusion and Students with Mental Retardation: Theoretical Perspectives and Implications." Cook, Bryan G., and Melvyn I. Semmel. Co-published simultaneously in *Special Services in the Schools* (The Haworth Press, Inc.) Vol. 15, No. 1/2, 1999, pp. 49-71; and: *Inclusion Practices with Special Needs Students: Theory, Research, and Application* (ed: Steven I. Pfeiffer, and Linda A. Reddy) The Haworth Press, Inc., 1999, pp. 49-71. Single or multiple copies of this article are available for a fee from The Haworth Document Delivery Service [1-800-342-9678, 9:00 a.m. - 5:00 p.m. (EST). E-mail address: getinfo@haworthpressinc.com].

49

KEYWORDS. Inclusion, mental retardation, developmental disabilities, tolerance theory

Examination of the educational programming and placement of students with mental retardation (MR) is an insightful perspective from which to analyze the inclusion debate. The field of MR and individuals with MR have traditionally played a defining role in inclusion advocacy and legislation. For example, Dunn's (1968) seminal position paper questioning the segregation of students with mild MR lent critical support and legitimacy to a nascent inclusion movement. Soon after, the landmark *Pennsylvania Association for Retarded Citizens (PARC) v. Commonwealth of Pennsylvania* decision of 1972 focused on the need to provide an appropriate public education for students with more severe MR. This decision helped to create legislation such as Public Law 94-142, which in turn provided a basis for recent inclusion initiatives.

Despite this intermingling of inclusion advocacy and the field of MR, the 1997 Annual Report to Congress indicated that only 8.6% of students classified as mentally retarded were fully included in a general education class (compared to 39.3% of student with specific learning disabilities, 37.4% of students with orthopedic impairments, 20.5% of students with serious emotional disturbance, and 9.1% of students with multiple disabilities). It appears that many educators, parents, and students with MR feel that they require specialized and intensive educational services and training that is not commonly available in general classrooms.

The population of students with MR also serves as an instructive vantage point for investigating inclusion because of the extreme diversity of needs, characteristics, and severity of disability presented by students within this classification. Students with mild MR have traditionally comprised the vast majority of the category. These students appear to be "the hypothetical average child living next door" (Hallahan & Kauffman, 1997, p. 120) and are not perceived to be "retarded" in many contexts or upon initial contact. Therefore, many educators expect that students with mild MR should experience success in inclusive classrooms without requiring intensive supports. Indeed, Wang, Reynolds and Walberg (1988) indicated that inclusion of students with mild disabilities is likely to succeed because few meaningful differences exist between these students and their non-disabled classmates.

Students with mild MR are therefore included more often than students with more severe MR. However, they may be less likely to receive the special supports required for generating successful outcomes in that environment due to their modal appearance. Even students with mild MR whose disability is initially "invisible" require specialized instruction and supports to be successful in school due to their unique needs.

Many students who previously would have been categorized at the mild end of the continuum of MR are now classified as slow learner or as having a learning disability (or are not found eligible for special education) due to changes in how MR is defined (i.e., a drop in the IQ cutoff from 80-85 to 70-75 and dual requirement of substantially sub-average adaptive behavior) and in attitudes toward the term mental retardation (which is typically viewed as more pejorative than other disability categories). In recent years, then, students with MR tend to have more severe and often multiple disabilities (Forness & Polloway, 1987). The increasingly large proportion of students with severe or profound MR poses unique challenges to inclusive educators because of the relatively large discrepancies between their needs, ability levels, and social functioning in comparison to their classmates. However, teachers, specialists, and peers are likely to immediately recognize these needs, adjust their expectations, and provide specialized treatment.

Subsequent sections of this article examine (a) the terminology of inclusion, (b) new definitional changes within the field of MR and their relation with inclusion reforms, (c) the impact of inclusion on the academic outcomes of students with MR–by employing tolerance theory and a model of joint outcome production (Gerber, 1988; Cook, Gerber, & Semmel, 1997), and (d) the impact of inclusion on the social outcomes of students with MR–by employing a model of differentiated expectations (Cook & Semmel, 1998).

CONCEPTUAL ISSUES
REGARDING INCLUSION TERMINOLOGY

We use the term inclusion to generically denote the placement of students with disabilities in general education classrooms. For our purposes, full inclusion occurs when all students with disabilities are placed in the general class for the entire school day. It is curious, and perhaps indicative of the often rhetorical manner in which these issues are debated, that the term *full* inclusion is sometimes used to describe less than what the phrase seems to imply. For example, it was recently reported that in, " . . . a model full-inclusion school, . . . students with disabilities spend almost all of their days in regular classes. . . . Here, mainstreaming will carry through after the assembly disperses" (Sack, 1998, p. 32).

Another important distinction lies in the amount of support assumed to be present in inclusive arrangements. For example, S. Stainback, W. Stainback, and Ayres (1996) define inclusion as, "providing all students within the mainstream with . . . any support and assistance they or their teachers require" (p. 35). While this definition provides an ideal, it departs from the reality of how inclusion is often implemented. General education teachers typically report that they do not feel prepared and do not receive enough support to carry out appropriate inclusion (Cook, Semmel, & Gerber, 1998; Scruggs & Mastropieri, 1996; Semmel, Abernathy, Butera, & Lesar, 1991). Such ideal definitions may be of little use in analyzing the implications of inclusion for actual students. For our purposes, inclusion refers only to physical placement in a general education classroom–which does not guarantee that students with disabilities are receiving sufficient supports or are meaningfully participating in the classroom.

DEFINITIONS OF MENTAL RETARDATION

The current definition for mental retardation put forth by the American Association on Mental Retardation (AAMR) refers to,

> substantial limitation in present functioning. It is characterized by significantly subaverage intellectual functioning existing concurrently with related limitations in two or more of the following adaptive skills areas: communication, self-care, home living, social skills, community use, self-direction, health and safety, functional academics, leisure, and work. Mental retardation manifests itself before the age of 18. (Luckason, Coulder, Polloway, Russ, Schalock, Snell, Spitalnick, & Stark, 1992, p. 1)

It is important to note that students categorized as having MR are characterized by significantly subaverage intellectual function in addition to limitations in adaptive skills thought to be necessary for successful independent functioning. The concomitant nature of these critical deficit areas make it unlikely for students with MR to experience academic success or achieve desired socio-emotional outcomes without significant supports, modifications, and accommodations.

Distinctions within the general category of MR have traditionally distinguished between the widely varied characteristics and needs of this population. For example, many experienced school personnel still use the terms EMR (educably mentally retarded) and TMR (trainable mentally retarded) to respectively distinguish between students with more mild and severe MR. The AAMR later adopted the classification scheme of mild, moderate, severe, and profound retardation–which correspond with measures of IQ–that is used in most contemporary schools (Hallahan & Kauffman, 1997).

The most recent changes in AAMR's system of categorization reflect, and are likely intended to influence, inclusion reforms. The 1992 classification scheme is not based on degree of disability exhibited by the child as were previous systems. Instead, students are classified by the level of support they require to function as competently as possible. Luckason et al. (1992) describe the four classifications as follows:

- *Intermittent*-Supports are not always needed, are typically short term, and may be of high and low intensity.
- *Limited*-Supports are time-limited but needed consistently over time.
- *Extensive*-Supports are needed regularly and frequently in at least some environments and are not time-limited.
- *Pervasive*-Supports are of high intensity, are needed constantly across environments, and may be of a life-sustaining nature.

The usefulness of this new classification has been called into question (MacMillan, Gresham, & Siperstein, 1993) and it is yet to be seen whether it will be widely adopted or exert substantial influence. Yet Luckason et al. (1992) suggest that the new classification is more meaningful because it results in labels that specify the environmental supports which enable competent functioning. By implying that disability is caused in large part by lack of appropriate supports, not solely by individual characteristics, this classification scheme may be interpreted to mean that *with the appropriate supports* students with

MR can be successful in any environment–including inclusive placements. Alternatively, advocates of traditional special education may interpret these same definitions as meaning that the specified levels of support necessitate a separate environment.

ACADEMIC OUTCOMES AND INCLUSION

Students classified as MR have unique learning styles and needs that appear to necessitate special instruction. At issue is whether instruction that meets the unique needs of students with MR and promotes appropriate academic outcomes can be delivered in inclusive classrooms. Inclusion proponents typically assume that successful full inclusion can occur without significantly increasing resources and without decreasing the educational opportunities and outcomes of non-disabled classmates. Although this is an appealing ideal, it necessitates that one or more of the following assumptions are met: (1) students with MR do not differ significantly from non-disabled classmates and therefore do not require significant instructional adaptations, (2) new technologies of instruction have been developed and implemented that allow teachers to address the learning characteristics of included students with MR without decreasing the educational opportunities of their classmates, (3) the efforts and attitudes of teachers have previously been less than optimal and improvements in such will result in increased instructional efficacy, (4) supports and resources available in special classes can be applied with equal or greater potency in general classes, and (5) significant new resources have become available and are applied to included students with MR. The following section provides a brief introduction to tolerance theory (Gerber, 1988) and a model of joint outcome production (Cook et al., 1997), which are employed to examine the validity of the above "arguable assumptions" (see Kauffman, Gerber, & Semmel, 1988).

Tolerance Theory and a Model of Joint Outcome Production

Tolerance theory holds that teachers can optimally address only a limited range of student characteristics given finite resources (resources are defined here to include both material resources, but primarily refer to personnel and resources imbued within teachers such as knowledge and expertise). "Teacher tolerance" denotes the unique range of student characteristics that a teacher can simultaneously address with effectiveness. The range of students that any specific teacher can include within their tolerance boundaries depends upon their experience, expertise, and available resources. Students who fall within teacher tolerance receive instruction that is tailored to their specific needs and learning characteristics. However, because the learning needs and characteristics of students in a class vary and resources are limited, teachers are unable to simultaneously meet the unique needs of all their students. Teachers, then, must make difficult decisions regarding which students are included within, and excluded from, their instructional tolerance.

Application of a model of joint outcome production is used to explicate tolerance theory's implications for students in heterogeneous classrooms. As posited by tolerance theory, teachers cannot optimally meet the varied educational needs of all students in a typical classroom. Any given mode of instruction engaged in by the teacher is designed to meet the needs of a range of students with relatively similar learning characteristics, and, in all likelihood, produces optimal (or near optimal) performance from those students. However, because student outcomes are produced simultaneously, or jointly, with other students in the same classroom, the same instruction necessarily results in far less than optimal performance from other students in the same class who fall outside of teacher tolerance. Thus, decisions regarding which students to include within teacher tolerance carry grave consequences; because other students educated jointly–in the same class–are receiving that same instruction which is not tailored to address their specific needs. For example, if teachers decide to focus on increasing the performance of their highest achieving students, they are likely to include these students in their tolerance boundaries by focusing their instruction on advanced enrichment activities. However, this shift in instructional focus has the effect of excluding low and modal achievers–who will not profit from the enrichment activities–from teacher tolerance and reducing their achievement gains. Until resources are increased to allow a one-to-one instructional arrangement (see Bloom, 1984) or student variance is somehow eliminated in classrooms, teachers are forced to make difficult decisions that benefit some of their students to the relative detriment of other students in the same class (Gerber & Semmel, 1985).

While scarce resources, student variance, joint outcome production, and limited teacher tolerance boundaries exist in special education classes as well, their consequences are often less severe. When a teacher devotes time to a group of students with similar needs, fewer students are left out of instructional tolerance because of the reduced number of students. Additionally, one or more instructional aides are typically available to work directly with the small group of remaining students. Although their instruction is typically not of the same quality as that provided by a well trained teacher, it is a better arrangement than being left to struggle without any assistance. The resource room provides an even closer approximation to the optimal one-to-one instructional arrangement, and is typically designed to group students with similar needs and learning styles together for instruction–thus allowing teachers to include all of the students within teacher tolerance.

Do the Learning Characteristics and Needs of Students with MR Differ?

If students with MR do not present significantly different instructional needs and styles from their nondisabled classmates, they fall within typical boundaries of teacher tolerance and receive instruction that is focused on their needs.

In contrast to this assumption, it appears somewhat obvious that students with severe to profound MR present significantly different educational needs and characteristics. In fact, students with severe and profound MR hold different education and life goals than most students, such as semi-independent living and supported employment. These different goals necessitate a different curriculum. Many students with more severe and profound MR engage in little of the traditional academics, but instead focus primarily on instruction designed to directly impact their post-school outcomes. For example, Snell (1988) suggested that teachers provide instruction in traditional academic subjects such as math and reading to students with severe and profound MR only in a functional capacity and only if the material is being learned. Functional and independent living skills such as dressing, cleaning one's clothes and living space, hygiene, communicating and socializing, paying bills, transportation, and job related skills take precedence over traditional subject matter. Separate curricula are a glaring example of how one teacher, with limited resources and a limited range of instructional tolerance, cannot simultaneously meet the needs of diverse students. When the teacher is engaged in teaching an academic curriculum, included students with severe MR receive less than optimal instruction in independent living, social, or job skills.

The claim that students with mild MR do not differ from non-disabled students is perhaps more plausible. Indeed, earlier mainstreaming efforts were driven by claims that instructionally relevant differences between students with mild disabilities and many of their non-disabled peers were artifacts of labeling, segregation, low expectations, and dead-end curricula in special classes (see Dunn, 1968, Wang et al., 1988). However, the academic characteristics of students with MR (problems in attention, memory, self-regulation and meta-cognition, language development, and motivation; Hallahan & Kauffman, 1997) suggest that they do not profit from typical instruction directed at modal and high achievers. Although students with mild MR and general students may receive instruction in similar academic areas, students with mild MR learn the material at a slower rate and have difficulty in *all* academic areas (Tarpley, 1997). Their knowledge base and academic progress typically resembles that of younger children (Lewis & Doorlag, 1995). Just as teachers cannot match their instruction to meet the needs of students from a variety of different grade levels, students with even mild MR present learning needs and characteristics that exclude them from typical boundaries of teacher tolerance.

Students with mild MR also frequently engage in distinct curricula to meet their unique needs and goals. One disturbing reminder of the need to directly address the unique needs of students with mild MR is their post-school outcomes. For example, Hasazi, Gordon, Roe, Hull, Finck, and Salembier (1985) reported that only 41 percent of students with mental retardation who had graduated from high school had full- or part-time jobs. The outcomes for individuals with disabilities who drop out is worse. To remediate these problematic outcomes, Patton, Polloway, Smith, Edgar, Clark, and Lee (1996) suggest that the education for students with mild MR focus on four outcomes: productive employment, self sufficiency and independence, life skills competence, and opportunity to participate successfully within schools and community. While some degree of inclusion is necessary to meet these goals, it appears that many of these critical outcomes are not adequately addressed in general education environments that typically stress academics. For example, Patton et al. stress the need for specific instruction related to home and family activities, social and interpersonal skills, health and safety skills, use of leisure time, and citizenship for students with mild MR. Given limited resources, general education teachers can not appropriately address these goals and curricula while simultaneously focusing on the needs of modal students.

Are New and Improved Instructional Technologies Being Employed?

Introduction of a new and improved instructional technology can expand or "elasticize" teacher tolerance without necessitating increased resources. Implementing an improved method of teaching enables instruction to meet the needs of a wider range of students at the same time. Students with MR may, under these circumstances, have their needs met in an inclusive environment without decreasing the quality of instruction offered to modal students.

Two popular instructional methods advanced to facilitate inclusion are peer tutoring and cooperative learning (S. Stainback & W. Stainback, 1996). The appeal of both methods is that other students can be employed as instructional agents, thus freeing the teacher to meet the unique needs of other students. However, the basis of appeal underscores the limitations of these methods. Regardless of how well they are trained and supervised, students should not be–except perhaps in the most unusual of circumstances–the instructional equivalent of a professional teacher. Further, peer tutoring and cooperative learning, when employed effectively, actually require increased commitments of teacher time (Gerber & Kauffman, 1981). Rather than freeing teachers, these techniques often constrict their availability to other students. Whereas these methods–when employed with fidelity–are superior to leaving students to flounder on their own, they do not constitute significantly improved teaching technologies capable of increasing academic outcomes for all students in inclusive classrooms.

W. Stainback, S. Stainback, and Moravec (1992) also suggested that constructivist instruction allows teachers to meet the needs of all students in inclusive classes. In this model, teachers facilitate learning and discovery rather than engage in direct instruction or traditional teaching. There are no pre-determined correct or incorrect reposes; true knowledge is gained only when the student discovers and constructs it themselves and is therefore inherently individualized.

Whatever response and learning that a student generates is a priori correct and meaningful for each individual student. The absence of correct answers and direct teaching may facilitate discovery and deeper acquisition of knowledge for some. Yet it leaves many without the fundamental knowledge and learning that is required for success in later life (Harris & Graham, 1996). There are correct and incorrect ways to perform on a job, balance a checkbook, and do your laundry. Use of constructivist models of instruction appears particularly troublesome for students with MR–who would not be in special education had they been able to discover appropriate solutions and responses given typical instruction or left to their own devices. Indeed, Scruggs and Mastropieri (in press) reported that students with mild MR did significantly worse on a science task that required discovery learning compared to same-age peers with learning disabilities and without disabilities. In fact, the students with MR typically learned nothing from the lesson until they received direct instruction. It appears that, rather than elasticizing teacher tolerance to include students with MR, constructivist methods actually restrict teacher tolerance, leaving included students with MR without appropriate instruction.

Can Teachers Perform Better?

If teachers have not been performing as well as they are capable, simply doing a better job expands teacher tolerance and increases the academic opportunities afforded to one group of students without decreasing opportunities for others. There undoubtedly exist specific teachers who can improve their performance and extend their instructional tolerance by increasing their effort. Yet it seems dubious to stake the success of childrens' education and a major reform initiative on the likelihood that teachers across the country are uniformly able to sustain a level of effort and efficacy substantially above that previously attained. The authors doubt whether teachers, on the whole, have done less than they are capable. And if perhaps they have, it appears that systemic changes in the institution of schooling–rather than pleas for harder work and longer hours–are required to maintain meaningful improvements.

Improved attitudes toward students with disabilities and inclusion are assumed to result in improved performance and are frequently cited as a necessary prerequisite for successful inclusion (Cook et al.,

1998; Villa & Thousand in this volume). Villa, Thousand, Meyers, and Nevin (1996) claim that attitudes toward inclusion are improving and may lead to improved efforts and instruction from general education teachers. However, while positive teacher attitudes may constitute a necessary condition for successful inclusion, they do not represent a sufficient condition. Positive attitudes alone will not produce appropriate academic outcomes in an inclusive class with significant student variance and limited personnel and resources. It is apparent that to meet the unique characteristics and needs of students with MR, inclusive teachers need increased resources or improved instructional strategies, or both, in addition to favorable attitudes.

Can Sufficient Resources Be Infused into General Classes?

Most of the potential problems with the inclusion of students with MR discussed above are rendered moot if special education resources (e.g., teachers and their expertise) follow students into general education environments without any loss of potency. Instruction is then simply delivered with equivalent support in a different setting.

However, resources are diluted as students with MR are dispersed upon implementation of inclusion if the tenet of natural proportions is followed. Natural proportions is an underlying assumption of the inclusion movement which holds that students with disabilities are placed in general education environments in naturally occurring proportions (S. Stainback et al., 1996). For example, let us assume that 10 students with MR previously attended a special day class with one teacher and two instructional aides. Upon the implementation of inclusion, one student is assigned to each of 10 general classes (approximating natural proportions). Each general education teacher requests that their class be team taught, and at the very least wants a full time instructional aide. Obviously, their desires cannot be met given constant resources. At any given time, the majority of students with MR receive no direct support from special education personnel in the new inclusive classes if personnel resources remain static. It should be recognized that the students with MR did not receive one-to-one instruction in the special day class. Yet the special education personnel were able to deliver instruction in small, relatively homogenous, groups at all times.

To solve this dilemma, many schools have gone to a "clustering" model of inclusion, placing many students with disabilities into one general education classroom (often the lowest achieving class). This arrangement allows one collaborating special education teacher (or instructional aide) to reach many students with special needs. Yet clustering may be interpreted by many inclusion advocates as a reinvention of special education and a violation of the spirit of inclusion (S. Stainback et al., 1996).

Of course, a significant increase that infuses all inclusive classrooms with sufficient resources to replicate or improve upon the instructional arrangements in special education environments also eliminates the problems discussed above. However, the magnitude of funds required is enormous (see above example of 10 students with MR applied on a national scale). The acquisition of such funding is highly unlikely, and made more improbable by claims of inclusion advocates that inclusion, rather than requiring additional funds, saves schools money (Lipsky & Gartner, 1996)–the money now spent on special education.

One final option exists that would allow included students with MR to receive undiminished instructional resources. Teachers or schools can elect to transfer resources from instruction aimed at higher achievers to instruction focused on students with MR. However, this option entails decreased educational opportunities for modal and high achieving students. It does not appear likely that taxpayers, teachers and schools will sacrifice mean outcomes to optimize the opportunities of students with MR. In fact, recent "world class" standards, proficiency testing (from which students with MR are often excluded), and rewards and sanctions demerits based on high mean achievement overtly pressure teachers to focus their instruction at the higher end of the achievement distribution (Cook et al., 1997). Gerber and Semmel (1997) relatedly cautioned that inclusion may be instituted primarily as a means to free resources previously devoted to special education for the purpose of raising mean achievement scores. It appears, then, that two of the strongest contemporary school reforms, inclusion and academic excellence, may lead to disastrous results for students with disabilities.

Conclusion

Based on applications of tolerance theory and a model of joint outcome production, full inclusion does not appear to lead to appropriate academic opportunities or outcomes for students with MR because (a) students with MR require significantly different instruction to meet their significantly different characteristics and goals, (b) significantly improved new technologies of instruction have not been developed, (c) teachers are already putting forth considerable effort given existing supports, (d) existing special education resources cannot be applied with equal or greater potency in general classes, (e) significant new resources have not become available, and (f) teachers are not likely to concentrate their instructional focus on students with MR to the relative detriment of non-disabled students.

A few caveats should be mentioned to qualify this analysis. Academic achievement is not the only consequential outcome of schooling, particularly for students with MR. Thus, if inclusion results in social benefits and enhances successful transition to life after school, it may still be a preferable option despite the problems associated with academic outcomes. Relatedly, although we feel that academics (and functional academics) play a vital part in the education of students with MR and are critical prerequisites of their ability to function successfully in post-school experiences, full-time segregation is not being advocated. On the contrary, we argue–as does federal law–for the amount of inclusion that maximizes the opportunity of students with MR to live independently and function as competently as possible (see Patton et al., 1996).

Recommendations. The most general recommendation derived from this analysis is that caution is warranted regarding, "the commitment to keep students with mental retardation within general education classrooms in spite of the frequent non-functionality of the curriculum in such programs" (Patton et al., 1996, p. 81). Typical general education programs simply do not and perhaps cannot meet the unique needs of students with MR. Unsuccessful inclusion is perhaps more of a danger for students with mild MR. School personnel may be more likely to believe that these students–who do not readily appear to have a disability–do not require special instruction or additional support to achieve appropriate academic outcomes. Alternatively, included students with more severe MR are likely to be accompanied by special education personnel in virtue of their apparent need for support. Paradoxically, then, students with mild MR may be at greater risk for failure in inclusive settings. It is recommended that school personnel make placement decisions for students with mild MR based on goals of productive employment, self sufficiency and independence, life skills competence, and opportunity to participate successfully within schools and community (Patton et al., 1996). These outcomes may be sacrificed if school personnel see inclusion as an end in and of itself.

SOCIAL OUTCOMES AND INCLUSION

Social outcomes such as acceptance and friendship have become primary goals of schooling, particularly for students with disabilities (Haring, 1991). This importance appears justified considering that loneliness, truancy, dropping out of school, juvenile delinquency, adult crime, psychopathology, poor job performance, and suicide have all been associated with low peer acceptance in childhood (see Parker & Asher, 1987). Inclusion was traditionally believed to result in improved peer acceptance for students with mild MR, due to their similarities with non-disabled peers (Christoplos & Renz, 1969; Dunn, 1968; Wang & Birch, 1984). However, decades of research indicate that students with mild MR are not well accepted in the general classroom (see Kaufman, Agard, & Semmel, 1985).

Research reporting that included students with mild MR are not well accepted was particularly foreboding because it was traditionally assumed students with mild disabilities were more likely to be accepted than students with severe disabilities (Burton & Hirshoren, 1979). Based on these assumptions and the importance placed on social outcomes for students with severe disabilities, placement in the general classroom was not considered a viable alternative for most students with severe MR until very recently (Grenot-Scheyer, 1994). However, a recent empirical literature base examining the acceptance of students with more severe disabilities indicated that many included students with severe disabilities were the most popular students in their class (Evans, Salisbury, Palombaro, Berryman, & Hollowood, 1992; Hall, 1994). Reflective of the traditional thinking regarding peer acceptance and severity of disability, Horne (1985) referred to findings that students with severe disabilities were better accepted than their peers with mild disabilities as inexplicable.

An Alternative Model of Acceptance and Severity of Disability

Labels such as MR are frequently denounced because of their presumed stigmatizing effects. However, Siperstein and Bak (1985) reported that peers use labels to adjust their expectations for students with disabilities, who receive less blame for atypical behavior. It appears that obvious indications of a severe disability serve a similar protective function. According to a model of differentiated expectations (Cook & Semmel, 1998) peers readily recognize the obvious cues presented by their included classmates with severe MR regarding their disability and adjust their expectations accordingly. Subsequently, rather than reject them for atypical behavior, classmates expect and excuse anomalous behaviors of their classmates with severe MR. In fact, atypical behavior may facilitate their acceptance. Dentler and Erikson (1959) theorized that group members who are consistently and obviously "deviant" actually enhance group functioning by exploring, testing, and demonstrating the limits of acceptable behavior. Because of this functional role, other group members protect, nurture, and accept individuals who fulfill the role of "protected deviant" (Dentler & Erikson). Students with severe MR are thus likely to receive some level of acceptance and protection *because* peers perceive them as being significantly different (see Cook, 1997; Cook & Semmel, 1998; Siperstein & Bak, 1985).

Appearing "normal"–as students with mild MR often do–has traditionally been interpreted as a factor that promotes acceptance. However, peers are likely to hold students with mild MR to modal and often unattainable expectations because their typical appearance does not excuse anomalous behavior or fulfill a functional role within the group. Thus, when students with mild MR display atypical and potentially threatening behavior, it leads to peer rejection, rather than being excused or disregarded. Paradoxically, students with mild MR are likely to be rejected in inclusive environments because they are *not* perceived by peers as consistently and obviously disabled (Cook, 1997; Cook & Semmel, 1998). Students with mild MR also typically have difficulty in initiating interactions from an early age (Kopp, Baker, & Brown, 1992; Pfeiffer & Baker, 1994), exacerbating the tendency for peers to reject them.

The Role of Contextual Group Characteristics

Sociologists posited that deviance is relative, determined by an interaction of individual characteristics with a particular group or audience (Dentler & Erikson, 1959; Erikson, 1962). Douglas (1971) provided the example that taking off your clothes can be perceived as deviant or extremely appropriate with different audiences. Cook and

Semmel (1998) proposed that the concept of relativity of deviance be applied to the case of inclusion to make predictions regarding the social outcomes of students with varying severity of disability included in classes with low and high student variance. We hypothesized that classrooms containing a great deal of student variance are less likely to perceive students as "deviant." For example, a classroom comprised of students reading from the first to the fourth grade level is likely to accept an incoming student reading at the second grade level as a modal member. Alternatively, a classroom with little student variance will have more rigid and narrow boundaries regarding acceptable behavior. Thus, the same student in the above example "stands out" in a low variance classroom composed of students reading solely at the fourth grade level.

The phenomenon of relativity of deviance appears to interact with the model of differentiated expectations presented above to yield recommendations for improving peer acceptance of included students with MR. The acceptance of students with severe MR was postulated to be a function of group recognition of consistent and extreme differences and the subsequent differentiation of classmates' expectations. The likelihood that peers recognize an included student with severe MR as qualitatively different, and subsequently differentiate their expectations, is heightened in a low variance classroom with relatively constricted tolerance boundaries regarding what is considered modal behavior.

Alternatively, the likelihood that students with mild MR are accepted in inclusive classes is theoretically associated with "fitting in" or not contradicting peers' initial expectations of modal behavior (based on their typical appearance). Thus, classes with greater student variance–which have more lax boundaries regarding what constitutes modal behavior–facilitate acceptance for students with mild MR. Cook and Semmel (1998) did indeed find significant classroom variance by severity of disability interaction effects on the peer acceptance of included students with disabilities. Students with severe disabilities received approximately the same proportion of acceptance nominations as non-disabled peers in low variance classrooms, but were significantly less accepted in high variance environments. Conversely, students with mild disabilities were better accepted in high variance inclusive classes.

Conclusion

Peer acceptance and social outcomes have been described as the most important outcome of schooling for students with disabilities (Grenot-Scheyer, 1994). It is also a frequent assumption that inclusion results in improved acceptance of students with mild MR in virtue of heightened contact with non-disabled peers (Dunn, 1968; Christoplos & Renz, 1969). However, students with MR, particularly those with mild MR, have typically experienced very low levels of peer acceptance in inclusive classes (Kaufman et al., 1985).

Recent research regarding a model of differentiated expectations and the interaction of classroom variance with severity of disability appears to generate direct recommendations for improving the peer acceptance of included students with MR. School professionals may facilitate acceptance of students with mild MR by placing them in high variance classrooms that contain students with widely varied achievement, behavior, and cultural characteristics. In these classrooms, peers are likely to accept a wider range of behaviors–including many exhibited by students with mild MR–as modal. Other interventions that lead to more relaxed peer tolerance without specifically calling attention to their disability (e.g., tolerance training) or that lead to more modal behavior of included students with mild MR (e.g., social skills training) may further increase opportunities for peer acceptance. Alternatively, initial findings indicate that the acceptance of students with severe MR is enhanced when they are placed in low variance classes in which they are more readily recognized as qualitatively different, subsequently excused for atypical behavior, and socialized into the role of a "protected deviant."

There is, perhaps, an inherent contradiction in the proposed strategy to increase the acceptance of included students with severe MR. Cook (1997) also found that included students with severe disabilities are more highly nurtured by classmates than students with mild disabilities, and that nurturance is associated with peer acceptance only for students with severe disabilities. Thus, it was speculated that acceptance of students with severe disabilities is based, at least to some degree, on peers' desires to take care of and parent them (see also Evans et al., 1992; Grenot-Scheyer, 1994; Hall, 1994; Stainback, W., Stainback, S., Moravec, & Jackson, 1992; Thousand & Villa in this volume). Placing students with severe MR in relatively homogenous groups in which their differences "stand out" even more markedly may result in increased peer acceptance, but is it a result of increased nurturance? If so, is it worth "purchasing" acceptance at the cost of a relationship based on nurturance and often void of extended interactions (see Evans et al., 1992)? Practices such as special friends programs or discussing a student with the class in their absence may improve peer acceptance by increasing feelings of difference and nurturance. While relationships devoid of nurturing are not desirable, it would appear to be in the best interest of students with and without disabilities to seek acceptance of students with severe MR without accentuating differences and heightening nurturance. It is suggested that school personnel prepare their students to accept and value diversity in general, and to be aware that some degree of rejection may, in fact, be a very normalized relationship.

CONCLUSION

Inclusion is, undoubtedly, one of the "hottest" reforms in contemporary education and is being implemented with increasing frequency. Rather than make a "leap of faith" regarding the merits of inclusion as Biklen (1989) suggests, inclusion initiatives appear to require increased scrutiny to ensure that we are providing students with disabilities the most appropriate education possible. The present analysis of inclusion and students with MR affords an insightful vantage to examine inclusion because of the historic involvement of the field in inclusion and the range of student characteristics and needs that fall within the category of MR.

The analysis focused on the impact of inclusion reforms for the academic and social outcomes of students with MR by employing concepts associated with tolerance theory, a model of joint outcome production, the relativity of deviance, and a model of differentiated expectations. The authors cautioned that full inclusion is not likely to yield appropriate academic outcomes for students with MR, particularly in the context of current demands for academic excellence, high standards, and high stakes testing. These concerns are magnified for students with mild MR, who may not initially appear to need significant supports. Although some degree of inclusion appears warranted to ensure that skills are generalizable, some form of traditional special education is required to meet the unique learning characteristics and needs of students with MR. With regard to social outcomes, it was recommended that simultaneous consideration of the severity of disability and classroom variance can result in improved acceptance in inclusive environments. Application of a model of differentiated expectations also raised question regarding the relation of peer acceptance and nurturance for students with severe disabilities. The special education community should strive to provide the maximum amount of inclusion that allows for appropriate academic and social outcomes. Yet inclusion, as an educational strategy, should not–in our view–be seen as an end in itself. An education that leads to productive and fulfilling lives includes a balance of experiences that meet the unique needs of the individual. For students with MR, we posit that an appropriate balance includes some amount of special education. To the degree that education prepares one for post-school life, full inclusion in school may paradoxically lead to reduced opportunities for inclusion in the community and a normalized post-school life.

Many proponents of inclusion claim that the reform initiative does not require, and cannot wait for, empirical justification (Biklen, 1991; S. Stainback & W. Stainback, 1996). However, the dangers of determining educational policy based on what feels good rather than what we know, to the best of our knowledge, to work are grave and far reaching (Wolfensberger, 1994). The theoretical and empirical work presented here represent one small part of what we hope is a large and ongoing movement to improve the quality of education for students with MR and other disabilities.

REFERENCES

Biklen, D. (1989). Making difference ordinary. In S. Stainback, W. Stainback, & M. Forest (Eds.), *Educating all students in the mainstream of regular education.* Baltimore: Paul H. Brookes Publishing Co.

Bloom, B. S. (1984). The 2 sigma problem: The search for methods of group instruction as effective as one-to-one tutoring. *Educational Researcher, 13,* 4-16.

Burton, T. A. & Hirshoren, A. (1979). The education of severely and profoundly retarded children: Are we sacrificing the child to the concept? *Exceptional Children, 45,* 598-602.

Christoplos, F., & Renz, P. (1969). A critical examination of special education programs. *Journal of Special Education, 3,* 371-380.

Cook, B. G. (1997). *The relationship of classroom variance and severity of disability to peer acceptance, self esteem, and quality of relationships of students integrated in general education classrooms.* Unpublished doctoral dissertation, University of California at Santa Barbara.

Cook, B. G., Gerber, M. M., & Semmel, M. I. (1997). Are effective schools reforms effective for all students? The implications of joint outcome production for school reform. *Exceptionality, 7*, 77-95.

Cook, B. G., & Semmel, M. I. (1998). *Peer acceptance of integrated students with disabilities as a function of severity of disability and classroom composition.* Manuscript submitted for publication.

Cook, B. G., Semmel, M. I., & Gerber, M. M. (1998). *Attitudes of principals and special education teachers toward integration: Critical differences of opinion.* Manuscript submitted for publication.

Dentler, R. A., & Erikson, K. T. (1959). The function of deviance in groups. *Social Problems, 7*, 98-107.

Douglas, J. D. (1971). *American social order: Social rules in a pluralistic society.* New York: Free Press.

Dunn, L. M. (1968). Special education for the mildly retarded–is much of it justifiable? *Exceptional Children, 35*, 5-22.

Erikson, K. T. (1962). Notes on the sociology of deviance. *Social Problems, 9*, 307-314.

Evans, I. M., Salisbury, C. L., Palombaro, M. M., Berryman, J., & Hollowood, T. M. (1992). Peer interactions and social acceptance of elementary-age children with severe disabilities in an inclusive school. *Journal of the Association for Persons with Severe Handicaps, 17*, 205-212.

Forness, S. R., & Polloway, E. A. (1987). Physical and psychiatric diagnoses of pupils with mild mental retardation currently being referred for related services. *Education and Training in Mental Retardation, 22*, 221-228.

Gerber, M. M. (1988). Tolerance and technology of instruction: Implications for special education reform. *Exceptional Children, 54*, 309-314.

Gerber, M., & Kauffman, J. M. (1981). Peer tutoring in academic settings. In P. S. Strain (Ed.) *The utilization of classroom peers as behavior change agents* (pp. 155-187). New York: Plenum Press.

Gerber, M. M. (1988). Tolerance and technology of instruction: Implications for special education reform. *Exceptional Children, 54*, 309-314.

Gerber, M. M., & Semmel, M. I. (1985). The microeconomics of referral and reintegration: A paradigm for evaluation of special education. *Studies in Educational Evaluation, 11*, 13-29.

Gerber, M. M., & Semmel, M. I. (1997). Why do educational reform commissions fail to address special education? In R. Ginsberg & D. N. Plank (Eds.), *Commissions, Reports, Reforms, and Educational Policy.* West Port, CT: Praeger.

Grenot-Scheyer, M. (1994). The nature of interactions between students with severe disabilities and their friends and acquaintances without disabilities. *Journal of the Association for Persons with Severe Handicaps, 19*, 253-262.

Hall, L. J. (1994). A descriptive assessment of social relationships in integrated classrooms. *Journal of the Association for Persons with Severe Handicaps, 19*, 302-313.

Hallahan, D. P., & Kauffman, J. M. (1997). *Exceptional learners: Introduction to special education* (7th Ed.). Boston: Allyn and Bacon.

Haring, T. G. (1991). Social relationships. In L. H. Meyer, C. A. Peck, & L. Brown

(Eds.) *Critical issues in the lives of people with severe disabilities.* Baltimore: Paul H. Brookes Publishing Co.

Harris, K. R., & Graham, S. (1996). Memo to constructivists: Skills count, too. *Educational Leadership, 53,* 26-29.

Hasazi, S. B., Gordon, L. R., Roe, C. A., Hull, M., Finck, K., & Salembier, G. (1985). A statewide follow-up on post-high school employment and residential status of students labeled "mentally retarded." *Education and Training of the Mentally Retarded, 20,* 222-234.

Horne, M. D. (1985). *Attitudes toward handicapped students: Professional, peer and parent reactions.* Hillsdale, NJ: Lawrence Erlbaum Associates.

Kauffman, J. M., Gerber, M. M., & Semmel, M. I. (1988). Arguable assumptions underlying the Regular Education Initiative. *Journal of Learning Disabilities, 21,* 6-11.

Kaufman, M., Agard, J. A., & Semmel, M. I. (1985). *Mainstreaming: Learners and their environment.* Cambridge, MA: Brookline Books.

Kopp, C. B., Baker, B. L., Brown, K. W. (1992). Social skills and their correlates: preschoolers with developmental delays. *American Journal on Mental Retardation, 96,* 432-441.

Lewis, R. B., & Doorlag, D. H. (1995). *Teaching special students in the mainstream* (4th Ed.). New York: Merrill/Macmillan.

Lipsky, D. K., & Gartner, A. (1996). Inclusive education and school restructuring. In W. Stainback & S. Stainback (Eds.), *Controversial issues confronting special education: Divergent perspectives* (2nd Ed.) (pp. 3-15). Boston: Allyn and Bacon.

Luckason, R., Coulder, D., Polloway, E., Russ, S., Schalock, R., Snell, M., Spitalnick, D., & Stark, I. (1992). *Mental retardation: Definition, classification, and systems of support.* Washington, DC: American Association on Mental Retardation.

MacMillan, D. L., Gresham, F. M., & Siperstein, G. N. (1993). Conceptual and psychometric concerns about the 1992 AAMR definition of mental retardation. *American Journal of Mental Retardation, 98,* 325-335.

Parker, J. G., & Asher, S. (1987). Peer relations and later personal adjustments: Are low-accepted children at-risk? *Psychological Bulletin, 102,* 357-389.

Patton, J. R., Polloway, E. A., Smith, T. E. C., Edgar, E., Clark, G. M., & Lee, S. (1996). Individuals with mild mental retardation: Postsecondary outcomes and implications for educational policy. *Education and Training in Mental Retardation and Developmental Disabilities, 31,* 77-85.

Pfeiffer, S. I., & Baker, B. (1994). Psychiatric disorders in mentally retarded children and adolescents: Diagnostic and treatment issues. In J. Blacher (Ed.). *When there's no place like home.* Baltimore: Paul H. Brookes.

Sack, J. L. (1998, March, 25). Side by side. *Education Week, 17* (28), 32-37.

Scruggs, T. E., & Mastropieri, M. A. (1996). Teacher perceptions of mainstreaming/inclusion, 1958-1995: A research synthesis. *Exceptional Children, 63,* 59-74.

Semmel, M. I., Abernathy, T. V., Butera, G., & Lesar, S. (1991). Teacher perceptions of the Regular Education Initiative. *Exceptional Children, 58,* 9-24.

Siperstein, G. N., & Bak, J. J. (1985). Effects of social behavior on children's attitudes toward their mildly and moderately mentally retarded peers. *American Journal of Mental Deficiency, 90,* 319-327.

Snell, M. E. (1988). Curriculum and methodology for individuals with severe disabilities. *Education and Training in Mental Retardation, 23,* 302-314.

Stainback, S., & Stainback, W. (1996). *Inclusion: A guide for educators.* Baltimore, MD: Paul H. Brookes Publishing Company.

Stainback, S., Stainback, W., & Ayres, B. (1996). Schools as inclusive communities. In W. Stainback & S. Stainback (Eds.), *Controversial issues confronting special education: Divergent perspectives, 2nd edition* (pp. 31-43). Boston: Allyn and Bacon.

Stainback, W., Stainback, S., & Moravec, J. (1992). Using curriculum to build inclusive classrooms. In S. Stainback & W. Stainback (Eds.), *Curriculum considerations in inclusive classrooms: Facilitating learning for all students* (pp. 65-84). Baltimore, MD: Paul H. Brookes.

Stainback, W., Stainback, S., Moravec, J., & Jackson, H. J. (1992). Concerns about full inclusion: An ethnographic investigation. In R. A. Villa, J. S. Thousand, W. Stainback, & S. Stainback (Eds.), *Restructuring for caring and effective education.* Baltimore: Paul H. Brookes.

Tarpley, P. L. (1997). Suggestions for teaching students with mental retardation in general education classrooms. In D. P. Hallahan, & J. M. Kauffman, *Exceptional learners: Introduction to special education* (7th Ed.). Boston: Allyn and Bacon.

U.S. Department of Education (1997). *Nineteenth annual report to Congress on the implementation of the Individuals with Disabilities Education Act.* Washington DC: Author.

Villa, R. A., Thousand, J. S., Meyers, H., & Nevin, A. (1996). Teacher and administrator perceptions of heterogeneous education. *Exceptional Children, 63,* 29-45.

Wang, M. C., & Birch, J. W. (1984). Effective special education in regular classes. *Exceptional Children, 50,* 391-398.

Wang, M. C., Reynolds, M. C., & Walberg, H. J. (1988). Integrating the children of the second system. *Phi Delta Kappan, 70,* 248-251.

Wolfensberger, W. (1994). A personal interpretation of the mental retardation scene in light of the "signs of the times." *Mental Retardation, 32,* 19-33.

Inclusion:
Welcoming, Valuing, and Supporting the Diverse Learning Needs of All Students in Shared General Education Environments

Jacqueline Thousand

California State University, San Marcos

Richard A. Villa

Bayridge (VT) Consortium Inc.

SUMMARY. In a growing number of schools in the United States, it now is possible to walk into elementary, middle, and secondary classrooms and observe students who could be identified as having moderate and severe cognitive, physical, and emotional disabilities successfully receiving their education together with similar-aged classmates who have no identified special education needs (Falvey, 1995; Lipsky & Gartner, 1997; Schrag, 1998; Villa & Thousand, 1995). This practice of welcoming, valuing, and supporting the diverse learning needs of all students in shared general education environments is referred to as inclusive education, inclusive schooling, or inclusion. This article examines inclusive education along a number of dimensions. First, the evolution of the inclusion moment is briefly examined. After the construct of "severe disability" is considered in the context of inclusive education, various rationale for inclusion are examined along with outcome

Address correspondence to: Dr. Jacqueline Thousand, College of Education, California State University, San Marcos, San Marcos, CA 92096-0001 (e-mail: jthousan@mail host1.csusm.edu).

[Haworth co-indexing entry note]: "Inclusion: Welcoming, Valuing, and Supporting the Diverse Learning Needs of All Students in Shared General Education Environments." Thousand, Jacqueline, and Richard A. Villa. Co-published simultaneously in *Special Services in the Schools* (The Haworth Press, Inc.) Vol. 15, No. 1/2, 1999, pp. 73-108; and: *Inclusion Practices with Special Needs Students: Theory, Research, and Application* (ed: Steven I. Pfeiffer, and Linda A. Reddy) The Haworth Press, Inc., 1999, pp. 73-108. Single or multiple copies of this article are available for a fee from The Haworth Document Delivery Service [1-800-342-9678, 9:00 a.m. - 5:00 p.m. (EST). E-mail address: getinfo@haworthpressinc.com].

data, legislation, and legal and U.S. Department of Education decisions which forward inclusive policy. Next, eight factors most frequently associated with successful inclusive education are described and discussed. In describing the factors, examples are provided of specific assessment, planning, and communication processes that support the inclusion of students with intensive cognitive, physical, and emotional disabilities. The article ends with a discussion of the implications of inclusive education for a 21st Century democracy. *[Article copies available for a fee from The Haworth Document Delivery Service: 1-800-342-9678. E-mail address: getinfo@haworthpressinc.com <Website: http://www.haworthpressinc.com>]*

KEYWORDS. General education, least restricted environment, in support of inclusion, factors of successful inclusion

HISTORICAL TREND TOWARD INCLUSIVE EDUCATION

For over a decade, researchers, policy-makers, parents, consumers, and educators have discussed changing the predominant delivery of special education services, using such terms as "mainstreaming," "integration," "regular education initiative," and "inclusion." These discussions have highlighted some of the perceived requirements for these new types of service delivery to be successful, including restructuring, merging general and special education, creating a unified educational system, and developing shared responsibility for students (Gartner & Lipsky, 1987; Lipsky & Gartner, 1997; Reynolds, Wang, & Walberg, 1987; Villa, Thousand, Stainback & Stainback, 1992; Wang, Reynolds, & Walberg, 1987).

The "regular education initiative" (REI), first proposed under that name by Madeline Will (1985), was the term originally used to convey the notion that students with mild disabilities could be served within the regular education setting. It was not long before advocacy efforts expanded the REI concept to incorporate serving all students, including those with severe and profound disabilities in general education classrooms in neighborhood schools (Biklen, 1988; Strully & Strully, 1985; Thousand et al., 1986; Villa & Thousand, 1988). By the 1990s, the concept had grown to one in which the focus was on "heterogeneous" schooling (frequently called "inclusionary schooling"), where all children are educated with necessary supports in general education environments in their local neighborhood schools (Villa & Thousand, 1988). In these schools, the traditional schooling paradigm was altered, with curriculum and instruction modified for *all* students (Falvey, 1995; Lipsky & Gartner, 1997; Neary, Halvorsen, Kronberg, & Kelly, 1992; Stainback & Stainback, 1990, 1992; Villa et al., 1992). During the past several years the movement toward inclusion has gained unparalleled momentum. By 1993, almost every state was implementing inclusion at some level (Webb, 1994).

Inclusion as Part and Parcel of Educational Reform

Tremendous attention at the federal, state, and local level is focused on educational reform. Policy makers are emphasizing the establishment of national and state standards, greater flexibility in the use of funds used to support categorical programs, and new more authentic forms of assessment. Until recently, the inclusive education movement was viewed as a separate initiative running parallel or even counter to concomitant general education reform efforts (Block & Haring, 1992). In contrast, as Udvari-Solner and Thousand (1995) illustrated, established and emerging general education theories in education actually emulate the principles and practices underpinning inclusionary education. General education school reform initiatives they identify as offering great promise for facilitating inclusive education include multicultural education, outcome-based education, multiple intelligence theory, interdisciplinary curriculum, constructivist learning, authentic assessment of student learning, multi-age groupings, use of technology in the classroom, forms of peer mediated instruction such as cooperative group learning, teaching responsibility and peacemaking, and collaborative teaming among adults and students.

Today the inclusion debate has expanded beyond special education and become part of the total school reform movement. Reports like *Winners All* by the National Association of State Boards of Education (NASBE) (1992) support the concept of inclusionary schools and urge states to create a new belief system of inclusion and to retrain teachers and revise funding formulas to support inclusive practice. Major educational organizations (e.g., Association of Supervision and Curriculum Development, 1992) have passed resolutions supporting the same notions.

In 1995, ten of the most prominent national educational associations (i.e., National Association of State Directors of Special Education, National Association of Elementary School Principals, National Association of Secondary School Principals, Council of Great City

Schools, American Association of School Administrators, National Association of State Boards of Education, National State Boards Association, Council for Exceptional Children, National Education Association, American Federation of Teachers) acknowledged schools successfully implementing inclusive schooling practices and identified their characteristics (Council for Exceptional Children, 1995):

- Diversity is valued and celebrated;
- The principal plays an active and supportive leadership role;
- All students work toward the same educational outcomes based on high standards;
- There is a sense of community in which everyone belongs, is accepted, and is supported by his or her peers and other members of the school community;
- There is an array of services;
- Flexible groupings, authentic and meaningful learning experiences, and developmentally appropriate curricula are accessible to all students;
- Research-based instructional strategies are used, and natural support networks are fostered across students and staff;
- Staff have changed roles that are more collaborative;
- There are new forms of accountability;
- There is access to necessary technology and physical modifications and accommodations; and
- Parents are embraced as equal partners.

It doesn't take much to notice that the characteristics of inclusive schools listed above are really modern day versions of the attributes of democratic schooling forwarded by John Dewey (1916) at the beginning of this century. Further, as many have noted, most current reform efforts are derived from and reviving Dewey's (1916) notions of education in a democratic society. Inclusive education is simply one thrust in the reform effort. Apple and Beane (1995), in *Democratic Schooling,* nicely explain the disposition of all of those involved in the democratic schooling movement (including those involved in inclusive schooling).

> Those involved in democratic schools see themselves as participants in communities of learning. By their very nature, these communities are diverse, and that diversity is prized, not viewed

as a problem. Such communities include people who reflect differences in age, culture, ethnicity, gender, socioeconomic class, aspirations, and abilities. These differences enrich the community and the range of views it might consider. Separating people of any age on the basis of these differences or using labels to stereotype them simply creates divisions and status systems that detract from the democratic nature of the community and the dignity of the individuals against whom such practices work so harshly. . . . In an authentically democratic community, all young people are also considered to have the right of access to all programs in the school and to the outcomes the school values. For this reason, those in democratic schools seek to assure that the school includes no institutional barriers to young people. (pp. 10-11)

WHO ARE STUDENTS WITH "SEVERE DISABILITIES"? WHY ARE THEY CONSIDERED SO CHALLENGING TO EDUCATE?

Whether or not a student is considered as having a severe disability often depends upon the idiosyncratic definition adopted by the state and community in which the student resides. The U.S. federal definition identifies students with severe disabilities as those who:

because of the intensity of their physical, mental, or emotional problems need highly specialized education, social, psychological, and medical services in order to maximize their full potential for useful and meaningful participation in society and for self-fulfillment. The term includes those children with disabilities with severe emotional disturbance (including schizophrenia), autism, severe and profound mental retardation, and those who have two or more serious disabilities such as deaf-blindness, mental retardation and blindness, and cerebral-palsy and deafness. (CFR chapter III, Sec. 315.4, 7-1-95, p.176)

At the local school level, such formal definitions oftentimes have little functional meaning or use. What is considered a "severe disability" varies from one school to the next and is contingent upon each school community's beliefs about and experience with students whose educational needs go beyond the school's standard curriculum or instructional practices (Thousand & Villa, 1993). For example, a school community with little experience accommodating for individual students may think of a new student with Down Syndrome as "severely disabled." A second school, with extensive experience accommodating for individual students who have a broad range of needs, may view a much more challenged student as "just another student" with unique needs that must be met. Given this phenomenon of "relativity," the term, *students with severe disabilities,* will be used throughout this article to represent those students with moderate and severe cognitive, physical, health and emotional/social disabilities described in the previous paragraphs as well as other students who, for whatever reason, are perceived by school personnel as "most challenging" to the current school culture or ecosystem.

As this volume illustrates, there has been and continues to be disagreement as to whether students with severe disabilities belong in general education classrooms, despite the fact that entire texts have been devoted to describing strategies that have been successful for including these and all students, regardless of their perceived exceptionalities, within general education and community environments (e.g., Falvey, 1995; Lipsky & Gartner, 1989, 1997; Stainback & Stainback, 1996; Thousand, Villa, & Nevin, 1994; Villa & Thousand, 1995). Years ago, Williams, Villa, Thousand, and Fox (1990) suggested that the special versus regular class placement debate was inappropriate for a number of reasons. The successful placement and education of students with intensive educational challenges in regular classes has been occurring for years in schools throughout the United States (e.g., Thousand et al., 1986). Furthermore, the Individuals with Disabilities Education Act (IDEA) clearly specifies placement of any student must be based upon the individual's identified needs, not the student's handicapping condition or categorical label. To even raise the question of whether regular class placement is appropriate for a category of learners (i.e., students with intensive educational needs) "assumes that placement can be made based upon handicapping condition without documentation, of an individual student's identified needs and examination of whether the needs could be met in a regular class-based placement" (Williams et al., 1990, p. 333). Finally, as will be elaborated later in this article, learning and social benefits in inclusive settings for students with and without disabilities have been documented (National Study of Inclusive Education, 1994, 1995; Stainback & Stainback, 1996; Villa, Thousand, Meyers, & Nevin, 1996), as have benefits for teachers, when educators collaborate to invent individualized responsive educational programs (Villa, Thousand, Nevin, & Malgeri, 1996).

The "Who belongs in general education?" placement question for students with severe disabilities may be inappropriate for all of the above reasons. Yet the norm within most schools is still for intensively challenged students to be educated in separate schools and classrooms for all or most of their day. Why? Gartner and Lipsky (in press) identify potential perceptual, cultural, and emotional barriers which cause people to balk at the idea of the inclusion of students with severe disabilities:

- Attitudes of disdain and prejudice;
- The belief that only those closer to "normal" can be/should be included;
- The belief that the needs of students with severe disabilities are unique and beyond the capacity of general educators;
- The "severity" of the disability;
- The need for more extensive related services to enable these students to benefit from instruction;
- The need for access to particularized expertise to support the student's academic and social learning;
- The relationship of educational goals for students with severe disabilities to the general education curriculum;
- Concern that the behavior of students with severe disabilities might be disruptive to the learning of other students in the general education classroom;
- Unfamiliarity with students with severe disabilities because the vast majority of them are served in settings apart from the district's general education population of teachers and students;
- The cost of providing special education and related services to students with severe disabilities; and
- The belief that functional life skills cannot be addressed in general education settings.

Nonetheless, despite these potential barriers, models of inclusive education for students with severe disabilities do exist and, in some places, have for some time. These living demonstrations have taught us much about how to facilitate systems change in the structure of the school and the school day, the everyday operation of the classroom, and the roles of educators, students, and community members, so that students with severe disabilities have equal educational opportunities, meaningful access to the general education curriculum, and effective educational and related services in neighborhood schools. Before sharing the "hows" of inclusive education learned in these schools, let us first examine the "whys" of inclusion–the data and related rationale for including students with disabilities in general education. Adults and students alike are more likely to learn *how* to do something (read "inclusive education") if they understand *why* doing so is important.

RATIONALE AND DATA IN SUPPORT OF INCLUSIVE EDUCATION

What leads people to get beyond their perceptual, cultural, and emotional barriers and shift their beliefs, attitudes, values, practices, and policy making toward more inclusive educational opportunities for students with identified learning differences? This section presents some of the rationale associated with the growing advocacy for inclusive schools where all students are welcomed, valued, supported, and learning in shared environments. For a more complete articulation of various rationale, examine Chapter 3 of Villa and Thousand's (1995) *Creating an Inclusive School.*

Efficacy Data: How Good Is Separate Special Education?

Over a decade ago, research reviews and meta-analyses known as the special education "efficacy studies" already showed that placement outside of general education had little or no positive effects for students regardless of the intensity or type of their disabilities (Lipsky & Gartner, 1989). Reviewing the findings, Lipsky and Gartner (1989) observed

> the basic premise of special education was that students with deficits will benefit from a unique body of knowledge and from smaller classes staffed by specially trained teachers using special materials. But there is no compelling body of evidence demonstrating that segregated special education programs have significant benefits for students. (p. 19)

A 1994 review of three meta-analyses concerned with the most effective settings for educating students with special needs concluded that regardless of the type of disability or grade level of the student, "special-needs students educated in regular classes do better academically and socially than comparable students in non-inclusive settings" (Baker, Wang, & Walberg 1994, p. 34).

Hunt, Farron-Davis, Beckstead, Curtis, and Goetz (1994) found that students with disabilities in inclusive settings had higher-quality individualized education programs (IEPs) and higher levels of engaged time compared to students with disabilities who were educated in separate classes.

Specifically, for students with severe disabilities, Keefe and Van Etten (1994) found higher levels of "active academic responding" and lower levels of competing behavior in general education settings as compared to segregated classes and schools. Hollowood, Salisbury, Rainforth, and Palombaro (1994) found the inclusion of students with severe disabilities not to be detrimental to classmates. Others found inclusion to enhance classmates' (Costello, 1991; Kaskinen-Chapman, 1992) as well as their own learning (e.g., Cole & Meyer, 1991; Hollowood, Salisbury, Rainforth, & Palombaro, 1994; Strain 1983; Staub & Peck, 1994) and to yield social and emotional benefits for all students, with self-esteem and attendance improving for some students considered "at risk" (Kelly, 1992). Burchard and Clark (1990) noted that for a child with severely maladjusted behavior it is considerably more cost effective to individualize services in the community than to place the child in a segregated residential program and that services provided in local schools and community are considered to be better.

In response to the fear that students with disabilities would have a detrimental effect on nondisabled classmates, Staub and Peck (1994) found in an analysis of studies using quasi-experimental designs, "no deceleration of academic behavior for nondisabled children" (p. 36) when children with mild, moderate, or severe disabilities were placed full time in general education. Sharpe, York, and Knight (1994) found no decline in the academic and behavioral performance on standardized tests and report card measures of the classmates of students with disabilities.

As for post-school employment data for graduates of separate special education programs, Wagner and colleagues (1991) found high levels of unemployment (over 50% one year post-graduation) and under-employment. In contrast, Ferguson and Ash (1989) found that the more time children with disabilities spent in regular classes, the more they achieved as adults in employment and continuing education. This held true regardless of the gender, race, SES, or type of disability of the child or the age when the child was afforded access to general education. In 1995, the United States Department of Education reported that "across a number of analyses of post-school results, the message was the same: those who spent more time in regular education experienced better results after high school" (p. 87).

Federal Legislation and Case Law

In response to current increases in advocacy for the inclusion of children with disabilities in general education, many ask whether the law regarding the education of children with disabilities has recently changed. The answer is both "no" and "yes." The answer is "no," because the Education of All Handicapped Children Act, promulgated in 1975, and all subsequent reauthorizations and amendments–have reflected Congress' preference for educating students with disabilities in regular classrooms with their peers. The answer is "yes," in that the June 1997 reauthorization of the law has shifted the burden of proof for exclusion to schools, so much so that Alan Gartner and Dorothy Lipsky (personal communication, December 6, 1997) suggested that the 1997 IDEA reauthorization and its amendments could be referred to as the *I*nclusion *D*evelopment and *E*xpansion *A*ct. Gartner and Lipsky (in press) explain.

> Indeed the Congress shifted the burden of school districts from specifying the extent to which a child with disabilities would participate with non-disabled children to requiring in the student's IEP an explanation of the extent to which the child will not participate. In effect, the Congress is saying that such participation is to be the norm, and exclusion needs to be explained and justified. The basic presumption becomes that children with disabilities are to be educated in general education classrooms with their same-aged peers unless there is a compelling educational justification for educating the child with a disability in a non-inclusive setting.

As for case law, since 1975, federal court cases have and continue to clarify the intent of the law in favor of the inclusion of students with disabilities in general education. For example, in 1983, the Roncker v. Walter case addressed the issue of "bringing educational services to the child" versus "bringing the child to the services." The case resolved in favor of integrated versus segregated placement and established a *principle of portability;* that is, "if a desirable service currently provided in a segregated setting can feasibly be delivered in an integrated setting, it would be inappropriate under P.L. 94-142 to provide the service in a segregated environment" (700 F. 2d at 1063). The 1988 U.S. Court of Appeals ruling in favor of Timothy W., a student with severe disabilities whose school district contended he was "too disabled" to be entitled to an education, clarified school districts' responsibility to educate all children and specified that the term *all* included in IDEA meant *all* children with disabilities, without exception. In 1993, the U.S. Court of Appeals for the Third Circuit upheld the right of Rafael Oberti, a boy with Down Syndrome, to receive his education in his neighborhood regular school with adequate and necessary supports, placing the *burden of proof* for compliance with the IDEA's mainstreaming requirements squarely upon the school district and the state rather than the family. In 1994, the U.S. Court of Appeals for the Ninth Circuit upheld the district court decision in the Holland v. Sacramento Unified School District case in which Judge Levi indicated that when school districts place students with disabilities, the presumption and *starting point is the mainstream.*

Philosophical Rationale

A third compelling rationale for inclusive education is moral, philosophical, and ethical in nature and compliments the data-based and legal rationale discussed above. This rationale is that categorical segregation of any subgroup of people is simply a violation of civil rights and the principle of *equal citizenship.* Many believe what Chief Justice Earl Warren clarified in the landmark *Brown v. Board of Education* decision over four decades ago, that is, that separateness in education can

> generate a feeling of inferiority as to [children's] status in the community that may affect their hearts and minds in a way unlikely ever to be undone. This sense of inferiority . . . affects the motivation of a child to learn . . . [and] has a tendency to retard . . . educational and mental development. (Warren, 1954, p. 493)

Many advocates of inclusive education see the parallels to other struggles for human and civil rights and recall images of school personnel of the 1950s and 60s blocking "white" schoolhouse doors in order to keep out African American children. In far too many communities, administrators, teachers, and other school personnel (e.g., social workers, school psychologists) figuratively still block the doors, but this time to keep out children with disabilities. The number one determinant of whether or not a child with disabilities has access to regular education is *where* the child's family happens to live.

Finally, Kozol (1991) and others, including the National Association of State Directors of Education (1994), remind us of the gross overrepresentation of minorities in special education and, thus, the racist aspect of separate education programs. For example, African American children are two to three times more likely to be placed in special education classes than European American children; while they are only half as likely to be placed in advanced or gifted programs (Gartner & Lipsky). Furthermore, more than a third of African American students in special education have stigmatizing labels of "retarded" or "emotionally disturbed," compared with fewer than a fifth of European American students.

EIGHT FACTORS
FOR SUCCESSFUL INCLUSIVE PRACTICE:
CHANGING ROLES OF SPECIAL SERVICES PERSONNEL

What have nearly 25 years of the implementation of P.L. 94-142/IDEA taught us about what facilitates successful inclusive education? Analysis of the reports from some 1000 school districts on their inclusive education efforts in the National Center on Educational Restructuring and Inclusion's *National Study* (1994, 1995) identifies at least eight factors for success: visionary leadership, collaboration, refocused use of assessment, support for staff and students, effective parental involvement, the implementation of effective program models, effective classroom practices, and funding. What follows is a description of the eight factors and specific National Center findings as well as suggestions for the role of special educators' and related services personnel in promoting each of the factors.

Factor 1: Visionary Leadership

Villa, Thousand, Meyers, and Nevin (1996), in a study of 32 inclusive school sites in five states and one Canadian province found the degree of administrative support and vision to be the most powerful predictor of general educators' attitude toward full inclusion. While traditionally leadership is viewed as emanating from the school superintendent or principal, in districts across the country the initial impetus for inclusive education has come from many sources. Visionaries may be educators, related services personnel (e.g., psychologists, occupational therapists), parents, students, and on occasion from a university or state-level project. The issue is less the initiator but more a recognition that for inclusive education to be successful ultimately all stakeholders must become involved. Who better to plant the seed and nurture the growth of an inclusive philosophy (and the accompanying practices) than the educational specialists who work with children and classroom teachers every day and whose training and background more likely has been in the areas in communication, human relations, and conflict resolution so critical to developing consensus for a vision.

Factor 2: Collaboration

Reports from school districts across the nation clearly indicate that the achievement of inclusive education presumes that no one person can or ought to be expected to have all the expertise required to meet the educational needs of all the students in the classroom. Having the *opportunity* to collaborate and to learn about and develop the *skills* to be effective and efficient collaborative team members (Thousand & Villa, 1992; in press) is a minimum requirement for inclusive education to work. In a study of over 600 educators, collaboration emerged as the only variable across general and special education teachers and administrators that predicted positive attitudes toward inclusion (Villa, Thousand, Nevin, & Meyers, 1996). Building planning teams, scheduling time for teachers to work together, recognizing teachers as problem solvers, conceptualizing teachers as front-line researchers–these means were all reported to the National Center on Educational Restructuring and Inclusion (1994, 1995) as critical for successful collaboration.

An example of role redefinition: The psychologist as collaborative team member. To illustrate the collaborative nature of special educators and related service providers in an inclusive school, let's examine how the role of the psychologist, one of the many specialists who provide student support, changes in a collaborative, inclusive school culture. Consider the case of Amy who is eligible for special education in the serious emotional disturbance category and who also has a diagnosis of Attention Deficit Hyperactivity Disorder (ADHD). Amy is preparing to transition from her local middle school to the district high school. The psychologist, having worked with Amy during her middle school years, attended her transition meetings along with Amy's mother, two current 8th grade teachers, her special education support teacher, the school nurse, two of the ninth grade high school teachers who would have Amy as a student in the coming year, the ninth grade special educator, and of course, Amy and her best friend, Heather.

In years past the high school staff might have looked to the school psychologist for "expert" opinions on the student's disability, questions about her behavior, and suggestions regarding how she should be taught. This day, the meeting took a different course as the current classroom teachers and special educator outlined Amy's learning strengths as well as areas that challenge her. Her mother shared feelings regarding Amy's prior school experience and described some of the challenges she faces in the home. Most importantly, Amy and Heather described learning situations and activities which Amy enjoyed and others which were difficult for her. This fact-finding was used with other assessment information to help the team identify learning priorities for Amy's IEP goals and to clarify general support needs and expectations for her participation within the general education curriculum.

Once these foundational decisions were made, the team asked the question, "What kind of supports will Amy need to be successful at the high school and to pursue her IEP objects?" The team decided that Amy and the school psychologist together would provide staff with general information regarding ADHD.

Amy's mother informed the team that she and Amy's physician had decided to try medication to see if it would counter the effects of ADHD. The team agrees that the school psychologist develop a behavioral data collection system for use by Amy's teachers and parents. This data would allow the physician to make informed decisions regarding dosage adjustments for optimal effect. In addition, the psychologist would meet with Amy regularly for social/emotional counseling and support and to obtain Amy's insights into her own academic and social functioning.

Amy's mother and 8th grade teachers both raised concerns regarding her peer relationships, which they both characterized as strained and often confrontational. The team agreed that the school psychologist and the ninth grade teachers would work together to develop a process for resolving conflicts (Johnson & Johnson, 1991). This process would be team taught to all incoming freshman students by teachers and the school psychologist. They also would instruct Amy and her classmates in these and other social skills within contexts in which they would need to be demonstrated, such as the classroom, lunchroom, hallways, study hall, and school bus. Aware of community resources, the school psychologist recommended that Amy participate in a week-long summer outdoor adventure learning program organized by the local social service agency with the community recreation program. This experience was aimed at enhancing important social skills such as teamwork, communication, problem-solving, and trust-building. A number of Amy's new classmates would be attending. The psychologist agreed to facilitate Amy's referral to the sponsoring agencies and ensure adequate supervision and crisis management plans and personnel were in place, should such supports be needed.

Factor 3: Refocused Use of Assessment

Historically, the practice of special education led to an overwhelming amount of special educators' and school psychologists' time being spent in assessment activities related to the determination of special education eligibility of a student (Levinson, 1990). Up to 50% of the special educator's and even more of a psychologist's time has been spent in non-instructional assessment and paperwork activities. This left little time for the special services personnel to offer other types of services which fall within their purview.

As a screening device for special education determination and classification, numerous studies have documented the inadequacy of the present system of assessment. According to assessment leader, James Ysseldyke, given one or another state's definition of learning disabilities, a substantial majority of all students would be so classified; indeed, he says, the determination is "little better than a flip of the coin." With regard to assessment as a measure of student progress, inclusive education schools and districts are reporting moving toward more "authentic assessment" designs, including the use of portfolios of students' work and performances, and generally working to refocus assessment. The 1997 reauthorized IDEA establishes dramatically new standards for assessment of *all* students, that requires the inclusion of students with significant disabilities.

Family-friendly assessment: The example of MAPs. Special services personnel also are in the position to introduce *family-friendly* tools for gathering information about an individual child and translating that information into a plan for future student goals as well as day-to-day instruction. Making Action Plans (MAPs) (Falvey, Forest, Pearpoint, & Rosenberg, 1995) is just such a process. It is particularly useful with students with severe disabilities whose needs and lives may be so complex that it is not always clear which directions are the "correct" ones to take. The MAPs process is initiated by gathering a team that includes the student, peers, family members, friends, and anyone else the student wants to attend, including school staff. With the help of a "neutral" facilitator, the team addresses a sequence of key questions in order to visualize creative schemes, short-term outcomes, and long-term goals for the student.

To illustrate the MAPs process in action, let's examine Juan's MAP, initiated at the start of his sophomore year in order to plan for his secondary and post-secondary life. Juan has Down Syndrome and is eligible for special education in the categorical area of mental retardation. Attending Juan's MAPs meeting were his family members (i.e., mother, father, brother, sister), two high school students (i.e., a football player and second friend); a counselor from the Department of Rehabilitation, and his advisor/counselor who represented the school staff. Together, they addressed the following questions:

1. What is Juan's history?
2. What are dreams for Juan?
3. What are nightmares for Juan?
4. Who is Juan? What are Juan's strengths, gifts, and abilities?
5. What are Juan's needs? What do we need to do to address those needs?
6. What do we need to do to achieve the dreams and avoid the nightmares?

Specifically, what would Juan's ideal education look like to make dreams happen?

In his MAPs meeting of approximately 90 minutes, Juan made clear to his family and team members that his priority dreams were to have a job, live in his own apartment, and have a family some day. It was discovered that Juan enjoys sports and dancing. He wants to live close to his family, yet be on his own. Community College was identified as a possible post-school option. Job exploration is needed. Thus far, Juan has worked at four different fast-food restaurants and no longer wants to work around food.

From the MAPs session, Juan's strengths were noted and IEP objectives were crafted that related to the global goals identified by Juan and his team in the session. Figure 1 shows a "Program-at-a-Glance" format for communicating this information. In their extensive work with educators in inclusive settings, Giangreco, Cloninger, and Iverson (1993) promote the use of this communication medium to enable all adults and peers who interact with a student to quickly and readily understand and act on a student's strengths and motivators, priority objectives, and critical management needs for ensuring safety, comfort, and success. The Individual Education Program/ General Education Matrix shown in Figure 2 extends this information by meshing a student's IEP goals with the classes, courses, and other daily activities available to students during, before, and after school (Giangreco et al., 1993). The matrix, when completed by a student's support team, suggests which classes or activities would most likely address priority objectives and helps to determine a student's schedule. Once the schedule is determined, it also offers educators a quick overview of which activities and classes priority objectives may be addressed.

One final communication tool for facilitating support is the Inclusive IEP Adaptation Checklist, completed for Juan in Figure 3. The checklist represents what Juan's IEP team considers reasonable and needed accommodations to facilitate Juan's learning and success. This checklist as well as Juan's Program-at-a-Glance is shared with any and all of the adults or youth who support Juan. Juan carries these summaries with him as well, so he can readily inform others and "advocate for" his interests and needs.

The vehicles for translating long-term dreams into specific goals and objectives, daily schedules, and individualized accommodations

FIGURE 1. Sample

Program-at-a-Glance

Student's Name: *Juan Sebastian*

Age 16

	Staff	Rm.
1	Copps	SC 123
2	Haggard	A 206
3	Eshilian	Study Skills
4	Bovette	L 123
5	Lablane	Voc. Skills
6	Miller	Study Skills

Lives with: Mother and father . . . (Sister and brother have moved out)

Positive Student Profile:	**IEP Objectives:**
Friendly	Self-regulate for behaviors
Stays with a Task	Type or say messages/communication
Good Sense of Humor	Deal with change
Very Motivated	Eye contact with students and adults
Very Artistic	Functional math
	Initiate conversations
	Vocational awareness
	Class participation
	Participate in Support Group
	Self-advocacy
	Use of mass transportation

Management Needs:

Needs support to maintain attention

Needs support to maintain behaviors in class

If necessary, have Juan leave class & not interrupt others while he goes to the Study Skills room or the Guidance Office.

Medical Needs: Has 1-2 seizures/year. Knows when they are coming.

Grading Accommodations: May need more time, large print, support from other students for note taking, or support at times from staff and students.

Other Comments:

Service Coordinator Elaine Easton   Extension 123

Parent/Guardian Adel and Roberto   Phone 888-555-1234

FIGURE 2. Individual Education Program/General Education Matrix

Matrix of Juan's IEP Objectives and the Schedule

Name *Juan Sebastian*   Grade/Age *Sophomore/16*   School Year *1998-1999*

IEP Objectives	World Civics	Geo- metry	English	P.E.	Biology	Coun- seling	Lunch	Assem- blies	Club Mtgs.	Pass- ing Periods	Peer Support Groups
1. Self-regulate impulsive behaviors	X	X	X	X	X	X	X	X	X	X	X
2. Type out a message for emotional					X						
3. Self- regulate to make changes	X	X	X	X	X	X	X	X	X	X	X
4. Eye contact with persons	X	X	X		X	X	X		X		X
5. Functional math	X	X	X	X	X	X	X	X	X	X	X
6. Initiate conversation	X		X	X		X	X		X	X	X
7. Vocational awareness exploration	X	X	X	X		X	X			X	
8. Member of class discussions											
9. Peer support group										X	
10. Public transportation											

suggested in this section are based upon three fundamental assumptions: (1) the student has a *caring support team* that meets regularly, communicates often and effectively with one another using these and other strategies, and holds the long-range dreams and nightmares in mind when making more short-term decisions with and on behalf of the student, (2) the *student* as well as peers and family members are *included as team members* at every step of the way (Villa & Thousand, 1996) and that their voices are heard and are as valued as the voices of the professionals (Thousand & Villa, 1992), and (3) the process used for futures planning

FIGURE 3. Sample Inclusive IEP Adaptation Checklist Which Identifies Appropriate and Needed Adaptations for Juan

INCLUSIVE IEP ADAPTATION CHECKLIST

STUDENT: Juan Sebastian   DOB: 4-25-82   DATE: 10-1-98
COMPLETED BY: RR

The following adaptations are appropriate and necessary for this student. Check all that apply.
(SEE STUDENT'S "PROGRAM-AT-A-GLANCE" FOR MORE INFORMATION)

Pacing
- **X** Extend time requirements
- ___ Allow breaks
- ___ Vary activity often
- ___ Omit assignments w/time situations
- **X** Texts sent home for summer preview
- ___ Home set of texts/materials

Environment
- ___ Preferential seating
- **X** Planned seating __**X**__ Classroom
  ___ Bus __**X**__ Lunchroom ___ Auditorium
- ___ Alter physical room arrangement
- ___ Define areas concretely
- ___ Reduce/minimize distractions:
  ___Visual _____ Auditory
  ___Spatial _____ Movement
- **X** Teach positive rules for use of space

Presentation of Subject Matter
- **X** Teach to student's learning style
  ___ Linguistic _____ Logical/Math
  __**X**__ Musical _____ Spatial
  ___ Bodily/Kinesthetic
  __**X**__Interpersonal _____ Intrapersonal
  ___Naturalistic
- **X** Model experiential learning
- **X** Utilize specialized curriculum
- **X** Tape lectures/discussions for replay
- **X** Teacher provide notes
- **X** NCR paper for peer to provide notes
- **X** Functionally apply academic skills
- **X** Present demonstrations (model)
- ___ Utilize manipulatives
- **X** Emphasize critical information
- **X** Preteach vocabulary
- **X** Make/use vocabulary files
- ___ Reduce language level of readings
- ___ Use total communication
- **X** Use facilitated communication
- ___ Use visual sequences

Materials
- **X** Arrangement of material on page
- **X** Taped texts and class materials
- ___ Highlighted texts/study guides
- ___ Use supplementary materials
- **X** Note-taking help: Xerox peer's notes
- **X** Large print
- ___ Special equipment:
  ___Calculator __**X**__ Computer _____ Other
  ___Video recorder ___ Adapted Phone
  ___Augmentative communication device

Assignments

- ___ Give directions in small, distinct steps
- ___ Use written backup for oral directions
- **X** Lower difficulty level; alter assignment
- **X** Shorten assignment
- ___ Reduce paper- and-pencil tasks
- ___ Read or tape-record directions to student
- **X** Use pictorial directions
- ___ Give extra cues or prompts
- **X** Allow student to record or type assignment
- ___ Adapt worksheets, packets
- ___ Avoid penalizing for spelling/penmanship

Self-Management/Follow Through
- **X** Visual daily schedule __**X**__ Calendars
- ___ Check often for understanding/review
- ___ Request parent reinforcement
- **X** Have student repeat directions
- ___ Teach study skills
- **X** Use study sheets to organize material
- **X** Use long-term assignment time lines
- **X** Review and practice in real setting
- **X** Teach skill in several settings/environments

Testing Adaptations
- **X** Oral _____ Short Answer __**X**__ Modify format
- **X** Multiple choice __**X**__ Pictures _____ Taped
- **X** Read test to student __**X**__ Apply in real setting
- **X** Preview language of test questions
- **X** Extend time frame __**X**__ Shorten length
- **X** Test administered by resource person

Social Interaction Support
- **X** Peer advocacy __**X**__ Peer tutoring
- **X** Structure activities to promote social interactions
- **X** Focus on social process, not activity/product
- **X** Cooperative learning groups

Teach social communication skills
- **X** Greetings __**X**__ Conversation turn taking
- **X** Sharing _____ Negotiation Other _____

Motivation and Reinforcement
- **X** Reinforce initiation __**X**__ Offer choice
- **X** Use strengths/interest often
- **X** Concrete reinforcement (e.g., tokens, stickers)
- ___ Plan motivating sequences of activities

(e.g., MAPs) is dynamic, meaning that *priorities*–dreams and nightmares–are *reexamined regularly.*

Role expansion and job satisfaction with refocused use of assessment. Both Juan's and Amy's scenarios offer snapshots of how the time, skills, and efforts of special services personnel can be shifted from formal assessment to curriculum-based, and family-centered assessment when students with disabilities are considered a part of the general education community. Assessment and evaluation remain important aspects of a special educators' and related service providers' (e.g., psychologist, speech and language therapist) role. However, as the above example of Amy's transition from middle school and Juan's MAPs illustrate, in inclusive schools the emphasis shifts to program development, curriculum-based and personalized student monitoring, and the provision of support and training (e.g., conflict resolution, peer mediation, self-management) to teachers as well as students. Further, Levinson, Fetchkan, and Hohenshil (1988) point out that school psychologist's can experience greater job satisfaction when they are able to expand their work efforts beyond the traditional assessment role boundaries. The same holds true for special educators and other related services personnel.

Factor 4: Support for Students and Staff

From the student vantage point, support for inclusion may mean integrating needed therapy services into the general school program; peer support such as "buddy systems" or "Circles of Friends" (Falvey et al., 1995); supplementary aids and services (including short- or long-term, part- or full-time paraprofessional support); and effective use of computer-aided technology and other assistive devices as classroom tools rather than fancy gadgets in a special room. Best practices in support provision are based upon an "only as much as needed" principle, in order to avoid inflicting "disabling help" on students who do not need or necessarily want the human or material support that could be provided. Thus, paraprofessionals are assigned to a class as a member of a teaching team, rather than "velcroed" to an individual child. The "only as much as needed" principle recognizes that related services are supposed to be educationally *necessary* (not all that might be to meet a child's other-than-educational needs) to enable the student to interact with the curriculum. It goes without saying that related services need to be coordinated, so that supports don't pull in opposite directions and actually pull the student away from the general education classroom and curriculum. See Giangreco, Prelock, Reid, Dennis, & Edelman (in press) for an in-depth treatment of these and other issues in delivering support services in inclusive schools.

Two support factors which are repeatedly identified as essential for the adults in the school to successfully implement inclusive education are (1) systematic staff development and (2) flexible planning time for special and general educators, classroom and other personnel, to work together. With regard to staff development, special services personnel have rich and diverse sets of skills which can shared through formal and informal methods to develop teachers' competence and confidence. Because many special service providers are not tied to a classroom like their general education teacher colleagues and because they have connections with many of the personnel in the school district, they have the flexibility to work with a broad range of people to identify, design, deliver, and evaluate training initiatives. As for flexible planning time, special service providers can support teachers by relieving them for meetings by taking over as the teacher to deliver social skills lessons, run class meetings, and focusing on other academic- or affect-related dimensions of the curriculum.

Schools attempting to include, support, and empower all students have expanded the potential list of collaborators and support personnel to include *students* themselves. Table 1 provides examples of ways in which students have provided support as instructors, decision-makers, and advocates for themselves and others in inclusive schools.

Factor 5: Effective Parental Involvement

Inclusive schools report the importance of parental participation. They encourage parental involvement by providing family support services, as well as the development of educational programs that engage parents as co-learners with their children. Programs that bring a wide array of services to children in the school settings report at least two sets of benefits–direct benefits to the children and the opportunities for parents and other family members to become involved in school-based activities. As the child in an inclusive school becomes a part of the fabric of the school along with her/his nondisabled peers, so, too, the parents of children with disabilities become less isolated.

The 1997 IDEA renewal also enhances parental participation. It does so by requiring their participation in all eligibility and placement

TABLE 1. Collaborative Support Roles for Students

- Students as instructors in cooperative group learning, partner learning, and adult-student teaching team arrangements.
- Students as members of collaborative planning teams that determine accommodations for themselves and other classmates experiencing academic or behavioral challenges.
- Students supporting a peer through a "peer buddy" system or Circle of Friends (Forest & Lusthaus, 1989).
- Students as coaches for their instructors offering feedback regarding the effectiveness and consistency of their instructional and discipline procedures.
- Students who are troubled or troubling serving on a student council or principal advisory committee to help set school rules and consequences for students and teachers and make recommendations on how to improve the school climate (Curwin & Mendler, 1988).
- Students trained to serve as peacemakers in conflict situations on the playground, in the school building, and in life outside of the school (Johnson & Johnson, 1991; Kreidler, 1984; Schrumpf, 1994).
- Older students teaching violence prevention information to younger students.
- Students establishing a violence-or-crime-prevention club in which they identify crime problems and develop strategies to reduce them (Pitcher & Poland, 1992).
- Students as members of curriculum, inservice, and other school governance committees, such as the school board or student-operated "Jury of Peers" for dealing with student behavioral infractions.

decisions involving their child(ren) and by requiring that they be informed about their child(ren)'s progress no less frequently than is the district's practice for nondisabled children. What IDEA 1997 does for special service providers is set a common national standard for minimal parent participation which in the past represented "best practice." What exemplary educational specialists did for families in the past, now must be done by all.

Factor 6: Implementation of Effective Program Models

There are many partnership and shared responsibility models of inclusion that have been successful (National Study, 1994; 1995). They include:

- a co-teaching model, where the special educator (and other support personnel such as the psychologist) co-teaches alongside the general education teacher;
- parallel teaching, where the special educator (and other support personnel such as the psychologist) works with a small group of students from a selected special education population in a section of the general education classroom;

- co-teaching consultant model, where the special educator (and other support personnel such as the psychologist) provides assistance to the general educator, enabling her/him to teach all the students in the inclusive class;
- a team model, where the special educator (and other support personnel such as the psychologist) joins with one or more general education teachers to form a team, sharing responsibility for all the children in the inclusive classroom;
- methods and resource teacher model, where the special educator (and other support personnel such as the psychologist), whose students have been distributed in general education classes, works with the general education teachers, providing direct instruction, modeling of lessons, and consultation; and
- a dually-licensed teacher, who holds both general and special education certification and, thus, is equipped to teach all of the students in an inclusive classroom (with the support of other support personnel such as the psychologist).

Schools have had success with each of these designs or variations of the designs. Factors in adopting a particular model are local decision-making and educators' preferences. Basic to any design is a strong professional development component that includes formal training and ongoing technical assistance both prior to and during the initiation of the model. As previously noted, special services personnel can play a central role in organizing and providing training and technical assistance. They can model for others role redefinition and role release as they "hand over" their diagnostic, instructional, behavior management, counseling, and other "discipline-specific" skills through modeling, coaching, and support in the classroom. Perhaps, most importantly, they can provide emotional support to classroom teachers and one another as they all go through the process of role transformation.

Factor 7: Effective Classroom Practices

Effective classroom practices, as reported by districts implementing inclusive education, have two over-arching characteristics. The first is that the adaptations appropriate for students with disabilities benefit all students. The second is that the instructional strategies used in inclusive classrooms are practices recommended by educational reformers and researchers for general education students. Cooperative learning is the most important instructional strategy supporting inclusive education. Well over half of the districts implementing inclusive education included in the National Center on Educational Restructuring and Inclusion's *National Study* (1994, 1995) reported using cooperative learning. Additional instructional strategies cited by a quarter or more of the districts include curricular adaptations; students supporting other students; paraprofessional support, and use of instructional technology. See Thousand, Villa, and Nevin (1994) and Villa and Thousand (1995) for descriptions of ways to implement these and other instructional strategies that support inclusive education.

Additional effective practices for students with severe emotional/behavioral challenges. Inevitably, when asked "Which are the most difficult students for you to have in your classroom?" the vast majority of teachers will reply "Those students who have severe behavioral and emotional challenges; those students who repeatedly violate the rules; and those students who might pose a danger to me and the other students." Clearly, it is not possible to guarantee that every classroom is completely safe. Aggression and violence is a problem found in all aspects of North American society–at home, on the streets, and in restaurants, malls, and workplaces. Concomitantly, an increasing number of children are perceived as troubled or troubling to their teachers, community, or family. Clearly, this is a societal problem that is not solely education's responsibility. *Permanent* solutions to student and societal violence will only emerge through community, interagency, and school collaboration. Yet, there are some emerging school-based solutions to make schools safer and more welcoming learning environments and to address the needs of students with severe behavioral/emotional challenges as well.

Clearly, the most effective and first "line of defense" against student rule-violating behavior is effective instruction, personalized accommodations, and motivating learning. However, a constellation of additional resources and services needs to be developed and brought to students experiencing behavioral/emotional challenges. This constellation includes, but is not limited to, strategies for promoting and teaching responsibility; social skills instruction; teaching students anger management and impulse control strategies; strategies for involving, empowering, and supporting students; strategies for involving, supporting, and empowering family members; increasing collaboration among and personal support to students from the adults of the school; and, getting creative in developing alternatives to what constitutes a student's day (see Villa, Udis, & Thousand, 1994 for a detailed description of these resources).

It is critical to emphasize that these and other supports and services for assisting students who are "troubled or troubling" can be brought *to* the school setting. It is not necessary to send students away and immerse them in classrooms or separate programs exclusively for children identified emotionally or behaviorally challenging; it is counter-productive to send students with emotional/behavioral needs to a climate and culture of dysfunction and disturbance, where they will have limited access to prosocial models of behavior and be given the message that they do not belong with their peers (Kunc, 1992). Children tend to live up to expectations, positive and negative. Isolation, incarceration, and exclusion provide explicit messages to students about expectations and sets up a heartbreakingly viscous cycle. A person who feels a sense of alienation and exclusion is punished for giving evidence of lack of belonging through disruptive behavior by being further excluded and alienated, which then gives rise to accelerated rule violating behavior.

A basic responsibility of every school is to attempt to ensure students and adults freedom from physical harm. No student has the right to harm another person. We know there will be times when a student will place him or herself and others in jeopardy of being harmed. In anticipation of this, every school must have a well-articulated and well-understood crisis management system that promotes student responsibility and choice at each stage of a crisis. Choices within a crisis management system may include: (a) allowing a student to "calm down" in a predetermined alternative setting in the school; (b) allowing students, with parental permission, to leave school grounds for a period of time; (c) in-school or out-of-school suspension for a short period of time until a team can convene and identify the "next steps"; (d) removal from school by a parent, mental health, social service, or police personnel; and (e) the use of passive physical restraint by trained personnel. It is imperative that if a student is asked to leave school, he or she has a safe and supervised place to go (Villa et al., 1995).

There is no denying that meeting the complex psychological and educational needs of students who are troubled or troubling is a difficult task. Matching intervention and support strategies to the life cir-

cumstances, stresses, and context from which an individual child oper-
ates requires thoughtful and careful consideration by teams of
educators, parents, and students who care about and are committed to
the child's survival and success.

*Additional effective practices for students with severe cognitive,
physical, and health challenges.* Students with severe cognitive,
physical, and health challenges are another set of students for whom
many teachers question the value of general education classroom experiences. A frequently asked question is why students who have very
different learning objectives from the majority of class members
would be included in activities that, at first glance, don't seem to relate
to the students' needs. Sometimes people don't realize just how rich
the general education environment is, particularly for a student with
intensive challenges. The variety of people, materials, and activities is
endless and provides an ongoing flow of opportunities for communication and human relationship building, incidental learning in areas
not yet targeted as priority objectives, and direct instruction in a student's high priority learning areas.

Key to ensuring a student's meaningful participation is the creative
thinking of the members of the student's educational support team.
The team always has at least four options for arranging a student's
participation in general education activities (Giangreco, Cloninger, &
Iverson, 1998). A student can do the *same* as everyone else (e.g.,
practice songs in Music). *Multi-level curriculum and instruction* can
occur; that is, all students are involved in a lesson in the same curriculum area, but are pursuing varying objectives at multiple levels based
upon their unique needs. For example, in math students may be applying computation skills at varying levels–some with complex word
problems, others with one-digit subtraction problems, and yet others
with materials that illustrate counting with correspondence. *Curriculum overlapping* involves students working in the same lesson, but
pursuing objectives from different curricular areas. For example, Bob,
a teenager with severe disabilities, was working in a cooperative group
in science class with two other students, using the lap tray attached to
his wheelchair as the team's work space. Most students were dissect-
ing frogs for the purpose of identifying body parts. Bob' objectives
came from the curriculum areas of communication and socialization.
One communication program (e.g., discrimination of objects including his blue drinking cup) was simple for Bob's teammates to carry out

along with their dissection throughout the activity. Another communication objective of vocalizing in reaction to others and events was frequently and readily achieved as Bob giggled and vocalized to teammates' wiggling of frog parts in the air. *Alternative activities* may be needed in a child's schedule to allow for community-based or work options or to address management needs (e.g., catheterization in the nurses office). Alternative activities also may be considered when a regular education activity cannot be adapted.

Extreme caution is advised in ruling an activity "impossible to adapt" or the general education classroom as inappropriate for a student with severe disabilities. Experience has taught the authors that general education (e.g., science class for Bob) can meet most needs of children with severe disabilities, given creative thinking and collaboration on the part of the adults and children of the school and greater community. Current theories of learning (e.g., Multiple Intelligences, constructivist learning), teaching practices which make subject matter including science more relevant and meaningful (e.g., cooperative group learning, project or activity-based learning, community-referenced activities), and authentic alternatives to paper and pencil assessment (e.g., artifact collection for a portfolio, role playing, demonstration) are now available to empower and equip educators to adapt instruction for any student, including one with a severe disability.

Finally, to make assumptions about an individual based upon a classification of disability is dangerous, as it can lead to tunnel vision. Specifically, it can blind others to an individual's strengths and abilities and cause them to see only the person's disability–a phenomenon Van der Klift and Kunc describe as "disability spread" (1994, p. 399). Without a student's strengths and abilities in view, it is easy to limit expectations, "over-accommodate," or ignore ways in which strengths and abilities can be employed to motivate and support a student's learning.

Factor 8: Funding

Historically, special education funding formulas favored restrictive placements for students in special education. The 1997 IDEA renewal now requires states to adopt policies that are "placement neutral"; that is, ones that do not contravene the law's program mandate as to least restrictive environment placement. Funds must follow the student, regardless of placement, and must be sufficient to provide the services necessary. Districts report that, in general, inclusive education programs are no more costly than segregated models ("Does inclusion cost more?" 1994; McLaughlin & Warren, 1994; Parrish, 1997). However, districts must anticipate one-time "conversion" costs, especially for necessary planning and professional development. Although special services personnel cannot single-handedly influence funding decisions, they certainly can play an important part in advocating for adequate financial support and in orchestrating the necessary planning and professional development activities needed at local school and district level.

IMPLICATIONS OF INCLUSION
FOR A 21st CENTURY DEMOCRACY

"Student diversity is only a problem because of the kind of school organization we have."

Nearly a decade ago the authors ended an article on strategies for educating learners with severe disabilities with this observation from a Holmes Group (1990) report and further noted that school organizations could and were changing so that diversity would *not* be the problem (Thousand & Villa, 1990). In this article we further proposed a united advocacy effort to promulgate national policy prohibiting segregated education for any youth by the year 2000. Advocacy in the 1990s led to a reauthorization of IDEA in 1997 which brings us much closer to a policy of no exclusion.

That same article ended with a call for research and a refinement of strategies for inclusive and personalized instruction, not only for students with severe disabilities, but for all students. We too have witnessed the implementation of assessment, instructional, and systems change strategies which have transformed schools, lives, and educational practice in communities that have chosen to embrace inclusive or democratic schooling. In terms of research, prominent journals (e.g., *Exceptional Children, Remedial and Special Education)* have devoted entire issues and regularly featured data-based articles which clarify the conditions under which inclusive education can be successful.

Sadly, despite the increasing knowledge base regarding inclusive practice, inclusive or democratic schools are not yet the norm in most communities in this country. Families still struggle to have their children with disabilities attend the local school and be welcomed and valued as members of the same classrooms as their nondisabled brothers and sisters. Why? Tom Skrtic offers one answer that has nothing to do with the skill or will of the educators of the school. Dr. Skrtic describes traditional school in the United States as professional bureaucracies that diminish teachers' ability to individualize for a great many students. He explains:

> The biggest problem is that schools are organized as professional bureaucracies . . . a contradiction in terms: Professionalization is intended to permit personalization; bureaucratization is intended to assure standardization. To blame the inability to individualize instruction totally on the capacity or will of professionals is misguided in that it blames the teacher for the inadequacies and contradictions of the organizational structure. This is the same kind of distortion of reality we make when we blame particular students for not learning from the existing standardized programs of the school organization. These students are the ones we call "handicapped," which is what I mean when I say that school organizations create "handicapped students." In both cases our tendency is to blame the victims–teachers who fail to individualize and students who fail to learn–for the inadequacies of the system. (Thousand, 1990, p. 31)

What we recommended at the time to counter this professional bureaucracy was the formation of adhoc teams or "adhocracies" within schools where educators could "mutually adjust their collective skills and knowledge to invent unique, personalized programs for each student" (Thousand, 1990, p. 32). This, in effect, is what educators do when they reorganize into the various teaching team models described in the previous section concerning effective program models. What happens when educators redefine their roles and relationships in ad hoc collaborative teaching and problem solving teams is they free themselves to be *inventors* who have an implicit understanding that educational programs must and always will be:

> . . . continuously invented and reinvented by teachers in actual practice with students who have unique and changing needs. . . . The value of the adhocracy is that it is configured for diversity whereas the professional bureaucracy is configured for homo-

geneity, and so must remove diversity from the system through means like special education and other pull-out programs. (Thousand, 1990, p. 32)

What Skrtic is suggesting is organizational restructuring of the nature that inclusive schools accomplish. Inclusive school communities succeed because they structure multiple ad hoc groups (including teaching teams of general and special services personnel), which form and dissolve as needed to address the instructional and organizational barriers to the invention of personalized learning opportunities. Members of inclusive school communities take responsibility and work to slay the "bureaucratic" dragons of standardization, end the discussion of *where* students with severe or other disabilities can or should be educated, and, instead, focus upon documenting, further refining, and disseminating the instructional, organizational, and technological innovations that allow them to respond to the diverse educational and psychological needs of their learners. The members of these school communities act on John Dewey's (1916) proposition that in a democracy it is not enough to have education for democracy–there also must be democracy in education. Namely, these people meet, discuss, and figure out how to reorganize themselves and their students (and gain community support) so that democracy in education can be a reality for all children.

To expand inclusive or democratic schooling nationwide, we, who are in or who are interested in education, must push the limits of our abilities to learn new skills, ways of thinking, and ways of dealing with our own and our colleagues' struggles to make behavioral, cognitive, and attitudinal transformations. We also must document *how* we go about doing all of this; that is, we must conduct the kind of "stories from the field" research Udvari-Solner and Keyes (in press) performed to supplement the lists of critical elements for successful inclusion that now appear in the literature (and in this chapter). As Udvari-Solner and Keyes observe, "inventories of recommendation without examples of situations or real-life challenges . . . to reform status quo practices fall short of providing direction and support for those in the throes of the system's change." Pushing our limits to effect change in educational systems and to talk about that change in ways that make sense to educators, families, and community members will be a challenge. But, as Pierre Tielhard de Chardin observed, "our duty as [humans] is to proceed as if limits to our abilities do not exist."

REFERENCES

Apple, M., & Beane, J. (1995). *Democratic schools.* Alexandria, VA: Association of Supervision and Curriculum Development.

Association for Supervision and Curriculum Development. (1992). *Resolutions, 1991.* Alexandria, VA: Author.

Baker, E., Wang, M., & Walberg, H. (1994). The effects of inclusion on learning. *Educational Leadership, 52* (4) 33-35.

Biklen, D. (1988). (Producer). (1988). *Regular lives* (Video). Washington, DC: State of the Art.

Block J. & Haring T. (1992). On swamps, bogs, alligators, and special education reform. In R. Villa, J. Thousand, W. Stainback, & S. Stainback (Eds.), *Restructuring for caring and effective education: An administrative guide to creating heterogeneous schools* (pp. 7-24). Baltimore: Paul H. Brookes Publishing.

Burchard, J. D., & Clark, R. T. (1990). The role of individualized care in a service delivery system for children and adolescents with severely maladjusted behavior. *The Journal of Mental Health Administration, 17*(1), 48-60.

Costello, C. (1991). A comparison of student cognitive and social achievement for handicapped and regular education students who are educated in integrated versus a substantially separate classroom. Unpublished doctoral dissertation. Amherst: University of Massachusetts.

Council for Exceptional Children (1995). *Inclusive schools: Lessons from 10 schools.* Reston, VA: Council for Exceptional Children.

Curwin, R., & Mendler, A. (1988). *Discipline with dignity.* Alexandria, VA: Association for Supervision and Curriculum Development.

Dewey, J. (1916). *Democracy and education.* New York: MacMillan.

Falvey, M. (1995). *Inclusive and heterogeneous schooling: Assessment, curriculum, and instruction.* Baltimore: Paul H. Brookes Publishing.

Falvey, M., Forest, M., Pearpoint, J., & Rosenberg, R. (1994). Building connections. In J. Thousand, R. Villa, & A. Nevin (Eds.). *Creativity and collaborative learning: A practical guide for empowering students and teachers* (pp. 347-368). Baltimore: Paul Brookes.

Ferguson, P. & Ash, A. (1989). Lessons from life: Personal and parental perspectives on school, childhood, and disability. In D. Biklen, A. Ford, & D. Ferguson (Eds.), *Disability and society,* pp. 108-140. Chicago: National Society for the Study of Education.

Forest, M., & Lusthaus, E. (1989). Promoting educational equality for all students: Circles and maps. In S. Stainback, W. Stainback, & M. Forest (Eds.), *Educating all students in the mainstream of regular education* (pp. 43-57). Baltimore: Paul H. Brookes Publishing Co.

Gartner, A., & Lipsky, D. (1987). Beyond special education: Toward a quality education system for all students. *Harvard Educational Review, 57,* 367-395.

Gartner, A., & Lipsky, D. (in press). Inclusion and school restructuring: A new synergy. In R. Villa & J. Thousand (Eds.), *Restructuring for caring and effective education: Putting the pieces of the puzzle together* (2nd. ed.). Baltimore: Paul H. Brookes.

Giangreco, M. F., Cloninger, C. J., & Iverson, V. S. (1993). *Choosing options and accommodations for children (COACH): A guide to educational planning for students with disabilities* (2nd ed.). Baltimore: Paul H. Brookes Publishing.

Giangreco, M., Prelock, P., Reid, R., Dennis, R., & Edelman, S. (in press). Roles of related service personnel in general education classrooms. In R. Villa & J. Thousand (Eds.), *Restructuring for caring and effective education: Putting the pieces of the puzzle together* (2nd. ed.). Baltimore: Paul H. Brookes Publishing.

Hollowood, T. M., Salisbury, C. L., Rainforth, B., & Palombaro, M. M. (1994). Use of instructional time in classrooms serving students with and without severe disabilities. *Exceptional Children, 61*(3), 242-253.

Holmes Group, The. (1990). *Tomorrow's schools: Principles for the design of professional development schools.* East Lansing, MI: Author.

Hunt, P., Farro-Davis, F., Beckstead, S., Curtis, D., & Goetz, L. (1994). Evaluating the effects of placement of students with severe disabilities in general education versus special class. *Journal of The Association for Persons with Severe Handicaps, 19*(4), 290-301.

Johnson, D. W., & Johnson, R. T. (1991). *Teaching students to be peacemakers.* Edina, MN: Interaction Book Co.

Kaskinen-Chapman, A. (1992). Saline Area Schools and inclusive community concepts. In R. Villa, J. Thousand, W. Stainback, & S. Stainback (Eds.), *Restructuring for caring and effective education* (pp. 169-185). Baltimore: Paul H. Brookes Publishing.

Keefe, E., & VanEtten, G. (1994, December 8). *Academic and social outcomes for students with moderate to profound disabilities in integrated settings.* Paper presented at conference of The Association for Persons with Severe Handicaps, Atlanta.

Kelly D. (1992). Introduction. In T. Neary, A. Halvorsen, R. Kronberg, & D. Kelly (Eds.), *Curricular adaptations for inclusive classrooms* (i-iv). San Francisco: California Research Institute for the Integration of Students with Severe Disabilities, San Francisco State University.

Kozol, J. (1991). *Savage inequalities: Children in America's schools.* New York: Harper Collins.

Kreidler, W. J. (1984). *Creative conflict resolution.* Glenview, IL: Scott, Foresman.

Kunc, N. (1992). The need to belong: Rediscovering Maslow's hierarchy of needs. In R. Villa, J. Thousand, W. Stainback, & S. Stainback (Eds.), *Restructuring for caring and effective education* (pp. 25-39). Baltimore: Paul H. Brookes Publishing.

Levinson, M. E. (1990). Actual/desired role functioning, perceived control over role functioning, and job satisfaction among school psychologists. *Psychology in the Schools, 27,* 64-74.

Levinson, M. E., Fetchkan, R., & Hohenshil, T. H. (1988). Job satisfaction among practicing school psychologist revisited. *School Psychology Review, 17,* 102-102.

Lipsky, D. & Gartner, A. (1989). *Beyond separate education: Quality education for all.* Baltimore: Paul H. Brookes Publishing.

Lipsky, D. & Gartner, A. (1997). *Inclusion and school reform: Transforming America's classrooms.* Baltimore: Paul H. Brookes Publishing.

McLaughlin, M. J., & Warren, S. H. (1994). *Resource implications for inclusion:*

Impressions of special educators at selected sites. Palo Alto, CA: Center for Special Education Finance.

National Association of State Boards of Education Study Group on Special Education. (1992). *Winners All: A call for inclusive schools.* Alexandria, VA: Author.

National Association of State Directors of Special Education (1994). Disproportionate representation. Alexandria, VA: Author.

National Study of Inclusive Education. (1994). New York: The City University of New York, National Center on Educational Restructuring and Inclusion.

National Study of Inclusive Education (1995). New York: The City University of New York, National Center on Educational Restructuring and Inclusion.

Neary, T., Halvorsen, A., Kronberg, R., & Kelly, D. (1992, December). *Curricular adaptations for inclusive classrooms.* California Research Institute for the Integration of Students With Severe Disabilities.

Oberti v. Board of Education, 995F. 2nd 1204 (3rd. Cir. 1993).

Parish, T. (1997). Fiscal issues relating to special education inclusion. In D. K. Lipsky & A. Gartner (Eds.). *Inclusion and school reform: Transforming America's classrooms* (pp. 275-298). Baltimore: Paul H. Brookes Publishing.

Pitcher, G. D., & Poland, S. (1992). *Crisis intervention in the schools.* New York: Guilford Press.

Reynolds, J. C., Wang, M. C., & Walberg, H. J. (1987). The necessary restructuring of special and regular education. *Exceptional Children, 53,* 391-398.

Roncker v. Walter. (1983). 700F.2d 1058, 1063 (6th Cir.) cert. denied, 464 U.S. 864.

Sacramento City Unified School District v. Rachael H., 14 F 3d 1398 (9th Cir. 1994).

Schrag, J. (February, 1998). *The continuum of educational options: Past, present, future.* Alexandria, VA: National Association of State Directors of Special Education.

Schrumpf, F. (1994). The role of students in resolving conflicts in schools. In J. Thousand, R. Villa, & A. Nevin (Eds.), *Creativity and collaborative learning: A powerful guide to empowering students and teachers* (pp. 275-291). Baltimore: Paul H. Brookes Publishing.

Sharpe, M. N., York, J. L., & Knight, J. (1994). Effects of inclusion on the academic performance of classmates without disabilities. *Remedial and Special Education, 15* (5), 281-287.

Stainback, S., & Stainback, W. (1996). *Inclusion a guide for educators.* Baltimore: Paul H. Brookes Publishing.

Stainback, S., & Stainback, W. (1990). Inclusive schooling. In W. Stainback and S. Stainback (Eds.). *Support networks for inclusive schooling: Interdependent integrated education* (pp. 25-36). Baltimore: Paul H. Brookes.

Stainback, S., & Stainback, W. (1992). *Curriculum considerations for inclusive classrooms.* Baltimore: Paul H. Brookes Publishing.

Staub, D., & Peck, C. A. (1994). What are the outcomes for nondisabled students? *Educational Leadership, 52*(4), 36-40.

Strain, P. (1983). Generalization of autistic children's social behavior change: Effects of developmentally integrated and segregated settings. *Analysis and intervention in developmental disabilities, 3*(1), 23-34.

Strully, J., & Strully, C. (1985). Teach your children. *Canadian Journal on Mental Retardation, 35*(4), 3-11.

Thousand, J. (1990). Organizational perspectives on teacher education and renewal: A conversation with Tom Skrtic. *Teacher Education & Special Education, 13,* 30-35.

Thousand, J., Fox, T., Reid, R., Godek, J., Williams & Fox, W. (1986). *The homecoming model: Educating students who present intensive educational challenges within regular education environments* (Monograph No. 7-1). Burlington: University of Vermont, Center for Developmental Disabilities.

Thousand, J., & Villa, R. (1990). Strategies for educating students with severe disabilities in their local home schools and communities. *Focus on Exceptional Children, 23*(3), 1-25.

Thousand, J., & Villa, R. (1992). Collaborative teams: A powerful tool in school restructuring. In R. Villa, J. Thousand, W. Stainback, & S. Stainback (Eds.), *Restructuring for caring and effective schools: An administrative guide to creating heterogeneous schools* (pp. 73-108). Baltimore: Paul H. Brookes Publishing.

Thousand, J., & Villa, R. (1990). Sharing expertise and responsibilities through teaching teams. In W. Stainback & S. Stainback (Eds.), *Support networks for inclusive schooling: Integrated interdependent education* (pp. 151-166). Baltimore: Paul H. Brookes Publishing.

Thousand, J., Villa, R., & Nevin, A. (1994). *Creativity and collaborative learning: A powerful guide to empowering students and teachers.* Baltimore: Paul H. Brookes Publishing.

Udvari-Solner, A. & Keyes, M. W. (in press). We're on the train and we've left the station, but we haven't gotten to the next stop: Chronicles of administrative leadership toward inclusive reform. In R. Villa & J. Thousand (Eds.), *Restructuring for caring and effective education: Fitting the pieces of the puzzle together* (2nd. ed.), Baltimore: Paul H. Brookes Publishing.

Udvari-Solner, A. & Thousand, J. (1995). Exemplary and promising teaching practices that foster inclusive education. In R. Villa & J. Thousand (Eds.), *Creating an inclusive school.* Alexandria, VA: Association for Supervision and Curriculum Development.

U.S. Department of Education (1995). *Seventeenth annual report to Congress on the implementation of the Individuals with Disabilities Education Act.* Washington, DC: Author.

Van der Klift, E., & Kunc, N. (1994). Beyond benevolence: Friendship and the politics of help. In J. Thousand, R. Villa, & A. Nevin (Eds.), *Creativity and collaborative learning: A powerful guide to empowering students and teachers* (pp. 391-401). Baltimore: Paul H. Brookes Publishing

Villa, R., & Thousand, J. (1988). Enhancing success in heterogeneous classrooms and schools : The powers of partnership. *Teacher Education and Special Education, 11,* 144-154.

Villa, R. & Thousand, J. (1995). *Creating an inclusive school.* Alexandria, VA: Association for Supervision and Curriculum Development.

Villa, R. & Thousand, J. (1996). Student collaboration: An essential for curriculum delivery in the 21st century. In S. Stainback & W. Stainback (Eds.), *Inclusion a guide for educators* (pp. 171-192). Baltimore: Paul H. Brookes.

Villa, R., Thousand, J., Nevin, A., & Malgeri, C. (1996). Instilling collaboration for inclusive schooling as a way of doing business in public schools. *Remedial and Special Education, 7*(3),182-192.

Villa, R., Thousand, J., Meyers, H., & Nevin, A. (1996). Teacher and administrator perceptions of heterogeneous education. *Exceptional Children, 63*(1), 29-45.

Villa, R., Van der Klift, E., Udis, J., Thousand, J., Nevin, A., Kunc, N., & Chapple, J. (1995). Questions, concerns, and practical advice about inclusive education. In R. Villa & J. Thousand (Eds.). *Creating an inclusive school* (pp. 136-161). Alexandria, VA: Association for Supervision and Curriculum Development.

Villa, R., Thousand, J., Stainback, W., & Stainback, S. (1992). *Restructuring for caring and effective education: An administrative guide to creating heterogeneous schools.* Baltimore: Paul H. Brookes Publishing.

Wagner, M., Newman, L., D'Amico, R., Jay, E.D., Butler-Nalin, P., Marder, C., & Cox, R. (Eds.). (1991). *Youth with disabilities: How are they doing? The first comprehensive report from the National Longitudinal Transition Study of Special Education Students.* Menlo Park, CA: SRI International.

Wang, M. C., Reynolds, M. C., & Walberg, H. J. (1987). *Handbook of special education research and practice.* Oxford, England: Pergamon Press.

Warren, E. (1954). *Brown v. Board of Education of Topeka,* 347 U.S. 483, 493.

Webb, N. (1994). Special education: With new court decisions behind them, advocates see inclusion as a question of values. *The Harvard Educational Letter, 10* (4), 1-3.

Williams, W., Villa, R., Thousand, J., & Fox, W. (1993). Is regular class placement really the issue? A response to Brown, Long, Udvari-Solner, Schwarz, VanDeventer, Ahlgren, Johnson, Grunewald, & Jorgensen. *Journal of the Association for Persons with Severe Disabilities, 14,* 333-334.

Will, M. (1985, December). *Educating children with learning problems: A shared responsibility.* Wingspread Conference on The Education of Special Needs Students: Research Findings and Implications for Practice, Racine: Wisconsin.

Interagency Collaboration: Recurring Obstacles and Some Possible Solutions

Steven I. Pfeiffer

Duke University

Leigh Cundari

Carbon Lehigh Intermediate Unit
Schnecksville, Pennsylvania

SUMMARY. Interagency collaboration has been described in various ways as service coordination, service integration, and community-wide agency cooperation. Regardless of how it is described, interagency collaboration has as its overall goal improving services through better planning and coordination. Several impediments exist which reduce the effectiveness of interagency collaboration. A number of recommendations are made to enhance interagency collaboration, thereby increasing successful inclusive education for

Address correspondence to: Steven I. Pfeiffer, Duke Talent Identification Program, 1121 W. Main Street, Suite 100, Durham, NC 27701-2028.

Special thanks to Drs. Lynn Cook, Richard Hess, Nancy Neef, Walt Pryzwansky, Ed Shapiro, and the staff of the Devereux Foundation Institute of Clinical Training & Research for their considerable contributions to the interagency collaboration research project.

Preparation of this article was supported, in part, by Grant Award No. H237D20006, awarded to the first author from the U.S. Department of Education, Office of Special Education and Rehabilitative Services. The opinions and statements in this article are those of the authors and in no way are meant to represent positions of the U.S. Department of Education.

[Haworth co-indexing entry note]: "Interagency Collaboration: Recurring Obstacles and Some Possible Solutins." Pfeiffer, Steven I., and Leigh Cundari. Co-published simultaneously in *Special Services in the Schools* (The Haworth Press, Inc.) Vol. 15, No. 1/2, 1999, pp. 109-123; and: *Inclusion Practices with Special Needs Students: Theory, Research, and Application* (ed: Steven I. Pfeiffer, and Linda A. Reddy) The Haworth Press, Inc., 1999, pp. 109-123. Single or multiple copies of this article are available for a fee from The Haworth Document Delivery Service [1-800-342-9678, 9:00 a.m. - 5:00 p.m. (EST). E-mail address: getinfo@haworthpressinc.com].

many special needs students. *[Article copies available for a fee from The Haworth Document Delivery Service: 1-800-342-9678. E-mail address: getinfo @haworthpressinc.com <Website: http://www.haworthpressinc.com>]*

KEYWORDS. Interagency collaboration, inclusion, system of care, consultation

There is a burgeoning body of literature encouraging interagency collaboration in the provision of services to children (Barnett, 1995; Epstein, Culligan, Quinn & Cumblad, 1994; Epstein et al., 1993; Nelson & Pearson, 1991).This is based in large part on the increasingly complex and challenging needs of students and the failure of the current child care and educational systems to provide high quality, cost effective and comprehensive services to special needs students and their families (Cook & Friend, 1991; Epstein et al., 1994; Golin & Ducanis, 1981; Harbin & McNulty, 1990; Nelson & Pearson, 1991; Pfeiffer & Reddy, 1998). It is also based on the as yet untested belief that schools and agencies working in partnership will be able to join forces and combine their efforts to better address the challenging needs of today's youth. It is essentially a reflection of the philosophy advocated by many African tribes and popularized by Hillary Clinton that it "takes an entire village to raise a child" (Duchnowski & Friedman, 1990; Epstein et al., 1994; Harvey, 1995; Knitzer & Yelton, 1990).

Stroul and Friedman (1986) have advocated a "system of care" as an alternative to the current, less than adequate, traditional model of service delivery. They define system of care as "a comprehensive spectrum of mental health and other necessary services which are organized into a coordinated network to meet the multiple and changing needs of severely emotionally disturbed children and adolescents" (p. iv). Obviously the new system of care that they advocate is equally applicable for children with mental retardation and developmental disorders. Stroul and Friedman's model expands the conceptual base of service delivery by incorporating a comprehensive array of programs and services, to be provided in the least restrictive environment across all relevant service agencies (Jacobs, 1990; Pfeiffer & Reddy, 1998). In addition, the model is based on a philosophy that is child and family centered, community based, and culturally sensitive (Epstein et al., 1994; Jacobs, 1990).

The model proposed by Stroul and Friedman (1986) encourages five changes in the provision of services to children and their families:

(a) expand the array of helpful services offered, (b) increase the availability of services, (c) streamline access to needed services, (d) provide more integrated services, and (e) use existing services more effectively (Duchnowshi & Friedman, 1990; Elder, 1980; Jacobs, 1990; Kazuk, 1980). Central to an effective system of care is collaboration among professionals and agencies (Elder & Magrab, 1980; Epstein et al., 1993).

Collaboration is a form of consultation. It is a process or style of interaction among two or more co-equal parties with diverse expertise who are voluntarily engaged in shared decision-making as they work cooperatively toward generating creative and helpful solutions to mutually defined problems (Friend & Cook, 1990; Idol et al., 1995; Pfeiffer & Tittler, 1983). Collaboration requires the following seven conditions: (a) team ownership of the problem, (b) joint planning and implementation, (c) parity among the parties, (d) active participation, (e) shared accountability, (f) pooled resources, and (g) voluntariness (Friend & Cook, 1990; Hord, 1986).

Interagency collaboration combines the concepts of collaborative consultation and service coordination. Service coordination consists of trained professionals identifying and coordinating the programs and services of various agencies to facilitate and sustain the gains made during prevention and treatment interventions (Elder & Magrab, 1980; Pfeiffer & Reddy, 1998). Collaborative consultation, as described above, is a dynamic interpersonal process in which professionals from at least two agencies work together collaboratively, with the goal of planning programs and providing high quality, comprehensive and cost effective services to special needs children, youth and their families.

Numerous authors have advocated the need for a system of care predicated on interagency collaboration. The practice of inclusive education of special needs students benefits from interagency collaboration since it brings professionals from various community agencies and the schools together with the goal of supporting the child in the general education environment. Legislative mandates have given further impetus to interagency approaches (*Cordero v. Pennsylvania Department of Education,* 1992; Harbin & McNulty, 1990; Nelson & Pearson, 1991). Several comprehensive children's mental health service delivery systems which incorporate a coordinated, community-linked approach have been discussed in the literature (Nelson & Pearson, 1991; Polivka & Clark, 1994; for a review of several programs see Cole, 1993; Pfeiffer & Reddy, 1998).

Although it is generally accepted that interagency collaboration is a good idea, very little empirical research has been conducted on the effectiveness of various agencies voluntarily working together in joint problem-solving with the goal of generating creative and helpful solutions for the increasingly challenging needs of many students. Anecdotal experience from over twenty years of work as a consultant to schools and community agencies suggest, however, that a number of potential problems challenge the successful implementation of the collaborative planning and problem solving approach. This anecdotal experience is supported by a review of the extant literature on interagency collaboration completed as part of a grant awarded from the U.S. Department of Education.

The purpose of this paper is first to discuss obstacles to interagency collaboration. Second, the paper will suggest strategies to assist in overcoming the obstacles or impediments and thereby maximize the potential impact of interagency collaboration. One implication apropos to this special volume is that successful interagency collaboration can help to support inclusive education efforts.

OBSTACLES TO INTERAGENCY COLLABORATION

As might be expected, there exist a host of obstacles which can interfere with efforts to successfully implement interagency collaboration. To simplify the mine field of possible obstacles, the impediments will be conceptualized into three domains: informational/skill-set barriers, attitudinal barriers, and organizational/regulatory barriers.

Informational/Skill-Set Barriers

Informational and skill-set barriers relate to professionals' lack of knowledge about or familiarity with critical information, terminology and skills (Golin & Ducanis, 1981; Martinson, 1982). Information includes services and programs offered by other agencies (and even offered in different schools in the same school district), eligibility criteria required to receive services, and licensing regulations and procedures which govern agencies and schools (Harbin & McNulty, 1990; Swan & Morgan, 1993). Terminology includes agency specific and profession specific vocabulary as well as differential usage of common terms (Martinson, 1982). This lack of a common vocabulary among interagency personnel can result in misunderstanding and awkward communication (Beck, Bartel & Nelson, 1991; Golin & Ducanis, 1981). Finally, a lack of knowledge about collaborative approaches to service delivery and service coordination and uncertainty about roles, functions and responsibilities along with a lack of experience and skills in collaborative consultation and service coordination serve as deterrents to effective practices (Pollard, Hall & Keeran, 1979).

Professionals' lack of a common language and limited knowledge about other service providers who are represented on interagency teams speak in part to the segregated and insulated nature of the existing system of service delivery and the highly specialized expertise of the professionals who participate on these teams. A lack of a common vocabulary across disciplines and jargon specific to a particular agency can often result in incomplete and mistaken communication. And yet effective communication between team members is a key ingredient to effective team functioning (Elder, 1980; Pfeiffer, 1980, 1981).

Attitudinal Barriers

Attitudinal barriers arise in part from each participant's unique frame of reference, which is the sum of their beliefs, past experiences, fears, hopes and expectations (Friend & Cook, 1992). A person's frame of reference consists of personal, professional and organizational elements, any or all of which can filter, distort or obscure information or result in selective attention to information. This perceptual/cognitive gating mechanism affects one's perspective regarding problems experienced by children and the agencies that serve them (Nelson & Pearson, 1991). In addition, frame of reference moderates a person's views about the value of interagency collaboration (Barnett, 1995; Harbin & McNulty, 1990). For example, a not infrequent misconception among first-time participants is incorrectly assuming that one's responsibility increases and power decreases on interagency teams (National School Boards Association, 1991). Unfavorable opinions about interagency collaboration as a useful vehicle to service delivery will likely impede the effectiveness of the cooperative decision-making process, which is at the heart of interagency collaboration. Attitudinal barriers are often reflected in such behaviors as missing or showing up late to meetings, argumentative interactions, playing devil's advocate, insisting that everything reasonable has already been attempted and nothing new can come out of a problem-solving process, resisting change, and turf guarding (Friend & Cook, 1992; Pfeiffer, 1980, 1981).

Individuals who work with children vary tremendously in the perspectives and experiences that they bring to interagency meetings. These perspectives influence behavior and can have a profound impact on team members' interactions (Elliott, 1990; Golin & Ducanis, 1981). For example, the 1st author has observed at interagency meetings significant attitudinal differences among participants representing education, juvenile justice, social service, and mental health. The 1st author has also noted significant attitudinal differences among male and female participants with differing ethnic and racial backgrounds–particularly in interaction with the child's race/ethnicity and gender.

In addition, misunderstandings regarding the demands of differing professional roles (Phillips & McCullough, 1990) and the philosophical differences among disciplines and agencies (Barnett, 1995; Martinson, 1982) contribute to the existence of attitudinal barriers to effective collaboration. Taken together, these attitudinal barriers can adversely affect commitment to the collaborative process, and therefore the ultimate success of the team process.

Organizational/Regulatory Barriers

Organizational/regulatory barriers exist in part as a result of legislative mandates and regulatory requirements which define the policy and procedures under which systems must operate (Harvey, 1995; Humm-Delgado, 1980; Martinson, 1982). Barriers that result from these system-driven structures include constraints on information exchange (Swan & Morgan, 1993), absence of unified procedures for information dissemination (Johnson, McLaughlin & Christensen, 1982), lack of single point of entry to access services or programs, and fragmented financial support for interagency collaboration efforts (Harbin & McNulty, 1990). In addition, the emphasis on service categories and specific eligibility criteria–both inclusionary and exclusionary–for access to services is the result of policy promulgated by the agency.

Our experience has been that inflexible operating procedures or regulations can often hamper agencies and school systems from collaborating. These barriers are frequently policies or regulations imposed by external governing agencies (e.g., federal and state legislation). A few examples are constraints dealing with funding requirements (e.g., Medicaid, Aid to Families with Dependent Children), collective bargaining agreements (e.g., teacher union contracts), and policies on client rights (e.g., doctor-patient confidentiality and privileged communication) (Barnett, 1995). These existing policies can serve to obstruct efforts at interagency collaboration.

Differing eligibility criteria is yet another organizational challenge to interagency collaboration. Federal and state laws mandate public schools to provide a free and appropriate education to all. In contrast, community mental health, child welfare, developmental disability, juvenile justice, social service, and vocational rehabilitation agencies are not so mandated. Eligibility for the services provided by these agencies is not automatic and is dependent on meeting specific requirements. Eligibility criteria often varies from agency to agency. For example, department of education eligibility requirements differ from the criteria used by mental health agencies, who typically use the American Psychiatric Association criteria, and from the eligibility criteria used by other agencies such as juvenile justice and developmental disabilities (Harvey, 1995).

Time is another pernicious organizational barrier. Most school personnel (particularly teachers) and many service providers simply have neither the flexibility in their schedules nor the funding to attend interagency meetings. Relatedly, it is often a major challenge to find a mutually convenient meeting time. For example, school personnel find it difficult to meet during the school day, whereas mental health workers find it problematic breaking away from their agency after three o'clock (Harvey, 1995; Pfeiffer & Tittler, 1983).

Funding mechanisms also often create barriers. Some agencies are in direct competition with each other for public and/or private funds. It is the rare exception to find agencies sharing or pooling flexible funds (Jacobs, 1990). It is common for agency directors to feel competitively protective about "their" particular funding stream(s).

STRATEGIES FOR IMPROVING
INTERAGENCY COLLABORATION

As discussed in the preceding section, efforts at interagency collaboration may be compromised by a number of informational/skill-set, attitudinal, and organizational/regulatory barriers. The administrator or practitioner who sees value in interagency collaboration will want to be cognizant of how to best eliminate or at least minimize the influence of the various barriers. As part of a grant awarded by the U.S. Department of Education, my colleagues and I developed an interagency collaboration training program. What follows is a description of three sets of strategies for improving interagency collaboration. The strategies are based on a review of the extant literature, solicitation of expert opinion as part of the preparation of the federally funded training program, and the authors' own experiences participating on interagency teams.

Increasing Knowledge

Participants' lack of knowledge about other agencies and professional disciplines is an obvious and yet often overlooked impediment to working together as a cooperative team. To resolve this issue, professionals should learn about other agencies and other professions. It would seem important for providers embarking upon participating on an interagency team to review federal and state regulations and begin to build a common language. For example, at an initial meeting providers can share brochures and resource directories and take a few minutes to provide an overview of the purview of their respective agency (Happe, 1990). In addition, participants will want to discuss their respective roles and responsibilities within their agency and any fiscal, legal and/or programmatic limits to their full participation on the interagency team.

Familiarity with the perspectives, philosophic orientation, terminology, and fiscal and regulatory parameters of participating agencies can only serve to increase the understanding and cooperation among the providers. The sharing of this information can be achieved at the start of an interagency meeting, although it is best accomplished during preservice training at the university or as part of an ongoing professional development program (Allen-Meares & Pugach, 1982; Nelson & Pearson, 1991; Pugach & Allen-Meares, 1985).

Increasing Skills

Successful interagency collaboration requires that participants work together cooperatively to identify needs, plan programs and provide comprehensive services to high need children and their families. Much has been written about interdisciplinary teams and effective team functioning (Francis & Young, 1979; Friend & Cook, 1992; Maddux, 1992; Parker, 1990; Pfeiffer, 1980, 1981; Pfeiffer & Heffernan, 1984). Interagency teams bring together service providers with varied skills, levels of training, backgrounds, perspectives and areas of expertise, all of which contribute to both the potential value of the team as well as the likely ambiguity regarding the roles of the members and the responsibilities of the team (Pfeiffer, 1980).

Effective teams must balance efficient task completion with successful group process. Thus, members of interagency teams must possess several skills germane to both task completion and group process (Phillips & McCullough, 1990). Group process skills in particular, are critical to the development and maintenance of a collaborative process. Problem solving, communication, and decision making skills are all essential to task completion while skills in running meetings and facilitating productive levels of engagement are critical to productive group process. The interagency collaboration training program that we developed included the following ten curricular topics:

- Understanding Frames of Reference
- Sharing Information
- Identifying Client Needs
- Generating and Evaluating Alternative Solutions
- Selecting, Implementing and Monitoring Appropriate Solutions
- Running Effective Meetings
- Facilitating Productive Levels of Participation
- Identifying Nonverbal Language
- Listening Actively and Asking Questions
- Managing Resistance and Resolving Conflict

Our experience as part of evaluating the efficacy of our training program has been that professionals vary tremendously prior to training in their level of proficiency with these essential skills. It is essential, nevertheless, that providers who participate on interagency teams possess at least minimal mastery of these skills.

Building a Commitment to Collaboration

Schools and community agencies recognize that they are ill equipped, by themselves, to effectively meet the increasingly complex needs of many children within their communities. For example, consider the learning disabled-ADHD student with concomitant severe behavior problems who resides within a violent neighborhood and lives with one parent with significant financial and drug dependency problems. This youngster cannot be expected to function successfully in the regular classroom without the combined efforts of a host of school and community-based resources working together to provide an integrated network of treatment and support services. All too often, attempts to provide these services are piecemeal and fragmented–resulting in uncoordinated efforts of low impact.

For a coordinated effort of high impact to occur, agencies and service providers need to appreciate the value of interagency collaboration and commit their facilities and its resources to this approach. Agency support must be extended by the senior administrator with ultimate operational authority. Epstein et al. (1993) recommend that the directors of participating agencies develop an interagency agreement that addresses the parameters of their efforts. Such an agreement serves as a contract that outlines the respective commitments and responsibilities of each agency. It should be mentioned, however, that the interagency agreement is nothing more than a thoughtfully crafted inter-organizational legal document–and that, ultimately, productive group work does not occur between agencies, but between people (Bruner, 1992).

It seems evident, but nonetheless important to highlight, that interagency team members recognize the value of embracing a collaborative approach. However, this is not always the perspective of professionals who participate on interagency teams. For example, we have frequently observed participants who don't appreciate the benefits of a collaborative problem-solving approach. This is most poignantly illustrated in their disdain for collaborative behaviors such as brainstorming, group compromise, or the sharing of resources, and in their tendency to interrupt and overtalk, minimize or ignore the input of others, and need to "win" all disagreements.

An important first step in introducing the merits of a collaborative approach is to ensure that participants understand the nature of service coordination and collaborative consultation (Allen-Meares & Pugach, 1982). A second step is discussing with participants the benefits of interagency collaboration–specifically its goal of improving the quality of comprehensive services for high-need children. Unfortunately, at this early stage we have little empirical data that supports the efficacy of interagency collaboration. But the logic underlying the model is apparent as we await the research to document its effectiveness.

A third step in introducing the benefits of interagency collaboration is pointing out that participants will find the process professionally and personally satisfying and rewarding. When run well, interagency team meetings guided by collaborative problem-solving are enjoyable experiences in which participants feel part of a cohesive group marked by a culture of trust, innovation, empowerment, intrinsic motivation, open communication, and accomplishment. Participants quickly develop an "interagency attitude" in which they rethink how services are provided, understand at a deeper level the philosophy of interagency collaboration, and believe that their efforts will result in the provision of more effective, better coordinated and higher quality services (Nelson & Pearson, 1991).

For many professionals who work in the schools or in community agencies, interagency collaboration is a novel approach to service provision. It should be apparent from the previous discussion that the implementation of interagency collaboration efforts will require organized, ongoing training and supervision to be successful (Allen-Meares & Pugach, 1982; Nelson & Pearson, 1991). To be maximally beneficial, the training should be pedagogically collaborative to reinforce the benefits of collaborative consultation. For example, the interagency collaboration training program that we developed is a 30-hour curriculum that provides exposure to both group process and collaborative problem-solving skills. It is based on the principles of active learning and incorporates videotape vignettes, role play activities, team activities, and large and small group discussions.

UNANSWERED QUESTIONS

The promise of interagency collaboration is great. Proponents claim numerous advantages when multiple agencies work together cooperatively to provide a network of critical treatment and support services to children and their families. The model is consistent with Stroul and Friedman's (1986) often-cited, innovative "system of care." However, as of yet we don't have a substantial body of empirical data supporting the many purported benefits of interagency collaboration. Those of us in the field who are committed to interagency collaboration excitedly await the research that will help us better understand whether the promise of interagency collaboration has been realized. Six of the more pressing, unanswered questions include:

- Does interagency collaboration (IC) minimize duplication of services?
- Does IC increase the identification of resources and creative solutions?
- Does IC expand the availability of services to children and their families?
- Does IC streamline access to needed services?
- Does IC support inclusion education practices and reduce out-of-home placements?
- Does IC reduce overall expenditures per case?

DISCUSSION

Interagency collaboration combines service coordination and collaborative consultation with the goal of providing high quality, comprehensive services to special need children and their families. A number of hurdles challenge the full and successful implementation of interagency collaboration, including informational/skill-set, attitudinal, and organizational/regulatory barriers. Strategies were presented to prepare professionals for active participation on interagency teams, with the goal of eliminating or minimizing the barriers that prevent the full realization of the benefits of interagency collaboration. Future research opportunities were offered to encourage investigators to begin examining the validity of the purported advantages of interagency collaboration.

REFERENCES

Allen-Meares, P., & Pugach, M. (1982). Facilitating interdisciplinary collaboration on behalf of handicapped children and youth. *Teacher Education and Special Education, 5*(1), 30-36.

Barnett, B. G. (1995). Visioning for the future: What can educational leaders do to build a shared commitment to interagency collaboration? *Journal of School Leadership, 5*(1), 69-86.

Beck, J. A., Bartel, N. R., & Nelson, C. M. (1991). The growing need for multidisciplinary collaboration for students with disabilities. In L. M. Bullock & R. L. Simpson (Eds.), *Critical issues in special education: Implications for personnel preparation* (Monograph) (pp. 19-29). Denton, TX: University of North Texas.

Bruner, C. (1992, July). Education and human services consortium. In L. A. Boyd (Ed.), *Integrating systems of care for children and families: An overview of values, methods and characteristics of developing models, with examples and recommendations* (pp. 20-24). Tampa: Florida Mental Health Institute, University of South Florida.

Cole, R. F. (With Poe, S. L.) (1993). *Partnerships for care: Systems of care for children with serious emotional disturbances and their families* (Interim Report of the Mental Health Services Program for Youth). Washington, DC: Washington Business Group of Health.

Cook, L., & Friend, M. (1991). Collaboration in special education: Coming of age in the 1990's. *Preventing School Failure, 35*(2), 24-27.

Cordero v. Pennsylvania Department of Education, 795 F. Supp. 1352 (M.D. Pa. 1992).

Duchnowski, A. J., & Friedman, R. M. (1990). Children's mental health: Challenges for the nineties. *The Journal of Mental Health Administration, 17*(1), 3-12.

Elder, J.O. (1980). Essential components in development of interagency collaboration. In J. O. Elder & P. R. Magrab (Eds.), *Coordinating services to handicapped children: A handbook for interagency collaboration* (pp. 181-201). Baltimore: Paul H. Brookes.

Elder, J. O., & Magrab, P. R. (1980). Introduction and overview. In J. O. Elder & P. R. Magrab (Eds.), *Coordinating services to handicapped children: A handbook for interagency collaboration* (pp. 1-9). Baltimore: Paul H. Brookes.

Elliott, S. (1990). Training vocational rehabilitation counselors in group dynamics: A psychoeducational model. *Journal of Counseling & Development, 68*, 696-698.

Epstein, M. H., Cullinan, D., Quinn, K. P., & Cumblad, C. (1994). Characteristics of children with emotional and behavioral disorders in community-based programs to prevent placement in residential facilities. *Journal of Emotional & Behavioral Disorders, 2*(1), 51-57.

Epstein, M. H., Nelson, C. M., Polsgrove, L., Coutinho, M., Cumblad, C., & Quinn, K. (1993). A comprehensive community-based approach to serving students with emotional and behavioral disorders. *Journal of Emotional & Behavioral Disorders, 1*(2), 127-133.

Francis, D., & Young, D. (1979). *Improving work groups: A practical manual for team building.* San Diego: University Associates.

Friend, M., & Cook, L. (1992). *Interactions: Collaboration skills for school professionals.* New York: Longman.

Golin, A. K., & Ducainis, A. J. (1981). *The interdisciplinary team: A handbook for the education of exceptional children.* Rockville, MD: Aspen Systems.

Hall, H. B. (1980). The intangible human factor: The most critical coordination variable. In J. O. Elder & P. R. Magran (Eds.), *Coordination services to handicapped children: A handbook for interagency collaboration* (pp. 45-62). Baltimore: Paul H. Brookes.

Happe, D. (1990). Best practices in identifying community resources. In A. Thomas

& J. Grimes (Eds.), *Best practices in school psychology-II* (pp. 1009-1047). Washington, DC: The National Association of School Psychologists.

Harbin, G. L., & McNulty, B. A. (1990). Policy implementation: Perspectives on service coordination and interagency collaboration. In S. J. Meisels & J. P. Shonkoff (Eds.), *Handbook of early childhood intervention* (pp. 700-721). New York: Cambridge University Press.

Harvey, V. S. (1995). Interagency collaboration: Providing a system of care for students. *Special services in the schools, 10*(1), 165-181.

Humm-Delgado, D. (1980). Planning issues in local interagency collaboration. In J. O. Elder & P. R. Magrab (Eds.), *Coordinating services to handicapped children: A handbook for interagency collaboration* (pp. 163-178). Baltimore: Paul H. Brookes.

Illback, R. J. (1993, August). *Kentucky IMPACT: Changes for children. Making progress for young Kentuckians with severe emotional disabilities.* A two-year evaluation report. (Available from Sandra Noble Canon, State Coordinator, Kentucky IMPACT, 275 East Main Street, Frankfort, KY 40621)

Jacobs, J. H. (1990). Child mental health: Service system and policy issues. *Social Policy Report: Society for Research in Child Development, 4*(2), 1-19.

Johnson, H. W., McLaughlin, J. A., & Christensen, M. (1982). Interagency collaboration: Driving and restraining forces. *Exceptional Children, 48*(5), 395-399.

Kazuk, E. (1980). Development of a community-based interagency model. In J. O. Elder & P. R. Magrab (Eds.), *Coordination services to handicapped children: A handbook for interagency collaboration* (pp. 99-131). Baltimore: Paul H. Brookes.

Maddux, R. B. (1992). *Team building: An exercise in leadership* (Rev. ed.). Los Altos, CA: Crisp.

Martinson, M. C. (1982). Interagency services: A new era for an old idea. *Exceptional Children, 48*(5), 389-394.

National School Boards Association. (1991). *Link-up: A resource directory. Interagency collaborations to help children achieve.* Alexandria, VA: NSBA.

Nelson, C. M., & Pearson, C. A. (1991). *Integrating services for children and youth with emotional and behavioral disorders.* Reston, VA: The Council for Exceptional Children.

Parker, G. M. (1990). *Team players and teamwork: The new competitive business strategy.* San Francisco: Jossey-Bass.

Pfeiffer, S. I. (1981). The problems facing multidisciplinary teams: As perceived by team members. *Psychology in the Schools, 18,* 330-333.

Pfeiffer, S. I. (1980). The school-based interprofessional team: Recurring problems and some possible solutions. *Journal of School Psychology, 18,* 388-394.

Pfeiffer, S. I., & Heffernan, L. (1984). Improving multidisciplinary team functions. In C. A. Maher, R. J. Illback, & J. E. Zins (Eds.), *Organizational psychology in the schools: A sourcebook for professionals.* Springfield, IL: Charles C. Thomas.

Pfeiffer, S. I., & Reddy, L. A. (1998). School-based mental health programs in the United States: Present status and a blueprint for the future. *School Psychology Review, 27*(1), 84-96.

Pfeiffer, S. I., & Tittler, B. (1983). Utilizing the multidisciplinary team to facilitate a family systems orientation. *School Psychology Review, 12,* 168-173.

Phillips, V., & McCullough, L. (1990). Consultation-based programming: Instituting the collaborative ethic in schools. *Exceptional Children, 56*(4), 291-304.

Polivka, B. J., & Clark, J. A. (1994). A collaborative system of care for youth with severe emotional disturbances: An evaluation of client characteristics and services. *The Journal of Mental Health Administration, 21*(2), 170-184.

Pollard, A., Hall, H., & Keeran, C. (1979). Community service planning. In P. R. Magrab & J. O. Elder (Eds.), *Planning for services to handicapped persons: Community, education, health* (pp. 1-39). Baltimore: Paul H. Brookes.

Pugach, M. C., & Allen-Meares, P. (1985). Collaboration at the preservice level: Instructional and evaluation activities. *Teacher Education and Special Education, 8*(1), 3-11.

Stroul, B. A., & Friedman, R. M. (1986, July). *A system of care for severely emotionally disturbed children & youth.* (Available from CASSP Technical Assistance Center, 3800 Reservoir Road, N.W., Washington, DC 20007).

Swan, W. W., & Morgan, J. L. (1993). *Collaborating for comprehensive services for young children and their families: The local interagency coordinating council.* Baltimore: Paul H. Brookes.

West-Stern, J. (1984). Interagency intervention: A case study. In S. Braaten, R. B. Rutherford, Jr., & C. A. Kardash, (Eds.), *Programming for adolescents with behavioral disorders: Vol. 1* (pp. 44-51). Reston, VA: Council for Children with Behavioral Disorders.

Legal and Ethical Issues of Inclusion

Steven G. Little

The University of Alabama

K. Angeleque Akin Little

The University of Southern Mississippi

SUMMARY. The inclusion of children with disabilities in the regular classroom has become a controversial issue in the area of special education. Definitions range from selective placement of special education students in one or more "regular" education classes to full-time placement of students with disabilities in the regular classroom. A review of the U.S. Constitution, federal legislation (i.e., IDEA, Section 504, ADA), and federal court cases clearly indicate that there is no legal mandate for "full inclusion." Rather, the courts have consistently supported the key provisions of IDEA and other legislation that decisions be individualized for each student, that the "least restrictive environment" does not necessarily mean full inclusion in the regular classroom, and that decision making regarding children with disabilities needs to be based on sound reasoning about what is in the best interest of the child. There does, however, appear to be a clear preference for placing students in as mainstream an environment as possible. In addition to reviewing legal issues in inclusion, this paper reviews ethical issues regarding placement decisions of students with disabilities and presents an eight-step model of decision making to guide educators and psychologists in arriving at ethical (and legally sound) placement decisions. *[Article copies available for a fee from The Haworth Document Delivery Service: 1-800-342-9678. E-mail address: getinfo@haworthpressinc.com <Website: http://www.haworthpressinc.com>]*

Address correspondence to: Dr. Steven G. Little, Carmichael 306, University of Alabama, Tuscaloosa, AL 35487-0231.

[Haworth co-indexing entry note]: "Legal and Ethical Issues of Inclusion." Little, Steven G., and K. Angeleque Akin Little. Co-published simultaneously in *Special Services in the Schools* (The Haworth Press, Inc.) Vol. 15, No. 1/2, 1999, pp. 125-143; and: *Inclusion Practices with Special Needs Students: Theory, Research, and Application* (ed: Steven I. Pfeiffer, and Linda A. Reddy) The Haworth Press, Inc., 1999, pp. 125-143. Single or multiple copies of this article are available for a fee from The Haworth Document Delivery Service [1-800-342-9678, 9:00 a.m. - 5:00 p.m. (EST). E-mail address: getinfo@haworthpressinc.com].

125

KEYWORDS. Inclusion, IDEA, least restrictive environment, ethical decision making

Inclusion, and particularly "full inclusion" has become a controversial issue in the education of children with disabilities. Although the definition of inclusion can vary from selective placement of special education students in one or more "regular" education classes to full-time placement of students with disabilities in the regular classroom, proponents of inclusion give three general reasons in support of inclusive education (Little & Witek, 1996). The first is federal and state legislation calling for children with disabilities to be educated in the "least restrictive environment," which many have interpreted as calling for inclusive settings. The second reason is the belief that inclusion results in social, behavioral, academic, and developmental benefits for both children with disabilities and other, nondisabled, children in the classroom. The third rationale derives from philosophical beliefs about the right of full access to services for individuals with disabilities. The intent of this paper is to discuss inclusion, and definitions of inclusion, with regard to (a) legislative and judicial mandates and (b) ethical decision making. It is our perspective that although law supercedes ethics (Woody, 1998), judicial decisions pertaining to inclusion leave a great deal of decision making responsibilities to educators regarding placement decisions for individual students. It is our position that one must consider all aspects of an individual's functioning in relation to characteristics of the proposed placement environment in order to make ethical placement decisions, ones that will maximize the development of the individual student.

Unfortunately, research on the effectiveness of inclusion is equivocal. For example, Jenkins et al. (1994) reported that students placed in inclusive settings with appropriate accommodations achieved as much or more than students in noninclusive settings. Schneider and Leroux (1994), however, found that students with behavior disorders who were placed in a self-contained classroom demonstrated greater improvement than similar students in inclusive settings. We need more research on inclusion and until the time that a substantial body of empirical evidence exists supporting across the board full inclusion, inclusion decisions should be made on a case by case basis considering the needs of the included student in the classroom in which inclusion is intended. This is especially true of students with emotional and behavioral disorders (Coleman, Webber, & Algozzine in this volume; MacMillan, Gresham, & Forness, 1996) who may need more intense treatment than can be provided in most regular classrooms in most school districts. How an individual student's specific needs can be met in the regular classroom needs to be made prior to placement. To do otherwise is less likely to provide the student with a positive educational outcome.

LEAST RESTRICTIVE ENVIRONMENT AND INCLUSION: DIFFERING DEFINITIONS

The current emphasis on inclusion began with the passage of the Education of All Handicapped Children Act in 1975 (PL 94-142, since renamed Individuals with Disabilities Education Act-IDEA). While neither the term inclusion nor mainstreaming are mentioned in PL 94-142, IDEA, or the most recent version of IDEA (Individuals with Disabilities Education Act Amendments of 1997), the least restrictive environment clause states:

> Each State must establish procedures to assure that, to the maximum extent appropriate, children with disabilities . . . are educated with children who are not disabled, and that special education, separate schooling, or other removal of children with disabilities from the regular educational environment occurs only when the nature or severity of the disability is such that education in regular classes with the use of supplementary aids and services cannot be achieved satisfactorily. (20 U.S.C. § 1412 [5] [B])

Since the implementation of PL 94-142, the number of children and youth with disabilities who have been identified has increased dramatically. In the period between 1978 and 1993 the total school enrollment (K-12) in the United States increased by 1.88% (U.S. Department of Commerce, 1997). At the same time those identified with a disability increased 73.12%. Interestingly, the percentage of individuals receiving full-time special education services outside of the regular classroom has actually increased from 23% 1978 to 25% in 1993 (U.S. Department of Commerce, 1982, 1997). It is clear, however, that a large number of individuals are receiving services in the regular classroom during the majority of the school day. According to the most recent *Statistical Abstract of the United States* (U.S. Department of Commerce, 1997), 43.1% of children and youth with disabilities with non-residential placements receives special education and related services outside the regular classroom less than 21% of the school day, the *Abstract's* definition of "regular class" placement.

Data such as these provide some evidence of attempts to place children and youth with disabilities in the regular classroom to a large degree. The position of the most radical inclusionists, however, is that "least restrictive environment" means the "full inclusion" in regular classes in regular schools for all students, regardless of type or severity of the handicapping condition. Advocates of full inclusion such as Stainback and Stainback (1992), Gartner and Lipsky (1987), and The Association for Persons with Severe Handicaps (TASH) advocate such a position, often without empirical data (MacMillan, Gresham, & Forness, 1996). Fuchs and Fuchs (1994), in their critique of the inclusive schools movement, provide a good overview of this issue as do MacMillan, Gresham, and Forness (1996) and Reddy in this volume. As the intent of this paper is to review legal and ethical issues regarding inclusion and not to debate the efficacy of inclusion, readers are referred to these articles for an in-depth discussion of issues surrounding the debate. It is important, however, to recognize the differing perspectives regarding inclusion in understanding the meaning of legal decisions and in making ethical placement decisions.

The United States Constitution

The Constitution of the United States provides the framework from which all federal, state, and local legislation is based. The Constitution consists of the main document outlining the duties and powers of the federal government, 10 amendments made in 1791 and referred to as the "Bill of Rights," and 16 additional amendments enacted between 1795 and 1971. The Constitution does not guarantee individuals a right to an education, but it has formed the foundation for decisions pertaining to education including children's right to equal educational opportunity (Jacob-Timm & Hartshorne, 1998). The 14th Amendment to the Constitution is the portion of the Constitution that is most relevant to the inclusion issue. It states:

> . . . No state shall make or enforce any law which shall abridge the privileges or immunities of citizens of the United States; nor

shall any state deprive any person of life, liberty or property, without due process of law; nor deny any person within its jurisdiction the equal protection of the law.

It is the "equal protection clause" of the 14th amendment that has been interpreted as meaning that an appropriate public education be made available to all children. The Supreme Court initially upheld this interpretation of the 14th amendment in the 1954 *Brown v. Board of Education* decision when they ruled each state must provide equal educational opportunities to all citizens, regardless of race. Later rulings (*Pennsylvania Association for Retarded Children v. Commonwealth of Pennsylvania,* 1971, 1972; *Mills v. Board of Education,* 1972) extend *Brown* by ruling that excluding children with disabilities from public school education is a denial of the equal protection clause (Jacob-Timm & Hartshorne, 1998).

Federal Legislation

A philosophy similar to that conveyed by the 14th Amendment forms the basis for the "free appropriate public education" (FAPE) and "least restrictive environment" (LRE) provisions of IDEA. IDEA never specifically defines "appropriate" however. The debate regarding inclusion that was previously discussed involves the interpretation of what is "appropriate." IDEA stipulates that each public agency must ensure that the placement of every child with a handicapping condition be determined at least annually, be based on the child's individualized education program (IEP), and be as close as possible to the child's home. In addition, this legislation states that unless a child's IEP requires some other arrangement, the child should be educated in the school which he or she would attend if not handicapped; that documentation be provided about how the child's disability affects his/her involvement and progress in the general curriculum; and that attempts are made at meeting the child's needs resulting from the disability to best enable the child to be involved in and progress through the general curriculum.

IDEA also requires schools to prepare a continuum of placements, from least to most restrictive (20 U.S.C. § 1412 [5] [B]). This continuum can include, but is not limited to, regular class placement, special education resource services, a self-contained classroom, special schools, home instruction, or hospital or institution placement. It is then the responsibility of the IEP Team to determine which option is least restrictive. Although some individuals (i.e., Laski, 1991) have advocated the abolition of the continuum, this does not appear consistent with the IDEA directive for the establishment of a continuum (Thomas & Rapport, in press). The Supreme Court supported this in *Hendrick Hudson Central School District v. Rowley* (1982) when it observed that neither the IDEA nor its legislative history established a substantive standard definition of what level of education amounts to a FAPE. They wrote:

> Congress recognized that regular classrooms simply would not be a suitable setting for the education of many handicapped children. The act expressly acknowledges that "the nature or severity of the handicap [may be] such that education in regular classes with the use of supplementary aides and services cannot be achieved satisfactorily." (p. 3038)

Two other federal laws also address some issues of inclusive education. Section 504 of the Vocational Rehabilitation Act of 1973 states that children with disabilities cannot be discriminated against based on their disability. It states:

> A school system shall educate, or shall provide for the education of, each qualified handicapped person in its jurisdiction with persons who are not handicapped to the maximum extent appropriate to the needs of the handicapped person. A school system shall place a handicapped person in the regular educational environment unless it is demonstrated that the education of the person in the regular environment with the use of supplementary aids and services cannot be achieved satisfactorily. Whenever a school system places a person in a setting other than the regular educational environment, it shall take into account the proximity of the alternative setting to the person's home. (34 C.F.R. § 104.34 [a])

The Americans with Disabilities Act of 1990 (ADA, 42 U.S.C. § 12101, *et seq.*) states:

> No qualified individual with a disability shall, by reason of such disability, be excluded from participation in or be denied the

> benefits or the services, programs or activities of a public entity, or be subjected to discrimination by any such entity. (42 U.S.C. § 12132)

and

> A public entity, in providing any aid, benefit or service, may not, directly or through contractual, licensing or other arrangements, on the basis of disability, among other things: provide different or separate aids, benefits or services to individuals with disabilities or to any class of individuals with disabilities than is provided to others unless such action is necessary to provide qualified individuals with disabilities with aids, benefits or services that are as effective as those provided to others. (28 C.R.F. § 35.130 [b] [1])

It is clear from these laws that Congress has a preference for the placement of children with disabilities in environments with their nondisabled classmates (Havey, 1998).

Court Decisions

There have been a number of legal decisions over the last few years that deal with inclusion. It is important to remember that each court has a separate jurisdiction and that the decision may not apply to all locations. The federal legal system consists of U.S. District Courts, 11 Circuit Courts (Court of Appeals), and the Supreme Court. Decisions by the Circuit Courts have controlling authority within their jurisdiction only and decisions made by other Circuit Courts can be contradictory (Havey, 1998). Only Supreme Court decisions are controlling throughout the United States and there are no Supreme Court decisions that directly relate to inclusion.

Daniel R.R. v. State Board of Education. The first time the inclusion standard was applied at the appeals court level was in the Fifth Circuit Court (Louisiana, Texas) in *Daniel R.R. v. State Board of Education* (1989). This case involved a 6-year-old boy with Down Syndrome who, after receiving both general education and special education services, was recommended by the district for placement in a full-time special education class. His only contact with nondisabled peers would be at lunch and recess. The court decided in favor of the school district and asked two main questions with four sub-questions that need to be answered in determining placement:

1. Can education in the regular classroom, with the use of supplemental aids and services, be achieved satisfactorily for a given child?
   a. Has the state taken steps to accommodate children with disabilities in regular education, and if so, are these efforts sufficient and within reason?
   b. Will the child receive an educational benefit from regular education? The Court said that academic achievement is not the only purpose of mainstreaming. Integrating a child with a disability into a regular classroom environment may be beneficial in and of itself, even if the child cannot flourish academically.
   c. Is there any detriment to the child from the proposed mainstreaming?
   d. What effect will the child's presence have on the regular classroom environment and, on the education of the other students?
2. If education in the regular classroom for the entire school day cannot be achieved satisfactorily, has the child been mainstreamed to the maximum extent possible?

The decision in support of the district held that Daniel's education in the regular classroom was not succeeding satisfactorily and that the time the regular classroom teacher had to devote to his education detracted from the instruction she was able to provide other students. Full inclusion was therefore unfair to the rest of the class. In this case, the court ruled that a segregated special education program was the least restrictive placement for Daniel. This case has subsequently been cited as the basis for decisions in the Third Circuit Court (Delaware, New Jersey, Pennsylvania, Virgin Islands) in *Oberti v. Board of Education of Clementon School District* (1993) and *Carlisle Area School v. Scott P.* (1995) and the Eleventh Circuit Court (Mississippi, Alabama, Georgia, Florida) in *Greer vs. Rome City School District* (1991).

Oberti v. Board of Education of Clementon School District. Although using the precedent established in *Daniel R. R.,* the Third Circuit Court found for the parents in *Oberti v. Board of Education of Clementon School District* (1993). This case involved an 8-year-old child with Down Syndrome and severely impaired communication ability. The court observed that the school had not seriously considered accommodations in a regular classroom and ruled in favor of a placement that was more inclusive than that provided by the district's self-contained placement. Similar to *Daniel R. R.*, the court ruled that three factors must be considered:

1. Did the district make reasonable efforts to accommodate the child in regular education, considering the whole range of supplemental aids and services that may be available?
2. A comparison of the educational benefits the child would receive in regular education (with supplemental aids and services) contrasted with the benefits in a special education classroom.
3. Consideration of the effect the inclusion of the child with disabilities might have on the education of other children in the regular education classroom.

If, after considering these factors, the court determines that the child cannot be educated satisfactorily in a regular classroom, they must consider whether the schools have included the child in regular programs to the maximum extent appropriate. Although the opinion does not adopt inclusion as IDEA's goal, it requires greater efforts by schools to mainstream disabled students or explain why not.

Greer v. Rome City School District. In *Greer v. Rome City School District* (1991) the Eleventh Circuit Court decided in favor of parents who objected to the placement of their Down Syndrome daughter in a self-contained special education classroom. Expanding on *Daniel R.R.*, the court concluded that before the school district could reach a conclusion that a child with a disability should be educated outside of the regular classroom it must consider whether supplemental aids and services would permit satisfactory education in the regular classroom. In this case the district had considered only three options for the child: (1) a regular education classroom with no supplementary aids and services, (2) a regular classroom with speech therapy only, and (3) a self-contained special education classroom. The district argued that the costs of providing services in the classroom would be too high. The court said that although the district cannot refuse to serve a child because of added cost, they do not have to provide a child with his/her own full-time teacher. As with other cases, no clear distinction is made about what constitutes reasonable or excessive costs. The primary directive is that all options must be weighed before removing a child from the regular classroom. The Court also said school officials must share placement considerations with the child's parents at the IEP meeting before a placement is determined. *Sacramento City Unified School District v. Holland.* In a case in which parents challenged the districts decision to place their daughter with moderate retardation half-time in a special education classroom and half-time in a regular education classroom (*Sacramento City Unified School District vs. Holland*, 1992, 1994), the Ninth Circuit Court (Arizona, Alaska, Hawaii, Guam, California, Nevada, Idaho, Montana, Oregon, Washington) upheld the decision of the lower court in finding for the Holland family. The parents wanted their daughter in the regular classroom full-time. The court considered the *Daniel R. R.* test and established a similar, but distinct, test to determine whether a school district is complying with IDEA. The four factors to consider in making placement decisions were:

1. The educational benefits of placing the child in a full-time regular education program,
2. The non-academic benefits of such a placement,
3. The effect the child would have on the teacher and other students in the regular classroom, and
4. The costs associated with this placement.

Although this decision has only been implemented in the ninth circuit's jurisdiction, it is the first case that requires a weighing of monetary and nonmonetary costs in placement decision making (Thomas & Rapport, in press).

Clyde K. v. Puyallup School District, No. 3. In *Holland* the ninth circuit court ruled in favor of the parents in deciding that regular class placement was the least restrictive environment based on placement considerations set down by the court. The same court reached the opposite conclusion in *Clyde K. v. Puyallup School District, No. 3* (1994). This case involved a junior high school student with Tourette Syndrome and ADHD who had received services in both regular and special education classes. His maladaptive behavior had escalated to the point where the school had imposed an "emergency expulsion" and then proposed a temporary placement in a segregated off-campus program. While originally agreeing to this placement, his parents eventually removed him from the program and filed for a due process hearing. The hearing officer upheld the district and that ruling was subsequently upheld by both the district and circuit courts. In the ruling the court determined that the segregated program was the least restrictive environment because the student's behavior prevented him from learning when he was in a regular classroom placement, he had become socially isolated and there were no indications that he benefited from the presence of appropriate peer models, and that his presence in the regular classroom had a negative impact on teachers and other students.

Poolaw v. Bishop. In another ninth circuit court case, *Poolaw v. Bishop* (1995), the court ruled in favor of the district's offer of a residential placement for a 13-year-old boy who was deaf in spite of the family's desire that he be educated in a regular education classroom. The court asserted that the child's previous and current placements had adequately explored the effectiveness of regular education placement with supplemental aids and services. As a result, the district determined that the benefits of regular education placement were minimal and that the child's educational needs could be met appropriately only by the residential placement offered by the district. Specifically, they ruled that placement at the state school for the deaf better met his needs in the acquisition of American Sign Language and other communication skills and that these needs were greater than the nonacademic benefits that may result from a regular class placement (Thomas & Rapport, in press).

Conclusion from Legal Decisions

Although different outcomes arose from the various circuit court decisions discussed in the previous section, certain general conclusions can be drawn regarding inclusion and the placement of children with disabilities in the least restrictive environment. It is clear that the courts have upheld the notion of a continuum of placement and that placement decisions must be made based on the needs of the individual child. The position of certain inclusion proponents that we cannot ". . . justify subrogating students with disabilities or any other students from the mainstream of school and community life" (Stainback, Stainback, & Ayres, 1996, p. 39) has not been upheld by the courts, just as a return to the days of complete segregation of students with disabilities would also be ruled unacceptable. The court has made clear that a "one size fits all" (Borthwick-Duffy, Palmer, & Lane, 1996) approach is illegal.

In the six legal cases reviewed, the courts decided in the parents' favor for a less restrictive placement than the school had recommend in three cases and in favor of the school district in support of noninclusive placements in three cases. Although the decisions may have differed, the guiding principle was the same behind each decision. That is, the school must consider inclusive placements but numerous factors may mitigate against such placements. While a preference exists for educating the child in a regular classroom, the appropriate placement is the one that is appropriate for the child. The decisions that were decided in favor of more restrictive placements tended to involve students with emotional and behavioral disorders (Havey, 1998). The problems they present in the regular classroom (i.e., lack of learning, negative impact on teachers and other students) have been recognized by the courts as conditions that argue against inclusion and in favor of more restrictive settings. Legal issues related to inclusion are not completely clear, however, especially with regard to cost. It would be surprising if additional cases do not reach the circuit courts and possibly the Supreme Court in the near future. These cases may help clarify the remaining unresolved issues. A recent paper by Thomas and Rapport (in press) provides a more extensive review of court decisions regarding the concept of "least restrictive environment" and readers are referred there for a more in-depth analysis of legal issues with respect to inclusion.

Ethical Decision Making

The courts have clearly supported legislation affirming the concepts of "least restrictive environment," "continuum of placement," and "free appropriate public education." Exactly how these principles are implemented is still open for discussion, however. In this section we will offer a model for making ethical placement decisions that is consistent with law, the ethical standards of major professional organizations, and empirical data.

As was previously mentioned law supercedes ethics. It is clear that the courts have rejected the concept of full inclusion, "the inclusion of all students in the mainstream of regular education classes and school activities with their age peers from the same community" (Stainback & Stainback, 1990, p. 225). The courts have supported the concept of "least restrictive environment" in the context of a "continuum of placement" depending on the needs of the individual child, the impact on others in the classroom, and the costs and benefits of the placement. It is within conditions set by the law that school psychologists and educators rely on our ethical principles to make decisions. It is our perspective that we need to be guided by the ethical standards set by our respective professional organizations and by empirical data. Decisions that are based on emotion and philosophical biases need to be avoided and we should base our actions on a firm foundation of empirical research. For a more in depth discussion of ethical decision making as it relates to inclusion see Paul, Berger, Osnes, Martinez, and Morse (1997).

Professional Standards. For school psychologists the standards of the National Association of School Psychologists (NASP) and/or the American Psychological Association (APA) provide the basis of professional conduct to guide professional activities. Although neither organization's ethical principles specifically address the issue of making placement decisions, some general standards do apply. The NASP *Principles for Professional Ethics* (NASP, 1997) states that "School psychologists engage in continuing professional development. They remain current regarding developments in research, training, and professional practices that benefit children, families, and schools" (II, A, 5) and that

> School psychologists consider the students or clients to be their primary responsibility, acting as advocates for their rights and welfare. When choosing a course of action, school psychologists take into account the rights of each individual involved and the duties of the school personnel. (IV, A, 1)

Similarly, the APA's *Ethical Principles of Psychologists and Code of Conduct* (APA, 1992) declares that "Psychologists rely on scientifically and professionally derived knowledge when making scientific or professional judgments or when engaging in scholarly or professional endeavors" (p. 1600), and

> Psychologists work to develop a valid and reliable body of scientific knowledge based on research. They may apply that knowledge to human behavior in a variety of contexts. In doing so, they perform many roles, such as researcher, educator, diagnostician, therapist, supervisor, consultant, administrator, social interventionist, and expert witness. Their goal is to broaden knowledge of behavior and,

where appropriate, to apply it pragmatically to improve the condition of both the individual and society. (p. 1599)

In addition, as a result of the psychologist's role in performing assessment as part of the eligibility and subsequent placement decision making process, the standard that says "Psychologists refrain from misuse of assessment techniques, interventions, results, and interpretations and take reasonable steps to prevent others from misusing the information these techniques provide" (APA, 1992, p. 1603), is also relevant.

Each of these provisions of professional ethics requires that decision making be based on protecting the rights and welfare of the client and that decisions be based on current scientific research. The logic behind the full inclusion movement is that it promotes the development of social skills, helps nondisabled peers develop positive attitudes toward children with disabilities, and promotes friendships between students with and without disabilities (Snell, 1991). Sale and Carey (1995), however, found that fully included students with disabilities were the least liked and most rejected students in their classes. They concluded that "Putting students together for 100% of the day in this school did not change how they are reported to be liked or disliked by their same-age peers" (p. 17). Gresham and MacMillan (1997), in an extensive review of the literature on the social competence and affective functioning of children with mild disabilities, concluded that "these children are poorly accepted and more often rejected and have lower levels of social skills and higher levels of internalizing and externalizing behavior problems than their nondisabled peers" (p. 400). These difficulties complicate efforts to place them in regular education classrooms. As in the *Clyde K.* decision, in which the student's social isolation was one factor in the court's decision to uphold a noninclusive placement, research appears to support the notion that not all students will benefit from regular class placement. Professional ethical standards would therefore dictate that individual decisions be made based on the available research relevant to the student in question as well as promote the welfare of the client (i.e., the student) to the greatest extent possible Clearly, a "one size fits all" full inclusion model can not be ethically justified.

Model of Ethical Decision Making. Jacob-Timm and Hartshorne (1998) recognize that for psychologists, sound decision making involves many factors that are consistent with sound professional practice. They present an eight-step model of problem-solving (adapted from Keith-Spiegel & Koocher, 1985) which we further adapt to the making of ethical placement decisions. The following eight-step model is proposed as a guide to making ethical (and legally defensible) placement decisions:

1. Fully evaluate the cognitive, educational, affective, behavioral, and social-emotional functioning of the student. This should include parent, teacher, and student interviews, observation in classroom and social contexts, as well as norm-referenced assessment. Sattler (1992) offers a discussion of "Four Pillars of Assessment" which is a good model to follow.

2. Identify the placement options available. A continuum of placements, supports, and services should be made available for all students; but the first placement option to consider is in regular education. Remember, however, that top-down mandated full inclusion is inappropriate. Neither federal nor state law requires full inclusion of all students and ethical standards make it hard to justify.

3. Consult legal and ethical guidelines. Recognize the guiding principles behind IDEA and other federal legislation that has been upheld by the federal courts. All placement decisions should be based on a well developed IEP with an emphasis on the needs of the child, his/her peers, and the reasonable provision of services.

4. Evaluate the rights, responsibility, and welfare of all affected parties (e.g., pupil, teachers, classmates, other school staff, parents, siblings). To effectively do this it is important that the decision making process include regular and special education teachers (Lloyd, Martin, & Kauffman, 1995), parents (Duchnowski, Berg, & Kutash, 1995), and wherever possible the student him/herself.

5. Evaluate the research literature with regard to the efficacy of the various placement options with other students with similar exceptionalities.

6. Generate a cost-benefit analysis for each placement option (Little & Witek, 1996). Although monetary costs may be considered, the focus should be on nonmonetary factors. Consider the possible psychological, social, and economic costs and benefits

to all parties. This should be based on the specific placement options available for this particular student and not that placement in general. Using the questions generated by the courts in *Daniel R. R.* (1989), *Oberti* (1993), and *Holland* (1992, 1994) would provide a good framework.

7. Present evidence that the costs or benefits resulting from each decision will actually occur.
8. The IEP team should make its decision. This decision should be consistent with legal mandates and ethical principles. All individuals should agree that the placement is in the best interests of the child. When agreement cannot be reached a trial placement in the least restrictive alternative is suggested.

If the decision is to include the student in a regular classroom it is helpful if the district makes attempts at unifying the special education and regular education systems. There should be assurances that sufficient support services are available to address the social, emotional, and cognitive needs of all students. Appeal procedures should be developed that allow teachers and other professionals to challenge the implementation of IEPs and placements that they determine to be inappropriate for a child (parental appeal procedures are mandated by law). If these procedures are followed ethical and legal placement decisions will likely result.

CONCLUSION

The principles established by the courts are clear in spite of rulings favoring both parents and school districts. The courts have consistently supported the key provisions of IDEA and other legislation that decisions be individualized for each student, that the "least restrictive environment" does not necessarily mean full inclusion in the regular classroom, and that decision making regarding children with disabilities needs to be based on sound reasoning about what is in the best interest of the child. There does, however, appear to be a clear preference for placing students in as mainstream an environment as possible. When inclusion is not possible, the burden of proof is on the school to document why. Answering the two main questions proposed by the court in *Daniel R. R.* (1989) may be the safest way to proceed in making placement decisions. These questions are (1) Can education in the regular classroom, with the use of supplemental aids and services, be achieved satisfactorily for a given child? and (2) If education in the regular classroom for the entire school day cannot be achieved satisfactorily, has the child been mainstreamed to the maximum extent possible?

Reviews of the inclusion literature (Fuchs & Fuchs, 1994; Kauffman & Hallahan, 1995; MacMillan, Gresham, & Forness, 1996) clearly illustrate that many of the conclusions being drawn by advocates of full inclusion are not supported by research evidence and are more philosophically than empirically driven. Ethical decision making, however, must take into account more than just an individual's philosophical biases. APA's *Ethical Principles of Psychologists and Code of Conduct* support this position in stating: "Psychologists rely on scientifically and professionally derived knowledge when making scientific or professional judgments or when engaging in scholarly or professional endeavors" (APA, 1992, p. 1600). Similarly, ethical decision making places the needs of the client, in this case the child, above all other concerns. The NASP *Principles for Professional Ethics* (NASP, 1997) state this clearly when they say:

> School psychologists consider the students or clients to be their primary responsibility, acting as advocates for their rights and welfare. When choosing a course of action, school psychologists take into account the rights of each individual involved and the duties of the school personnel. (IV, A, 1)

If we strive to make decisions that are in the best interests of the children we serve and base those decisions on the best empirical research available, while considering legal mandates, legal and ethical placement decisions are likely to follow.

REFERENCES

American Psychological Association (1992). Ethical principles of psychologists and code of conduct. *American Psychologist, 47,* 1597-1611.

Americans with Disabilities Act of 1990 (P.L. 1010336), 42 U.S.C.A. § 12101.

Board of Education, Sacramento Unified School District v. Holland, 786 F. Supp 874, 73 Ed. Law Rep. 969 (E.D. Cal. 1992); *affd sub nom. Board of Education, Sacramento Unified School District v. Rachel H.,* 14F. 3d 1398, 89 Ed. Law Rep. 57 (9th Cir. 1994).

Borthwick-Duffy, S. A., Palmer, D. S., & Lane, K. L. (1996). One size doesn't fit all: Full inclusion and individual differences. *Journal of Behavioral Education, 6,* 311-329.

Brown v. Board of Education, 347 U.S. 483 (1954).

Carlisle Area School v. Scott P., 62 F. 3d 520 (3rd Cir. 1995).

Clyde K. v. Puyallup School District, No. 3, 35 F. 3d 1396 (9th Cir. 1994).

Daniel R. R. v. State Board of Education, 874 F. 2d 1036 (5th Cir. 1989).

Duchnowski, A., Berg, K., & Kutash, K. (1995). Parent participation in and perception of placement decisions. In J. M. Kauffman, J. W. Lloyd, D. P. Hallahan, & T. A. Astuto (Eds.), *Issues in educational placement: Students with emotional and behavioral disorders* (pp. 183-195). Hillsdale, NJ: Lawrence Erlbaum.

Fuchs, D., & Fuchs, L. S. (1994). Inclusive schools movement and the radicalization of special education reform. *Exceptional Children, 60,* 294-309.

Gartner, A., & Lipsky, D. K. (1987). Beyond special education. *Harvard Educational Review, 57,* 367-395.

Greer v. Rome City School District, 950 F. 2d 688 (11th Cir. 1991).

Gresham, F. M., & MacMillan D. L (1997). Social competence and affective characteristics of students with mild disabilities. *Review of Educational Research, 67,* 373-375.

Havey, J. M. (1998). Inclusion, the law, and placement decisions: Implications for school psychologists. *Psychology in the Schools, 35,* 145-152.

Hendrick Hudson Central School District v. Rowley, 458 U.S. 176 (1982).

Individuals with Disabilities Education Act of 1990, 20 U.S.C. §§ 1400-1485 (1990).

Jacob-Timm, S., & Hartshorne, T. (1998). *Ethics and law for school psychologists* (3rd ed.). New York: Wiley.

Jenkins, J. R., Jewell, M., Leicester, N., O'Connor, R. E., Jenkins, L. M., & Troutner, N. M. (1994). Accommodations for individual differences without classroom ability groups: An experiment in school restructuring. *Exceptional Children, 60,* 344-358.

Kauffman, J. M., & Hallahan, D. P. (Eds.). (1995). *The illusion of full inclusion: A comprehensive critique of a current special education bandwagon.* Austin, TX: PRO-ED.

Keith-Spiegel, P., & Koocher, G. P. (1985). *Ethics in psychology.* Hillsdale, NJ; Lawrence Erlbaum.

Laski, F. J. (1991). Achieving integration during the second revolution. In L. H. Meyer, C. A. Peck, & L. Brown (Eds.), *Critical issues in the lives of people with severe disabilities* (pp. 409-421). Baltimore: Paul H. Brookes.

Little, S. G., & Witek, J. M. (1996). Inclusion: Considerations from social validity and functional outcome analysis. *Journal of Behavioral Education, 6,* 283-291.

Lloyd, J. W., Martin, K. F., & Kauffman, J. M. (1995). Teachers' participation in decisions about placement of students with emotional or behavioral disorders. In J. M. Kauffman, J. W. Lloyd, D. P. Hallahan, & T. A. Astuto (Eds.), *Issues in educational placement: Students with emotional and behavioral disorders* (pp. 169-181). Hillsdale, NJ: Lawrence Erlbaum.

MacMillan, D. L., Gresham, F. M., & Forness, S. R. (1996). Full inclusion: An empirical perspective. *Behavior Disorders, 21,* 145-159.

Mills v. Board of Education District of Columbia, 348 F. Supp. 866 (1972).

National Association of School Psychologists (1997). *Principles for professional ethics*. Bethesda, MD: Author.

Oberti v. Board of Education of Clementon School District, 995 F 2d 1204 (3rd Cir. 1993).

Paul, J. L., Berger, N. H., Osnes, P. G., Martinez, Y. G., & Morse W. C. (Eds.), *Ethics and decision making in local schools: Inclusion, policy, and reform*. Baltimore, MD: Paul H. Brooks.

Pennsylvania Association for Retarded Citizens (P.A.R.C.) v. Commonwealth of Pennsylvania, 334 F. Supp. 1257 (D.C.E.D. Pa 1971), 343 F. Supp. 279 (D.C.E.E. Pa 1972).

Poolaw v. Bishop, 67 F. 3d 830 (9th Cir. 1995).

Sale, P., & Carey, D. M. (1995). The sociometric status of students with disabilities in a full-inclusion school. *Exceptional Children, 62*, 6-19

Sattler, J. M. (1992). *Assessment of children* (Revised and Undated 3rd ed.). San Diego: Jerome M. Sattler, Publisher, Inc.

Schneider, B. H., & Leroux, J. (1994). Educational environments for the pupil with behavioral disorders: A "best evidence" synthesis. *Behavioral Disorders, 19*, 192-204.

Snell, M. E. (1991). Schools are for all kids: The importance of integration for students with severe disabilities and their peers. In J. W. Lloyd, A. C. Repp, & N. N. Singh (Eds.), *The Regular Education initiative: Alternative perspectives on concepts, issues, and models* (pp. 133-148). Sycamore, IL: Sycamore.

Stainback, S., & Stainback, W. (1992). Schools as inclusive communities. In W. Stainback & S. Stainback (Eds.), *Controversial issues confronting special education* (pp. 29-43). Boston: Allyn & Bacon.

Stainback, S., Stainback, W., & Ayres, B. (1996). Schools as inclusive communities. In W. Stainback & S. Stainback (Eds.), *Controversial issues confronting special education* (2nd ed., pp. 31-43). Boston: Allyn and Bacon.

Stainback, W., & Stainback, S. (1990). *Support networking for inclusive schooling: Interdependent, integrated education*. Baltimore: Paul H. Brookes.

The Rehabilitation Act of 1973 (P.L. 93-112), 29 U.S.C.A. § 794.

Thomas, S. B., & Rapport, M. J. K. (in press). Least restrictive environment: Understanding the direction of the courts. *Journal of Special Education*.

U.S. Department of Commerce (1982). *Statistical abstract of the United States, 1982* (102nd ed.). Washington, DC: Author.

U.S. Department of Commerce (1997). *Statistical abstract of the United States, 1997* (117th ed.). Washington, DC: Author.

Woody, R. H. (1998, April). *Liability in school psychology: The interface between ethics and law*. Paper presented at the annual Trainers of School Psychologists Conference, Orlando, FL.

Achieving Effective
and Inclusive School Settings:
A Guide for Professional Development

Todd A. Gravois

Howard County (MD) Public Schools

Sylvia Rosenfield

University of Maryland, College Park

Lindsay Vail

Baltimore City (MD) Public Schools

SUMMARY. Skills underlying effective inclusion practices, especially for mildly handicapped students, should center on quality of instruction and the development of collaborative structures to support teachers' core competencies which also facilitate successful schools in general. However, ensuring professional growth in these competencies requires implementation of the best practices in staff development and adult learning. An example of how staff development is implemented in practice is described, using the example of one model program, Instructional Consultation Teams. *[Article copies available for a fee from The Haworth Document Delivery Service: 1-800-342-9678. E-mail address: getinfo@haworthpressinc.com <Website: http:// www.haworthpressinc.com>]*

Address correspondence to: Dr. Todd A. Gravois, 10306 Globe Drive, Elliott City, MD 21042.

[Haworth co-indexing entry note]: "Achieving Effective and Inclusive School Settings: A Guide for Professional Development." Gravois, Todd A., Sylvia Rosenfield, and Lindsay Vail. Co-published simultaneously in *Special Services in the Schools* (The Haworth Press, Inc.) Vol. 15, No. 1/2, 1999, pp. 145-170; and: *Inclusion Practices with Special Needs Students: Theory, Research, and Application* (ed: Steven I. Pfeiffer, and Linda A. Reddy) The Haworth Press, Inc., 1999, pp. 145-170. Single or multiple copies of this article are available for a fee from The Haworth Document Delivery Service [1-800-342-9678, 9:00 a.m. - 5:00 p.m. (EST). E-mail address: getinfo@haworthpressinc.com].

145

KEYWORDS. Consultation, teams, collaborative instruction teams, staff development

There remains a lack of agreement within the research as to the definition and practice of inclusion. Defining characteristics of successful inclusive settings include terms such as supportive, cooperative, individualized, and collaborative (Reed & Monda-Amaya, 1995). Inclusion assumes the development of programming that is directly related to the capabilities and needs of the student (Stainback & Stainback, 1990) and is delivered within the general education arena. The current inclusion debate focuses on the degree to which students with disabilities should be educated alongside their nonhandicapped peers within their community schools, as opposed to being mainstreamed into general education classes after first developing the skills and capabilities within segregated environments. This debate, grounded in philosophy and beliefs, and in some instances, empirical findings, will likely continue for years.

Proponents of least restrictive environment (LRE) cited in the Individuals with Disabilities Education Act (IDEA) imply that the intention of the law is for students with disabilities to be educated within the general education classroom within community schools (Stainback & Stainback, 1990; Wigle & Wilcox, 1996; also see Villa, Thousand, Stainback, & Stainback, 1992). Further, proponents suggest that "full" inclusion will provide not only educational benefits, but more importantly, the social and emotional connections that such students will require when they leave the safe haven of the structured and confined education arena and move into the less supportive and routinized work world (Villa & Thousand, 1988 in this volume as well). While acknowledging that the costs for such a goal are high, in terms of increased staff and time for joint planning, advocates for full inclusion believe that the costs will benefit individual students' and society's productivity (Villa, Thousand, Nevin & Malgeri, 1996).

An opposing view is that LRE is not necessarily mandated, but instead involves consideration of a continuum of educational services and a determination of appropriate placement on a student by student basis (see Wigle & Wilcox, 1996 for a review of the literature). While not opposed to fully including students who are deemed able to function successfully within the classroom, advocates of a continuum of services are concerned, justifiably so in some instances, that service and supports for students with disabilities will decrease, leaving individual students stranded within classrooms, unable to succeed and with little or no support and advocacy. Between these two views are a multitude of subtle, yet debatable, options of how to conceptualize and define inclusion.

THE HIDDEN DEBATE

However divergent the conceptualizations of inclusion may be, a central issue within the debate exists which is rarely explicitly acknowledged. Inclusion debaters, to a large extent, disagree about whether students who experience difficulty within the classroom suffer some student-centered disability which must be identified in order to provide specialized programming and instruction. That is to say, the current special education process largely centers around first *excluding* students from being normal, then arguing *where* to provide *specialized* instruction to these *disabled* students. In addition, there is the larger issue as to whether the current special education delivery system itself, especially in the case of mild disabilities (i.e., learning disabilities, mild mental retardation, behavior disordered and language impaired) is in fact defensible regardless of whether students are pulled out of or are provided specialized instruction within the general education classroom.

The criticisms of special education as a separate service delivery model (Wang, Reynolds & Walberg, 1986), of the negative impact of labeling students (Hobbs, 1975), a continuing disproportionate overrepresentation of minority students in special education (Heller, Holtzman, & Messic, 1982), and the lack of reliability and validity in the testing, identification and placement process (e.g., Aaron, 1997; Ysseldyke et al., 1983) remains largely unanswered from a system that is reaching its quarter-century mark (see also Brantlinger, 1997). In addition, research also does not appear to support the argument that students who are referred for learning problems often require highly specialized instruction. Slavin and his colleagues' (Slavin, Madden, & Karweit, 1990) review of the research on special education instruction did not find the uniqueness of special education instruction often described, nor did it support improved student outcomes in the categorical programs that have developed. Indeed, Slavin et al., much like Bloom (1976) and Brophy (1986), concluded that while some students will need more intensive instruction, there is no evidence that the type of instruction needed be different. More pointedly, it becomes clearer that it was not where services were provided, but the quality of the instruction that made the difference for students. Empirical evidence further suggests that the application of principles of effective instruction not only assists in creating success for low achieving and identified students within the classroom (Wigle & Wilcox, 1996), but in fact prevents student failure and avoids the need to consider special education services at all (Nevin & Thousand, 1987).

This research-based perspective that the skills underlying effective inclusion, especially for mildly handicapped students, should center on quality of instruction and the development of collaborative structures to support teachers, is the foundation for this article. The prevailing need for schools attempting to include students with disabilities, and more importantly to assist students' success without the need for special education, appears to be related to a better understanding of several core competencies that educators should possess to facilitate the creation of successful schools in general. These competencies include: the ability to build a shared understanding around several key issues; awareness and application of empirical research on effective instruction and student learning; skills in problem solving and data-based decision making; and skills in collaboration (see, for example, Alexander & Murphy, 1998, Fallen & Hargreaves, 1991; Pfeiffer & Cundari in this volume; Rosenholtz, 1989; Ysseldyke & Christenson, 1993). Successful schools must be defined according to the teaching and learning that occurs for *all* students, rather than the success of the highest or lowest achieving students.

Secondly, we will discuss the necessary steps that must be taken to ensure effective professional growth in each of the core competencies. The problem of limited research utilization continues to plague education, i.e., there is a large chasm between our knowledge of effective practice and our ability to implement those practices within the classroom. According to Alexander et al. (1996), the failure to translate knowledge into practice is because educators:

> Do not have a rich understanding of those innovations, leading to superficial solutions or implementation, or. . . . Do not have an extensive knowledge of the literature or research that underlie these innovations, resulting in the reinvention or recycling of old movements under new labels. (p. 31)

Making the transfer of skills and knowledge into school practice requires an understanding and appreciation of the research and practice for staff development and adult learning as well (e.g., Joyce & Showers, 1980; Showers & Joyce, 1996).

Finally, we will provide an example of how these practices have been employed to support the development of schools which are collaborative, focus on teaching and learning, and simultaneously, are inclusive. The training underlying one such model, Instructional Consultation Teams (Rosenfield & Gravois, 1996), will provide examples of structures that support schools to develop collaborative and data-driven problem-solving teams which help schools move from a conception of Least Restrictive Environment for individuals with disabilities to Most Enabling Environment for all students (Witkin & Fox, 1992).

COMPETENCIES OF PROFESSIONALS IN EFFECTIVE AND INCLUSIVE SCHOOLS

A review of the educational literature demonstrates a clear connection between the characteristics of effective schools and those considered inclusive. Terms such as common vision and goals, common conceptual framework, collaboration, shared technical culture, continuous monitoring, and increase student engagement continually emerge from both sets of literature (e.g., Pankake & Palmer, 1996; Fullan, 1991, 1993; Rosenholtz, 1985, 1989; Villa, Thousand, & Chapple, 1996; Villa, Thousand, Nevin & Malgeri, 1996; Wigle & Wilcox, 1996).

Based upon this review of the literature, we suggest effective and inclusive schools have four major and common processes upon which they both focus: conceptual vision and philosophy; teaching practices guided by empirically based research; norms of problem solving; and norms of collegial collaboration and teaming. These areas represent the "what" of effective and inclusive schools. Fullan and Hargreaves (1991) indicated that schools first must make decisions as to what is important and then work to achieve that focus. For example, curriculum and instruction remains a key focus for schools that are effective. This implies that school leadership and staff must agree that their energy, resources, staff development, and time will be devoted to selecting the best curriculum and developing the very best teaching skills to meet the needs of all students. "How" a particular school goes about creating such a focus is the issue of staff development, which will be a major discussion for the development of the four areas described below. These core areas represent content which educational professionals should be exposed to as part of both their pre-service and in-service training (Villa, Thousand, & Chapple, 1996; Wigle & Wilcox, 1996).

Shared Vision and Philosophy

"If there is any center to the mystery of schools' success, mediocrity, or failure, it lies deep within the structure of organizational goals and whether or not they exist, how they are defined and manifested, the extent to which they are mutually shared" (Rosenholtz, 1989, p. 13). Although this concept is widely shared in the organizational development literature, many times setting school goals is viewed as a meaningless exercise for staff members by leaders who themselves often do not truly believe in a shared vision of schooling. General school goals are not enough, however. Within schools seeking to practice inclusion, research supports the need to specify goals and vision around inclusion. For example, in investigating teacher concerns around including students with severe and multiple disabilities, Pankake and Palmer (1996) discovered that a major factor supportive of inclusion was staff development that helped frame the purpose and direction of the inclusion initiative in which they were involved. Considering the ongoing debate discussed earlier with regard to what is inclusion and how it should look, it is understandable that educators do not have a clear vision or expectation of inclusion, but instead must be assisted in creating one. The opportunity for staff members to dialogue, receive information and formulate a conceptual understanding of the change that they are about to undertake assists in addressing several basic concerns that have been studied across initiatives (Hall & Hord, 1987; Stokes & Howard, 1996). Stokes and Howard's study of concerns of individuals involved in inclusion suggested that initial concerns of participants focused upon personal and information needs. These concerns decreased with increased opportunities to build a common understanding around the definition and characteristics of inclusion, a common philosophy, to explore the types of supports that would be required and to gain an understanding of those supports that actually existed.

The competency required here is twofold. First, there needs to be a conceptual understanding for teachers, staff and leaders as to the scope, purpose and practical implications of inclusion. Second, some individuals within the school, most likely the school principal or other key player, must possess the skill to assist the staff in creating a vision and philosophy that focuses upon student learning and instruction for all students. Such a vision and philosophy will not be achieved unless the leaders of schools directly address and confront the basic beliefs, assumptions and attitudes of both professionals and community members about students with disabilities and effective practices for teaching and learning (see for example, Servatius, Fellows, & Kelly, 1992).

Empirically Based Instructional Practices

A large body of research supports the notion that the type, amount, and quality of instruction provided to students is a critical, if not *the* critical, determiner of student success (Wigle & Wilcox, 1996; Ysseldyke & Christenson, 1993). Professionals in successful and inclusive settings require an understanding of the empirical research surrounding effective instruction, student learning and classroom management. Whether a student has a disability or not, it is increasingly clear that what and how the teacher instructs makes a difference. In many instances, the type of instruction does not differ so much between disabled and non-disabled students (Slavin et al. , 1990). Instead, how instruction is delivered, including the frequency and focus of teaching practices, appears relevant.

Student-Teacher Interactions. In their review of the literature, Wigle and Wilcox (1996) summarized the research relating to the learning environment. Their review found that teacher-student interactions and students' opportunity to respond were both positively related to academic success. Research over the past twenty years demonstrates the connection between student interactions with teachers (i.e., being asked questions, responding during learning activities, receiving corrective feedback) and student achievement. While class size and composition certainly influence the number and quality of teacher-student interactions, teachers' expectations also play a part. Indeed, teachers tend to interact at higher levels with students expected to achieve than with students whom teachers expect to do poorly.

For disabled students to be successful within the general education classroom, teachers must develop competencies in managing the classroom environment so that teacher-student interactions are maximized. Teachers must master skills in questioning, providing wait time, cuing responses and coaching. Teachers must also develop a vigilance toward the tendency to have fewer interactions with students who are expected to do poorly. Pre-service teachers should receive classroom experience which focuses upon such teacher behaviors, and practicing professionals should form coaching pairs with a focus upon maximizing teacher-student interactions.

Student Responding. As with student-teacher interactions, the opportunity for students to respond appears highly related to achievement (Wigle & Wilcox, 1996). The creation of classroom environments in which students have multiple opportunities to respond to relevant tasks was found to benefit student learning. By increasing students' opportunity to respond, teachers are able to provide frequent corrective feedback and to assess and monitor student learning. Teachers who follow a traditional approach to instruction (i.e., the stand and deliver model) will likely not provide disabled students with maximum response opportunities. Likewise, such instructional practices will not maximize engagement of the average or above average student. However, teachers who are skilled at creating classrooms that engage students in cooperative models of participation (i.e., cooperative groups; think, pair, share, etc.) can increase student responding opportunities with little or no effort. Teachers who learn to monitor their own instructional behavior and, much like student-teacher interactions, recognize the potential for decreased response opportunities for low achieving and disabled students, can better search out alternative strategies to maintain high response rates.

The Non-Neutrality of Tasks and Curriculum. There remains a misconception in education that the task and curriculum demands that are placed upon students are neutral in terms of their impact on student learning. However, the task and curriculum that a teacher selects is not neutral and very much influences both actual learning and, equally important, a student's motivation to learn (Wigle & Wilcox, 1996). Research indicates that student success rates with tasks should remain fairly high (see, e.g., Gickling & Rosenfield, 1995; Wigle & Wilcox, 1996). It is suggested that for basic skills and topics, students should have a success rate within the 70-85% range. For application tasks, such as reading, doing homework and seatwork, success rates should range from 90-97% (Berliner, 1984, cited in Wigle & Wilcox, 1996; Gickling & Rosenfield, 1995; McGreal, 1985, cited in Wigle & Wilcox, 1996). To be clear, these ratios represent a predictor of student success on a particular task prior to attempting the task and prior to instruction.

A practical example of how success rates influence learning can easily be seen in a typical spelling program in which students learn ten words per week. According to this concept of high success rates, a student should already know 7 of the 10 words on the list that is presented on Monday. The student's learning then is focused upon three new words while successfully practicing the remaining seven. For any classroom teacher doubting this ratio, she/he is encouraged to critically review the spelling pre-test of all students on Monday. Invariably, average and high achieving students already know a large percentage of the words on Monday and only have to learn 3-4 words for Friday's test. However, low achievers and disabled students often score 1-2 words correct on Monday and in effect have to learn 2-3 times the number of words as their counterparts. While spelling programs represent a simple task to demonstrate the importance of maintaining high success rates, the concept applies to all tasks and curriculum demands. As such, teachers in pre-service and in-service programs not only require an awareness of task influence on learning, but also appropriate classroom and curriculum-based assessment strategies that allow them to assess students' prior knowledge, plan objectives based upon students' prior knowledge, and then select appropriate tasks which maintain high success rates.

The common question raised is whether a classroom teacher, with a class size of 25-30 students, can assess students prior to instruction, and then take the time to develop tasks that meet each student's needs. However, linking assessment and instructional planning is exactly what teachers in successful schools do. Just as increasing students' opportunities to respond implies restructuring instructional delivery to include cooperative peer interactions, teachers in inclusive classrooms have to rethink their conceptualization of how to gather critical assessment information about students' prior knowledge. To do so, teachers must utilize the most plentiful resource in the classroom—the students themselves. Gickling and Rosenfield (1995) provide an example of how teachers transferred the assessment process to their students in a completely restructured classroom. In this example, students were taught to assess for themselves what they knew about the upcoming assignment, and what they would need to know in order to be successful. The teacher utilized this information to maximize development of basic skills/ topics and then utilized cooperative groups to support the success rate during instruction. Not only does this student-driven assessment process assist the teacher, it represents a critical thinking skill for students–the ability to self-assess what they know and what they need to know about a learning task.

There are two critical comments that need to be made about understanding the awareness of task variables upon student learning. The first is that the desire of teachers is often counter-intuitive to the concept of high success rates. Teachers tend to want to give low achievers and disabled students more unknown information in an effort to "catch them up." However, as the research demonstrates, the learning process is driven more by understanding the student's learning rate than the teaching rate. More importantly, frustration associated with low success rates erodes long term motivation on the student's part. The second comment is to emphasize that the concept of high success rates is not the same as "watered down" or "slow paced" curriculum. Indeed, as teachers master the ability to assess a student's knowledge and skills on a frequent basis, they will be able to increase the student's rate of learning by adjusting and raising objectives in a timely fashion. Using the spelling test example, a teacher who utilizes pre-testing can quickly adjust the task if a student scores 9 out of 10 words on Monday by adding more words or extending the lesson to include application. Likewise, such assessment processes will assist teachers in analyzing the rate at which students are learning and flexibly adjust the success rate related to a particular student's own tolerance for challenge.

Student Academic Engaged Time. Wigle and Wilcox (1996) provide a valuable service by differentiating academic engaged time from instructional time, as well as differentiating the impact of both upon learning. Instructional time, the time that the teacher has allocated for the delivery of a selected lesson, has a low correlation with student learning. However, academic engaged time, the time in which students are actually involved in a learning task, has a strong relationship with learning. The research demonstrates that disabled and low achieving students typically experience low engagement rates and high frustration. In order to promote greater academic engagement, teachers must "be able to provide the support and structure necessary to facilitate engaged learning. . . . high level of student-teacher interaction, consistent and frequent monitoring of student activity, numerous opportunities to respond, and a great deal of effective teacher feedback" (p. 325).

Classroom Management and Student Behavior. Rosenfield (1987) frames the teacher's job as twofold: managing the learning process, which to a large extent is captured in the above sections and management of the learner. Professionals within inclusive and effective schools recognize that student behavior is influenced by many variables, including the instructional and management practices employed within the classroom. While this review has focused primarily on instructional strategies, a similar literature on behavioral interventions in the classroom documents essential principles which are helpful to teachers and parents, but less often found in practice. Munger (1998), for example, provides an overview of principles for mental health practitioners to assist them in understanding the impact of the environment on a child's functioning and ways to create supportive environments at school and at home. He stresses the application of these principles to children with serious emotional disturbance, as he reframes the issue of mainstreaming children with behavior problems from a focus on the child to a more inclusive approach based on providing environmental support for appropriate behavior. A solid grounding in behavioral and cognitive behavioral principles has also been found to be useful, provided they are implemented with integrity in the school setting (Rosenfield, 1985). The empirical literature on classroom management has grown "explosively" in the last quarter century, focusing increasingly on creating positive environments for learning rather than disciplinary techniques (Jones & Jones, 1998). However, Jones and Jones cite the research demonstrating the lack of knowledge about these strategies, even in teachers of special education.

As one reviews this brief summary of empirical findings related to effective instruction and student learning, it is easy to see how overwhelmed classroom teachers can feel. And yet, there is a clear message that such empirically based practices promote successful learning and behavior not only for high achieving students but also for low achieving and students with disabilities. The goal then for schools seeking to embed such practices into all professionals' functioning is to develop the final two competencies that are required for successful and inclusive schools: problem solving and collaboration.

Problem Solving

It is our position that the constructs of problem solving and collaboration should remain linked in practice. However, each represents a unique competency to be mastered by professionals in successful and inclusive schools, and deserves individual treatment. We will start with the competency of problem solving and the belief that professionals in successful and inclusive schools adopt, share and implement a common framework of problem solving that is grounded in the overall philosophy and vision of the school.

The *American Heritage Dictionary* defines a problem as "a situation, matter, or person that presents perplexity or difficulty . . . a question to be considered, solved or answered." In education, the ultimate problem or situation to be improved always remains the same–student achievement. As Rosenholtz (1985) suggests "school excellence lies in the direction of rational planning and action where principals . . . mobilize teachers against a single common enemy: low student achievement" (p. 381). With regard to successful and inclusive schools, then, problem solving represents an agreed upon approach directed toward improving learning for students. Specific to inclusive schools is the goal of improved student learning within the general classroom. Problem solving remains intimately linked to a school's norms of continuous improvement for students and staff.

Problem solving occurs on a daily basis in schools. Teachers regularly encounter one or more students who are not successful, assess the situation, make an adjustment in instruction and then evaluate whether there is improvement. Such processes can be isolated and closed to other teachers, or can be in the form of a participatory model (Huberman, 1995). School staff can make explicit the components of problem solving so that allocations can be made of resources and staff development for the skills necessary for every professional to successfully participate alone or with others in problem solving. These components include recognition of the difficulty and uncertainty of teaching, skill in a system of inquiry, a focus of problem solving on the teaching and learning process, and a repertoire of evaluation skills linked to instruction and management.

Recognizing Uncertainty. For problem solving to become a standard of the school culture and part of professional practice, there must be the recognition that every educational professional will at some point in their professional functioning experience uncertainty. Indeed, education as a profession is nonroutine and often unpredictable, thereby increasing teachers' uncertainty about their own and students' performance. However, unlike other professions (i.e., medicine and law) teaching is much more isolated. In her research of effective schools, Rosenholtz (1989) suggests that isolation and uncertainty become a vicious cycle whereby the isolated teacher experiences uncertainty and further isolates her/his professional functioning from other teachers, which in turn further increases the uncertainty. Such uncertainty will only be exacerbated for teachers in inclusive settings where they are now being asked to instruct students that they have previously been told need specialized instruction. When schools can promote an expectation that teachers, as professionals, will encounter problems, then problem solving will become an accepted competency to acquire.

Adopting a System of Inquiry. There is a dire need for schools to foster a common language by which professionals will approach problems. The explicit adoption of a system of inquiry effectively guides the type of staff development and support given to professionals so they may practice and master the necessary skills. Although many models of problem solving exist, they all have fairly common characteristics. Models typically rely upon steps or stages and are presented in a cyclical nature. For example, Huberman (1995) described an individual cycle of innovation used by lone teachers which includes (1) perceiving a problem, (2) assessing the problem, (3) experimentation and (4) applying new ideas. This process can occur repetitively until the perceived problem is resolved or until the teacher stops. In addition to individual processes of inquiry used by teachers, successful schools are found to have active processes and procedures by which teachers interact with colleagues to generate solutions to problems (Little, 1982; Rosenholtz, 1985; 1989). Professionals in successful and inclusive schools must forge a system by which they will address problems and are encouraged to review the school consultation literature (see, e.g., Kratochwill & Bergan, 1978; Parsons & Meyers, 1984; Rosenfield, 1987) for examples of problem-solving models. Whichever model is adopted, it is important to recognize that such inquiry is a circular and an on-going process in which educators remain engaged until student success is achieved.

Focusing Problem Solving. Adoption of a system of inquiry is not enough. Professionals in successful and inclusive schools must focus their problem solving efforts on their own professional functioning and practice in order to influence student performance–instead of focusing only on students' perceived deficits. This requires a knowledge of and skill in the empirically based instructional practices reviewed earlier, and an openness to examining the classroom ecology as part of the system of inquiry. Educators in inclusive schools in particular must recognize and understand that no learning has ever improved by simply labeling a student with a handicapping condition. Instead, we believe true improvement occurs when professionals identify a student's current functioning, set specific goals and then intervene–*adjust, modify, add, delete, embellish and change* [emphasis added] their own instructional practices in relation to the student's entry skills. Such focus is tied closely to the school's overall philosophy of continuous improvement and expectation that professionals analyze, evaluate and experiment in order to accomplish student achievement.

Evaluating Instructional Decisions. Problem solving that exists in most schools is often informal and lacks accountability. Time is often named as the bandit that robs teachers and support personnel of the ability to evaluate whether their instructional practices are indeed making a difference for students. However, professionals in successful and inclusive schools need to acquire and utilize skills in conducting frequent assessments of student performance (i.e., curriculum based assessment, direct behavioral observation, etc.) and become skilled in monitoring their own practice (via peer coaching, professional reflection). More importantly, evaluation should be built into the instructional process rather than seen as an extra part to be added or deleted depending upon time constraints. As Rosenfield (1987) suggests, "ongoing evaluation is a necessary ingredient of quality instruction. All instructional strategies are formulated as hypotheses to be tested for effectiveness in achieving desired outcomes rather than as carved-in-stone recommendations to be carried out . . . until the academic year ends" (Rosenfield, 1987, p. 18). The bottom line is that professionals engaging in problem solving must be skilled in formulating problems in measurable terms and collecting relevant data about students' performance within the classroom prior to, during and following instruction (see Gickling & Rosenfield, 1995).

Collaboration

The connection between the literature on effective schools and that of inclusive schools is nowhere more prevalent than with respect to the concept of collaboration. The proponents of inclusion promote collaboration among professionals as the foundation for achieving success for students with disabilities within the general education classroom (e.g., Pfeiffer & Cundari in this volume; Reed & Monda-Amaya, 1995; Thousand &Villa, 1992; Villa et al., 1996; Wigle & Wilcox, 1996). Research on effective schools repeatedly has found that schools which demonstrated increased student achievement were able to tear down the barriers of isolation and foster collegial collaboration (Fullan, 1991; Little, 1982; Rosenholtz, 1985; 1989). There is little question a major competency that professionals in successful and inclusive schools need is the ability to collaborate with peers.

However, many educators continue to confuse problem solving and collaboration, often implying that the two are the same or are always present together. It is, however, a reality that a teacher can problem solve without collaborating with others, and likewise collaborate with other professionals without actually engaging in a problem solving process. For example, Fullan and Hargreaves (1991) have delineated a hierarchy of collaboration ranging from comfortable collaboration, which includes "advice-giving, trick-trading and material-sharing of a more immediate, specific and technical nature" (p. 55) which "does not embrace the principles of systematic reflective practice" (p. 56) to contrived collegiality, in which administrators implement "a set of formal, specific, bureaucratic procedures to increase the attention . . . to joint teacher planning, consultation and other forms of working together" (p. 58) which at its worst "can be reduced to a quick, slick administrative surrogate for collaborative . . . cultures" (p. 58) to interactive professionalism, which adopts reflection about practice and norms of continuous improvement.

Although there are many definitions of collaboration within the literature that speak to the voluntary nature, mutual benefit, and creative solutions involved (e.g., Friend & Cook, 1992; Fullan & Hargreaves, 1991; Reed & Monda-Amaya, 1995; Villa et al., 1996), Rosenholtz's (1989) simple definition of collaboration as "requests for and offers of collegial advice and assistance" (p. 41) cuts to the core of the competencies that professionals must possess. Unlike other definitions of collaboration, Rosenholtz places onus on educators to approach other educators and offer assistance, rather than simply wait and receive it. Defined in this way, collaboration implies professionals must not only have adopted the mind set and/or skills of those competencies presented thus far–a shared perspective in which inclusive schooling is a given, a willingness to employ empirically based practices/evaluate effectiveness of practices, and a reflective, problem solving process–but must develop effective communication and interpersonal skills and be secure and articulate in their roles and responsibilities within the building as well.

In studying the inclusion of severe multiple disabled students, Pankake and Palmer (1996) found that a major barrier to effective collaboration and coordination of supports was unclear roles and responsibilities and under-developed interpersonal skills. Support given by paraprofessionals (i.e., classroom aides and assistants) was more favorably cited by classroom teachers than that offered by the special educators and resource personnel, largely due to unclear roles and responsibilities. "It is unwise to assume that special educators know how to serve as consultants," indeed special educators, are "also in need of staff development . . . regarding their new roles and relationships" (p. 29) when working in inclusive settings. Similar changes will be necessary in almost every role in a school striving to be effective and inclusive.

Given these findings, the "critical question becomes, then, how to develop patterns of interaction that will support innovation or commitment to more effective instructional policies for all students rather than an unconditional and nonreflective enthusiasm for collaboration" (Rosenfield & Gravois, 1996, p. 10). A major set of skills that must be mastered by professionals is a recognition of the importance of a good working relationship and competency in basic listening and communication skills. Because collaboration is inherently a relationship, professionals must be willing to negotiate parameters and boundaries, reciprocate when appropriate, and remain respectful of others' opinions and feelings. Most of all, professionals engaged in collaboration must be genuine and authentic in their offers of assistance. Mastery of basic listening and communication skills, such as paraphrasing, clarifying, summarizing, reflective listening and strategic questioning, provide tools with which to establish the collaborative nature of the relationship and to assist in the overall problem solving process described earlier.

PROMOTING PROFESSIONAL GROWTH AND DEVELOPMENT

Although there is increased agreement on the competencies educational professionals require to successfully participate in effective and inclusive schools, the dilemma remains how to transfer that knowledge into practice. It is now widely acknowledged by school change scholars that one-day, one-shot training, while useful to build awareness of new ideas and skills, does little to change professional functioning (Fullan, 1991, 1993). The same holds true for inclusion where "too much training and explaining early on and too little when the actual implementation is underway are typical errors" (Pankake & Palmer, 1996, p. 30). To fully appreciate the importance of thoughtful and strategic professional development, schools must give consideration to the vast literature on staff development and adult learning.

In the 1970s, educational researchers demonstrated that fewer than 10% of educators involved in workshop or inservice programs implemented what they learned (Showers & Joyce, 1996). Such lack of transfer represents a critical problem for schools attempting to assist professionals in changing their behaviors. However, recent attention to the practices and procedures utilized in training and inservice have significantly increased the likelihood of acquisition of new skills and knowledge, and the ultimate transfer of skills into practice. In their classic review of the literature, Joyce and Showers (1980) suggested five methods of training, each providing a different level of impact on professionals' skill, knowledge and practice.

The first method of training is presentation of theory. Through reading, discussion, and lectures, professionals gain greater intellectual awareness of a concept. While useful to increase professionals' knowledge of certain competencies, such as awareness of empirically based teaching practices, these type of presentations will do little to alter actual practice.

Modeling and demonstration is the second method of training reviewed by Joyce and Showers (1980). By observing a model or enactment of the skill or strategy through live action or film, professionals increase their awareness and gain some knowledge about a new skill. Again, professionals could develop a better understanding of how empirically based teaching practices look within a situation. However, as with presentation of theory, little if any change in practice occurs.

A third training method presented by Joyce and Showers (1980) is practice under simulated conditions. In this method, teachers try new skills or strategies in controlled or simulated conditions. Professionals may practice communication skills with one another during a training, or try to utilize a problem-solving framework to address a simulated problem. According to Joyce and Showers, a large percentage of professionals learn new behaviors in this fashion and begin to transfer these newly learned skills into the school and classroom setting. However, such transfer was thought to be limited with complex and unfamiliar skills such as those required for collaboration, problem solving and empirically based teaching practices.

A fourth method of training is the use of structured and unstructured feedback. Feedback represents the opportunity for professionals to observe one another and provide information about current behavior or about the use of a newly learned skill. Feedback can occur with other methods of training (e.g., within simulation exercises) and is seen as necessary for producing and maintaining changes in practice. Feedback that is structured involves a particular system of observation and reflection and is thought to result in more consistent changes in teacher behavior. Unstructured feedback, however, is thought to have an uneven impact in changing teacher behavior (Joyce & Showers, 1980).

The fifth and final method to foster professional development is coaching for application. Coaching involves helping professionals analyze the situation in which the new skill will be used, plan, implement and then evaluate the impact of using the new skill within the work environment (Joyce & Showers, 1980). A coaching relationship develops between two professionals–one attempting to utilize a skill and the other experienced in applying the skill in practice. It is within this relationship that the actual application of new skills or refinement of existing skills occurs.

For example, after learning about the importance of high student response rates in a lecture or workshop, teachers may choose to participate in a peer coaching relationship to increase student responding in their classrooms. The two professionals could analyze current practices for student responding, plan new strategies, and observe one another in the classroom implementing the strategy. Following the observation they would meet and provide feedback to each other as to the application of the strategy and its effectiveness upon student responding.

Showers and Joyce (1996) hypothesized and later demonstrated that the use of coaching produces significant transfer of newly acquired skills and knowledge into actual practice. However, it is critical to remember that coaching relies upon the other four methods of training to develop awareness, knowledge and skill. One cannot coach when an individual does not have an awareness or skill to be coached. If there is a deficit, then other methods of training will be needed to build the requisite knowledge and skills.

As would be expected, strategically and sequentially combining training methods produces greater impact than any one method alone (Joyce & Showers, 1980, Showers & Joyce, 1996). Likewise, the use of all training methods would provide greater assurance that professionals develop awareness, knowledge, and use of the professional competencies associated with successful and inclusive schools.

AN EXAMPLE
OF COMPREHENSIVE PROFESSIONAL DEVELOPMENT

The review of the literature presented thus far provides a comprehensive view of developing professionals' knowledge, skills and practices toward the creation of not only inclusive, but effective schools. Creating such a comprehensive professional development program, one that cuts across both competencies and processes of staff development, is a complex process. Without careful consideration of the available research, inclusion, much like previous efforts to change the general education setting to accommodate learning differences (i.e., REI), will fail to demonstrate effective outcomes. The broad literature on inclusion, effective schools, and professional development can be brought together in an effort to not only foster inclusion for students with disabilities, but to restructure schools to promote academic achievement for all students. While relatively rare in the literature, some models of effective professional development to prepare professionals for inclusive settings exist.

Instructional Consultation Teams (IC-Teams; Rosenfield & Gravois, 1996) is an example of an interdisciplinary model that incorporates key components of the effective schools literature and best practice in professional development. While not an inclusion model in the same frame as those offered by Villa et al. (1992, in this volume), IC-Teams focus upon many of the classroom instructional practices related to inclusion and use the educational change literature in its implementation and training. As a model of interdisciplinary problem solving, IC-Teams link school-based professionals (i.e., teachers, administrators, psychologists, guidance counselors, special educators, health providers, etc.) in a systematic delivery of services that supports classroom teachers who have requested assistance regarding a particular concern, be it with an individual student, classwide concerns or general instructional practices. Individual team members consult with the referring classroom teacher utilizing a systematic problem solving process that is data-based and relies heavily upon individual's collaborative and interpersonal skills. The team is a resource to support the teacher/team member dyad with more complex problems and address school-wide concerns (for further description of IC-Team model, see Rosenfield & Gravois, 1996). The complex skills and knowledge required for the IC-Team model parallels that required of best practices of inclusion and provides a practical example of how to design and deliver comprehensive training utilizing empirically derived professional development practices.

Currently, the IC-Team model is being implemented in over 30 schools in two school districts, one urban and one suburban. The support for the training process has been generated in-part by the continual presentation to district and school level decision makers of both formative and summative evaluation results demonstrating the efficacy of the model related to relevant district goals (e.g., presentation of changes in special education referral patterns, changes in inclusion practices for disabled students, and success in achievement of behavioral and academic student goals).

Initial Training of the IC-Team

A driving force of the IC-Team training model is the recognition that "a school team has to be carefully built if its members are going to be reasonably able to take on roles that are new to them" (Maeroff, 1993, p. 16). Hence, the purpose of staff development is twofold in the IC-Team process: (1) to build a collaborative team capable of positively influencing the school culture toward norms of collaboration and systematic problem solving, and (2) to provide the necessary skills and knowledge to individual team members so that they may effectively collaborate and solve problems presented by classroom teachers.

All teams involved in the IC-Team project participate in a 25 hour, week-long summer training institute (Gravois, 1995, 1996, 1997). As Maeroff (1993) indicates, "teamwork for any purpose is foreign to most teachers" (p. 7) and conscious efforts must be made if a functional team is to be achieved. The value of training an entire team–as a unit–cannot be overstated. Not only does a common training provide all members a shared understanding of the model, of the team's purpose, and of their own role as a member of the team, but such a training also provides the opportunity to begin developing working relationships and a shared philosophy about problem solving.

The second goal of the summer training is to create an awareness of the IC model among team members, assist team members in developing conceptual understanding and knowledge of the key components of IC and to develop basic skills and knowledge of the problem solving model. Throughout, there is respect for and understanding of educators as adult learners. Every effort is made to establish a climate of respect and a collaboration. Further, there is recognition that educators bring to each training their own knowledge and experience which, if understood and appreciated, can be maximized to ensure greater learning and ultimate transfer of new information into practice once they return to their school environment.

Team members actively diagnose their needs and their input is incorporated for the design of the training program whenever possible. For example, interactive, self-assessment activities (i.e., cooperative groups, table activities, etc.) are employed to assess team members' prior knowledge and then efforts are made to link such knowledge to newly introduced information. During the week of training, didactic presentation is utilized to introduce the theory and empirical bases underlying the IC-Team model while role plays, videotaped models and written activities assist team members in applying newly learned skills in the areas of communication, data collection and analysis, systematic problem-solving stages and curriculum-based assessment.

Since each area requires unique skills and knowledge, simulation activities are designed to target the practice of individual skills in the safe confines of a training environment. As an example, team members may participate within a role play of a case consultation in which they are to focus only on certain communication skills. While such application would be very difficult, not to mention uncomfortable, within the "real" world of school, team members are allowed the opportunity to see and hear themselves utilize a new skill or refine an existing one. Such practice is accompanied by structured feedback provided by both trainers and other team members.

On-Site Facilitation and Coaching

In order to support greater application of newly learned skills within the school by team members, each IC-Team project school is assigned a specially trained, on-site change facilitator. The change facilitator's time is allocated for the sole purpose of advancing the implementation of the IC-Team model. In the current implementation of IC-Teams the school psychologist serves as the on-site facilitator and is allocated an additional day and a half per school to facilitate and coach. The change facilitator's responsibility is to support the application of collaborative problem solving skills by team members through weekly one-hour meetings and periodic day-long training sessions focused upon developing and refining specific skills and knowledge introduced during the summer institute. By utilizing the various staff development methods, i.e., presentation of theory, simulations, coaching, etc., the change facilitator fosters a positive impact upon participants' acquisition and application of key skills. For example, if after the summer training the change facilitator assesses that team members continue to have difficulty utilizing curriculum based assessment (CBA), he/she may develop several simulation items for additional practice of skills. Likewise, team members may be encouraged to practice the use of CBA skills with several students within their own classroom before utilizing the skill as part of a case consultation.

While such continued team training remains a necessity, another crucial role for the on-site facilitator is to assist each team member in transferring the knowledge and skills they have learned into actual practice during consultation. The main method of staff development used is the coaching relationship between facilitator and team member (Joyce & Showers, 1980; Showers & Joyce, 1996). The change facilitator coaches individual members as they begin applying the problem solving model within actual consultations. The change facilitator meets individually with each team member and specifies skills to focus upon. The coaching process typically consists of a preconference, a data collection phase and a coaching conference (Rosenfield & Gravois, 1996). The preconference is used to specify a skill area that the team member will apply and a method by which the team member will collect data on the application of the selected skill. The data collection phase represents the actual application of the skill during a case consultation. Finally, the change facilitator and team member meet to review the application of the skill and review any changes in practice that are required. As would be expected the coaching process can be highly individualized to the particular needs of each team member and is applied for the development of the various skills required of the IC-Team model.

The on-site training and coaching of teams is mixed with one or two annual day-long trainings in which teams from multiple schools participate. In the early years of implementation of the IC-Team model, these one-day trainings allow the opportunity for teams from different schools to share successes and concerns in implementing the model. As implementation progresses, such trainings focus on key skills that have yet to be fully transferred into practice or upon new skills that are required to meet the demands of the particular school environment. Based on program evaluation results IC-Teams have re-visited skills in data-collection, charting and graphing of data, and the analysis of data as part of these day-long trainings. Likewise, teams have learned new skills that were directly related to the needs of their schools, such as the assessment of instructional factors that influence learning.

IC-Team Maintenance

The process of professional development of IC-Teams continues for three to five years. At the end of each year, the team and change facilitator schedule an end of year reflection meeting in which the progress of the preceding year can be reviewed and evaluated. Time is provided so that teams can review relevant data, assess their own functioning, and identify accomplishments and continued needs. Utilizing a structured problem-solving process, teams work together to develop specific goals and objectives to work on during the following year. Team members work collaboratively to specify training activities in which they, as a team, can engage in order to achieve established goals. They may design a training and professional development plan that meets the needs of their particular school. New team members receive training each summer and work with the on-site change facilitator to build their competence in the IC process. As team members' skills in and comfort with the data-based, problem-solving process increase, they assume more responsibility for monitoring the application of the model within their school.

CONCLUSION

The decision by schools and school districts to move toward the inclusion of students with disabilities is not a minor one given the history of segregating such students over the past 25 years. It requires both a shift in mindset as well as a shift in practice. Even those educators who themselves are supportive of the concept of inclusion, frequently do not have the necessary instructional and management skills to feel comfortable achieving success with such diverse learning needs, nor do many educators currently work in a school environment with established norms of collaboration and problem solving to support their individual efforts. The success of inclusion must be considered in light of the knowledge and skills derived from empirical research on teaching and learning, along with an appreciation and understanding of the research on effective professional development. The design and implementation of comprehensive staff development programs to support the creation of inclusive and effective schools is essential and possible when schools and systems make a clear commitment to effective inclusion practices.

REFERENCES

Aaron, P. G., (1997). The impending demise of the discrepancy formula. *Review of Educational Research, 67*, 461-502.

Alexander, P. A., & Murphy, P. K. (1998). The research base for APA's learner-centered principles. In B. L. McCombs & N. Lambert (Eds.) *Issues in school reform: A sampler of psychological perspectives on learner-centered schools.* Washington, DC: American Psychological Association.

Alexander, P. A., Murphy, P. K., & Woods, B. S. (1996). Of squalls and fathoms: Navigating the seas of educational innovation. *Educational Researcher, 25,* 31-36, 39.

Bloom, B. S. (1976). *Human characteristics and school learning.* New York: McGraw-Hill.

Brantlinger, E. (1997). Using ideology: Cases of nonrecognition of the politics of research and practice in special education, *Review of Educational Research, 67,* pp. 425-459.

Brophy, J. (1986). Research linking teacher behavior to student achievement: Potential implications for instruction of Chapter 1 students. In B. I. Williams, P. A. Richmond, & B. J. Mason (Eds.) *Designs for compensatory education: Conference proceedings and papers* (pp. IV-122-IV-179). Washington, DC: Research and Evaluation Associates.

Friend, M., & Cook, L. (1992). *Interactions: Collaboration skills for school professionals.* New York: Longman.

Fullan, M. (1993). *Change forces.* London, England: Falmer Press.

Fullan, M. G. (1991). *The new meaning of educational change.* New York: Teachers College Press.

Fullan, M. G., & Hargreaves, A. (1991). *What's worth fighting for? Working together for your school.* Andover, MA: Regional Laboratory for Educational Improvement of the Northeast and Islands.

Gickling, E. E., & Rosenfield, S. (1995). Best practices in curriculum-based assessment. In A. Thomas & J. Grimes (Eds.). *Best practices in school psychology, Vol. 3* (pp. 587-595). Washington, DC: National Association of School Psychologists.

Heller, K. A., Holtzman, W. H., & Messick, S. (Eds.). (1982). *Placing children in special education: A strategy for equity.* Washington, DC: National Academy Press.

Huberman, M. (1995). Professional careers and professional development. In T. Guskey & M. Huberman (Eds.), *Professional development in education: New paradigms and practices* (pp. 193-224). New York: Teachers College Press.

Jones, V. F., & Jones, L. S. (1998). *Comprehensive classroom management: Creating communities of support and solving problems* (5th ed.). Boston: Allyn & Bacon.

Joyce, B., & Showers, B. (1980). Improving inservice training: The messages of research. *Educational Leadership, 37,* 379-385.

Kratochwill, T. R., & Bergan, J. R. (1978). Training school psychologists: Some perspectives on a competency-based consultation model. *Professional Psychology, 9,* 71-82.

Little, J. (1982). Norms of collegiality and experimentation: Workplace conditions of school success. *American Educational Research Journal, 19,* 325-340.

Maeroff, G. I. (1993). *Team building for school change: Equipping teachers for new roles.* New York: Teachers College Press.

Munger, R. L. (1998). *The ecology of troubled children: Changing children's behavior by changing the places, activities, and people in their lives.* Cambridge, MA: Brookline Books.

Nevin, A., & Thousand, J. (1987). Avoiding or limiting special education referrals: Changes and challenges. In M. C. Wang, M. C. Reynolds, & H. J. Walberg (Eds.), *Handbook of special education: Research and practice* (Vol. 1, pp. 273-286). Oxford, England: Pergamon Press.

Pankake, A. M., & Palmer, B. (1996). Making the connections: Linking staff development interventions to implementation of full inclusion. *Journal of Staff Development, 17,* 26-30.

Parsons, R. D. & Meyers, J. (1984). *Developing consultation skills: A guide to training, development, and assessment for human services professionals.* San Francisco: Jossey-Bass.

Rosenfield, S. A. (1987). *Instructional consultation.* Hillsdale, NJ: Erlbaum.

Rosenfield, S. A. (1985). Teacher acceptance of behavioral principles. *Teacher Education and Special Education, 8,* 153-158.

Rosenfield, S. A., & Gravois, T.A. (1996). *Instructional consultation teams: Collaborating for change.* New York: Guilford.

Rosenholtz, S. J. (1985). Effective schools: Interpreting the evidence. *American Journal of Education, 93,* 352-388.

Rosenholtz, S. J. (1989). *Teachers' workplace: The social organization of schools.* New York: Teachers College Press.

Servatius, J. D., Fellows, M., & Kelly, D. (1992). Preparing leaders for inclusive schools. In R. Villa, J. Thousand, W. Stainback and S. Stainback (Eds). *Restruc-*

turing for caring and effective education: An administrative guide to creating heterogeneous schools (pp. 267-283). Baltimore, MD: Brookes.

Showers, B., & Joyce, B. (1996). The evolution of peer coaching. *Educational Leadership, 53,* 12-16.

Slavin, R. E., Madden, N. A., & Karweit, N. L. (1990). Effective programs for students at risk: Conclusions for practice and policy. In R. E. Slavin, N. L. Karweit, & N. A. Madden (Eds.), *Effective programs for students at risk* (pp. 355-372). Boston: Allyn & Bacon.

Thousand, J. S., & Villa, R. A. (1992). Collaborative teams: A powerful tool in school restructuring. In R. Villa, J. Thousand, W. Stainback, and S. Stainback (Eds.) *Restructuring for caring and effective education: An administrative guide to creating heterogeneous schools* (pp. 73-108). Baltimore, MD: Brookes.

Villa, R. A., & Thousand, J. S. (1988). Enhancing success in heterogeneous classrooms and schools: The power of partnership. *Teacher Education and Special Education, 12,* 173-276.

Villa, R. A., Thousand, J. S., & Chapple, J. W. (1996). Preparing teachers to support inclusion: Preservice and inservice programs, *Theory Into Practice, 35,* 42-50.

Villa, R. A., Thousand, J. S., Nevin, A. I., & Malgeri, C. (1996). Instilling collaboration for inclusive schooling as a way of doing business in public schools. *Remedial and Special Education, 17,* 169-181.

Villa, R. A., Thousand, J. S., Stainback, W., & Stainback, S. (Eds.) (1992). *Restructuring for caring and effective education.* Baltimore, MD: Brookes.

Wang, M. C., Reynolds, M. C., & Walberg, H. J. (1986). Rethinking special education. *Educational Leadership, 43,* 26-31.

Wigle, S. E., & Wilcox, D. J. (1996). Inclusion: Criteria for the preparation of educational personnel. *Remedial and Special Education, 17,* 323-328.

Witkin, S. L., & Fox, L. (1992). Beyond the least restrictive environment. In R. Villa, J. Thousand, W. Stainback, and S. Stainback (Eds.) *Restructuring for caring and effective education: An administrative guide to creating heterogeneous schools* (pp. 325-334). Baltimore, MD: Brookes.

Ysseldyke, J. (1983). Current practices in making psychoeducational decisions about learning disabled students. *Journal of Learning Disabilities, 16,* 226-233.

Ysseldyke, J. E., & Christenson, S. L. (1993). *The instructional environment scale (TIES)-II.* Longmont, CA: Sorpris West.

Ysseldyke, J. E., Thurlow, M. L., Graden, J. L., Wesson, C., Algozzine, B., & Deno, S. L. (1983). Generalizations from five years of research on assessment and decision making. *Exceptional Children Quarterly, 4,* 75-94.

Inclusion:
A Worthy Challenge
for Parents, Teachers, Psychologists
and Administrators

Thomas Lombardi

Diane Woodrum

West Virginia University

SUMMARY. Despite the growing support for inclusion, there are still many misconceptions and concerns. Is it a philosophy, a program, or a placement? A clear definition seems to be part of the problem since nowhere in the federal legislation is it defined. Can a school be considered inclusive and still have some of its students in resource rooms or special classes? How do those closest to the education of students with disabilities perceive inclusion? This article reports on the attitudes and perceptions of parents, teachers, psychologists and administrators. It also describes new roles and responsibilities each must meet if the challenges of responsible inclusion are to be realized. Finally, it provides checklists which may assist others in measuring support for responsible inclusion. *[Article copies available for a fee from The Haworth Document Delivery Service: 1-800-342-9678. E-mail address: getinfo@haworthpressinc.com <Website: http:// www.haworthpressinc.com>]*

Address correspondence to: Thomas Lombardi or Diane Woodrum, Department of Educational Theory & Practice, 608 Allen Hall, West Virginia University, Morgantown, WV 26506-6122.

[Haworth co-indexing entry note]: "Inclusion: A Worthy Challenge for Parents, Teachers, Psychologists and Administrators." Lombardi, Thomas, and Diane Woodrum. Co-published simultaneously in *Special Services in the Schools* (The Haworth Press, Inc.) Vol. 15, No. 1/2, 1999, pp. 171-192; and: *Inclusion Practices with Special Needs Students: Theory, Research, and Application* (ed: Steven I. Pfeiffer, and Linda A. Reddy) The Haworth Press, Inc., 1999, pp. 171-192. Single or multiple copies of this article are available for a fee from The Haworth Document Delivery Service [1-800-342-9678, 9:00 a.m. - 5:00 p.m. (EST). E-mail address: getinfo@haworthpressinc.com].

KEYWORDS. Inclusion education, perceptions and attitudes, parents, teachers, psychologists

Special education in the United States has a long history that reflects many changes in attitudes towards and perceptions of people with disabilities. Many diverse groups have contributed to this change process including parents, educators, psychologists, physicians, clergy, researchers and the disabled themselves.

Special education was established in the United States in the 1800s with students who had demonstrable disabilities such as blindness, deafness, crippling conditions as well as "idiotic and feeble-mindedness" (Smith & Luckkason, 1995) being taught in institutions. By 1917, most states had at least one institution in which children and adults were educated and lived for most of their lives (Scheerenberger, 1983). Although the basis for special education was founded in institutions, gradually public schools began to accept greater responsibility. This was a very slow process with only 12 percent of identified children and youth with disabilities receiving special education services in the schools, primarily in separate schools or classrooms by 1948 (Ballard, Ramierz, & Weintraub, 1982). The next twenty-five years saw major growth in terms of number of students with disabilities being served by both public and private schools and a wider range of service configurations. A combination of advocacy and litigation was responsible for these changes (see Reddy in this volume).

Special education, as we know it today, became institutionalized in our public schools with the passage, in 1975, of the Education for All Handicapped Children Act (P.L. 94-142) which is now known as the Individuals with Disabilities Education Act (IDEA) (P.L. 101-476). Over the years, students served under this act increased dramatically. For the first time in the history of education, all individuals, regardless of the severity or complexity of their disability were entitled to a free, appropriate education as well as increased attention to parental involvement in programming. Many states expanded the federal legislation by offering more special education programs and services to a wider age range and greater number of students with special needs. Special education became a big, expensive, unique business.

Despite the progress made in providing education to students with disabilites, a number of professionals began to quesion the outcomes and to explore ways for greater integration. New models for providing special education programs and services began to be explored. Pull out programs were being replaced by greater integration in general classes as the mainstreaming movement of the 80's was replaced by the inclusion movement of the 90's. All of this began occurring simultaneously as school reform of general education became a national priority.

For well over a decade, American education has been almost obsessed with school reform. Part of this alarm was a result of the much publicized *Nation at Risk* (U.S. Department of Education, 1983) report. By the early nineties, every person even remotely connected with our education systems was aware of the *America Goal 2000* challenge (U.S. Department of Education, 1991). Most of those goals continue to be part of the 90's educational agenda.

Many states had alread begun to address inclusion before President Clinton's dictates. For instance, in 1995, the West Virginia Legislature mandated that each school faculty senate develop a strategic plan to manage the integration of special needs students into regular classes in their respective schools.

As a result of this state legislation, major changes have been occuring in the state's teacher training program, special education classification, identification and assessment procedures, achievement testing, and service delivery models.

Despite the growing support for inclusion, there are still many misconception often generate by confusing data. One example is the 27th Annual Phi Delta Kappa Gallup Poll on the Public's Attitude Toward Public Schools (Elam & Rose, 1995). In that Poll one series of questions dealt with the issue of inclusion of special education students in regular classrooms. The conclusion cited in the summary report was that the public's clear preference is to educate students with learning and behavior problems in separate classrooms. This finding is very misleading. A review of the four questions asked on inclusion indicated the terms physically handicapped, mentally retarded, and learning disabilities were used interchangeable as if their special needs were the same. There was no acknowledgment of the level of disability as well as the range of options available on a continuum of service placements. Respondents had to choose either a regular class preference or special class preference. Clearly there are a series of placement options in between these extremes including part-time regular class placement, resource rooms for short periods of time, and itinerant services. A letter response from the senior author of this often quoted survey assured this senior author that the next time the area of special education or inclusion was addressed in a Phi Delta Kappa Gallup Poll, there would be greater consultation with special educators before drafting questions. It was also noted that in some states, students identified as gifted are part of the special education population as are students with speech disorders. Interestingly, in 1997 Phi Delta Kappa International sponsored a series of 15 regional leadership training institutes on inclusion in the United States and Canada.

A clear definition of inclusion seems to be part of the problem as we consider school restructuring. Nowhere in the federal legislation is the term defined. IDEA does require schools to place students in the least restrictive environment (LRE) to the maximum extent appropriate. For the most part agreement does exist that inclusion involves educating each student with a special education need in the school, and when appropriate, the class the student would have attended if he or she did not have a disability. A guiding principle is that services are brought to the student rather than the student to the services. Another, and perhaps of even greater significance, is that the student with a disability is fully accepted as part of the student body of that school with all the rights, privileges and responsibilities as every other student.

The senior author has advocated for the term responsible inclusion (Lombardi, 1994). Placing students with special needs in general classes without the necessary support services is not responsible inclusion. Expecting general teachers to make accommodations and modifications in their teaching without inservice or preservice training is not responsible inclusion. Exempting students with special needs from formalized achievement testing without providing for alternative equally effective assessments is not responsible inclusion. And limiting parental input to just signing an individualized education plan (IEP) is not responsible inclusion.

Advocates for and against inclusion are quite passionate (see Coleman, Webber, & Algozzine; Cook & Semmel; Thousand & Villa in this volume). If those who are responsible for the student's education do not believe inclusionary practices are appropriate or are unwilling to modify their own roles and responsibilities, then such efforts are doomed. The perceptions and attitudes of parents, teachers, students, psychologists and administrators concerning inclusion need to be addressed. How inclusion may effect their new roles and responsibilities needs to be described.

PERCEPTIONS AND ATTITUDES
OF PARENTS AND PROFESSIONALS

Parents

There has been extensive research that demonstrates the association of positive student outcomes and meaningful parental involvement in education. This is reflected in National Educational Goal 8: "By the year 2000, every school will promote partnerships that will increase parent involvement and participation in promoting the social, emotional, and academic growth of children" (National Educational Goals Panel, 1994, p. 11).

However, successful inclusion will never be achieved unless teachers and parents work together to achieve a common focus and vision about basic classroom realities. If schools are to change, teachers and parents need to change their perceptions and thinking about the educational process. The demographics of the traditional American family has changed considerably during the past several decades. This change has to also be reflected in our schools.

The history of the educational system during the past several decades emphasizes a separation between schools and communities, parents and teachers (see Reddy in this volume). Consequently, many social problems faced by communities today recognize that the system must change. In order for this to happen, a change must take place in the process for decision making. Many people believe that inclusion is primarily an issue of social justice (Tiegerman-Farber & Radziewicz, 1998). If this is true, it only stands to reason that educational decisions must be made within a collaborative structure that includes parents, teachers and administrators because the social problems of society have dramatically impacted the educational system. Collaboration in and between families and schools may possibly provide an opportunity to create a mechanism for decision making that will positively affect many other areas in education that need to be addressed.

Henderson and Berla (1994) report the results of 15 studies that demonstrate that student achievement increases directly with the duration and intensity of parental involvement. The research concludes that the more the relationship between schools and families is collaborative and comprehensive, the higher the student achievement.

Epstein's framework (1995) is a comprehensive program for parent involvement in education and shows that six types of involvement help families and schools fulfill their shared responsibilities for children's learning and development: parenting, communicating, volunteering, learning at home, decision making, and connections with the community.

Research during the past 15 years concludes that the degree to which families support students' learning contributes to the educational status of children. A national sample of 217 parents of school-age children participated in a parent interview study (Christensen, Hurley, Sheriden, & Fenstermacher, 1997) and rank-ordered the following partnership activities as the top five: (1) provide information on how schools function: (2) provide information on "how to's" for parents; (3) provide information on how to structure children's learning at home; (4) provide information on how children develop socially, emotionally, and academically: and (5) create time for parents and teachers to share information about children, school requirements, and family needs. Christensen's study strongly suggests that parents are interested in being involved in education to enhance student performance and that they desire more parental involvement in education. The data corroborate the finding that parents want to be involved in promoting the educational success of their children (Epstein, 1986) as well as indicating that they want to be more involved in education.

We cannot place children with disabilities in general education classrooms without the consent and support of *all* parents. Inclusive classrooms require that parents, teachers, and communities have to work in harmony to develop and implement inclusive changes and to work past traditional perceptions and viewpoints and think about the classroom with new ideas, expectations and goals. According to Tiegerman-Farber and Radziewicz (1998), inclusion provides the reality and mechanism for parents to become more involved in their child's education. Contributions of teachers, parents, administrators and psychologists, literally the whole of education, gradually shape the philosophy of inclusion, not only for the school, but for the whole district or system.

Historically parents have been relegated to a secondary role in education. In general education, parents have not been involved with planning or programming within the school. In contrast, by law, the last 25 years has assigned the role of participator to parents of children with disabilities. Still, these parents are not viewed as teachers when in reality, parents are their children's primary teachers. For the most part, they usually are not prepared in guiding a child with a disability. In fact, in many cases they are unaware their child has a disability until informed by school professionals. How they perceive disabilities has much to do in how they will treat their child. Parents of children with disabilities have a need to feel comfortable with their decision to place their child in the regular classroom.

However, inclusive classrooms cannot succeed without the support of parents of regular education children. These parents will have to be convinced that there is a benefit to their children in the inclusive classroom. They will have to have an understanding that the inclusive classroom is different and that, for the most part, their child will be positively affected by being in the class. Many of the outcomes will be different than those in the traditional class. Children in inclusive classes learn a great deal about individual diversity. Parents will come to the realization that the ideal of social justice will have to be balanced with the realities of educational programming.

Since inclusion requires that children with disabilities be placed in regular education settings, part of the inclusion process involves embedded programming for peers without disabilities. Kirchner (1994) states that educational goals and outcomes will have to be redefined for all children and that parents of regular and special education children will want to know how educational changes, both academic and instructional, will affect the learning and development of all children in the classroom.

Tiegerman-Farber (1997) conducted a study in 77 school districts in New York and Long Island. The study concluded that there are significant negative attitudes about inclusion from parents of children without disabilities. Part of the problem stems from the fact that there is no empirical research that defines whether or not a child will benefit from an inclusive classroom. The benefits for regular education children as well as children with disabilities need to be established. This entails that regular education students accept and receive the child and that *all* children in the classroom will benefit from the inclusive process.

The effects of parent participation in education on both teachers and parents has been documented. As parents become involved in education, teachers become more easily recognized by parents for better teaching, better interpersonal skills, and better grading practices. And the teachers themselves indicate greater satisfaction with their job (Christenson, 1995). Parental benefits include an increased sense of self-efficacy (Davies, 1993; Kagen & Schraft, 1982), and a greater appreciation of the role that they play in their child's education (Davies, 1993). IDEA has definitely increased positive parental involvement and has reinforced the importance of education in the LRE.

Teachers

People enter the teaching profession because they want to help students learn. When general teachers encounter students who have difficulty learning because of a disability, they may feel anxious, frustrated, and inadequate. These feelings can become compounded when it is a hidden disability such as a specific learning, emotional or attention deficit disorder. Unfortunately, many general teachers have received little or no training in teaching students with disabilities in their preparation programs (Stoler, 1992; Vidovich & Lombardi, 1998). Using a meta analysis, Scruggs and Mastropieri (1996) assessed 28 reports on general teachers' attitudes and perceptions on mainstreaming and inclusion conducted between 1958 and 1995. Overall, they found that while two-thirds of the 10,560 teachers surveyed supported the concepts, only one-fourth of those teachers felt they had the time, training or resources to implement them successfully. However, almost half did feel mainstreaming and inclusion could provide benefits to students with disabilities. Reported attitudes did not seem to vary based upon geographical region or time when studies were conducted. This later finding was particularly interesting since one might expect greater acceptance of inclusion with the more current studies. For the most part, the terms mainstreaming and inclusion were used interchangeably although some educators (Lombardi, 1997) comment on their differences. Mainstreaming has more to do with acceptance of students with disabilities in general classes providing they can adjust to methods, materials and curriculum being taught. Inclusion involves making necessary adaptations in methods, materials and curriculum so such integration can be successful. It should be noted that most of the studies in the Scrugg and Mastropieri review were surveys conducted with elementary level teachers. High school teachers, who are used to teaching specialized content subjects, view their roles in implementing an integration program sometimes differently than elementary teachers (Connard & Dill, 1984). In the Ravenswood Project (Lombardi, Kennedy, Nuzzo & Foshay, 1994), 36 high school teachers experienced a full year of inservice training, emphasizing the differences between a mainstreaming and inclusion philosophy. Results from the project indicated greater teacher acceptance of inclusion, more collaboration between the general and special education teachers in terms of program planning, and less discipline office referrals for special education students. Using both qualitative and quantitative methods to investigate the perspectives of both teachers and parents regarding inclusion of the disabled children in preschool programs, Bennett, Deluca and Bums (1997) found teachers less supportive of inclusion than parents. While parents felt positive attitudes toward students with disabilities as being essential for successful inclusion, teachers focused on the need for assistance and resources. In the future, it will be important to examine those variables and characteristics which allow teachers and their students to be successful in inclusive settings.

Psychologists

No other topic has garnered as much attention as has that of school reform in the educational literature in recent years. School psychology has played an active role in school reform during the last two decades. The discipline has contributed its skills to the knowledge of learning, program evaluation, problem solving, and mental health.

There is a dearth in the literature concerning school psychologists' perspectives on inclusive schooling. In a recent study of school psychologists in the state of West Virginia by Woodrum (1998) question five from the checklist (Appendix B) generated written responses that overwhelmingly agreed that children with disabilities should attend the same school that she or he would attend if they were not disabled. However, they also felt that the ability to accomplish this task within the schools depended in part on the disability, degree of severity, and geography. In a state that is as rural as West Virginia, geography appears to impact the realities of hiring possibly one teacher in a rural county for one autistic child or one deaf child. The responses further indicated that limited or responsible inclusion can work well in rural areas. All respondents agreed that inclusion is an option for most children with mild disabilities.

Helene Mermelstein, Psy.D., school psychologist for the School for Language and Communication Development which is located in North Bellmore, New York, when asked if inclusion is appropriate for all children with disabilities replied that: I believe inclusion is an exciting and necessary alternative for some children with disabilities. This alternative must be part of the continuum of services offered. It cannot be the only alternative offered. If this becomes a general practice, in effect, one abandons the notion of individual needs. Needs assessment for the individual, I believe is one of the most important processes when considering placement for handicapped children. Looking at the whole child, the team can make a realistic placement that can take into consideration not only the child's academic development, but also the child's social and emotional development. . . . The committee must consider many variables. For example: What are the support systems in place? How well are the teachers trained in handling certain disabilities? Are there guidance services or social skills training available? Will there be a way to help mainstream youngsters accept and interact with youngsters with disabilities? (Tiegerman-Farber & Radziewicz, 1997, p. 215)

Although the examples cited are from two diverse sections of the U.S., both sectors imply that inclusion should be an individual decision and that the goal should be the same for all children and that is to help the child reach his or her own potential.

Administrators

Historically, as special education became part of every school in every school system, the need to administer and supervise these programs had to be met. In most cases, special education administrators and special education supervisors were hired to guide these functions. Unfortunately, few states had a requirement for even basic knowledge of special education within their administrative endorsements (Valesky & Hirth, 1992). On a more positive note, these researchers did report that 75% of the states at that time were offering inservice training programs for all school administrators. Not unlike teaching, for the most part, general education administrators relied upon special education administrators when problems arose in identification, programming, evaluations and transportation. They did not perceive special education students and special education teachers as their responsibility. However, by the fall of 1993, almost every state was beginning to implement inclusion at some level (Webb, 1994). As inclusion increasingly becomes the accepted model for meeting the needs of students with disabilities, administrator involvement becomes critical because the attitude of school personnel and students towards inclusion frequently mirror those of the administrator. A national survey conducted by Arick and Krug (1993) analyzed 1,468 special education directors' perceptions regarding inclusion practices. Results indicated that those administrators who had course work or special education teaching experience were more supportive of inclusion than those who did not. Another study (Villa et al., 1996) had similar findings emphasizing that administrative support collaboration was a powerful predictor of positive attitudes toward full inclusion. In a very recent study conducted in Pennsylvania, Vidovich and Lombardi (1998) assessed parents', teachers' and administrators perceptions on the inclusion movement. Using a ten item questionnaire developed by the co-author (Lombardi, 1997, Appendix A), administrators scored in the most supportive range (87%), followed by parents (76%) and then teachers (67%). All of the administrators agreed that students should be recommended for special education services based upon need rather than any categorical label. They all had plans for promoting physical integration such as locker assignments, homeroom locations and lunch schedules. Almost all agreed they were responsible for encouraging social integration such as dances, clubs, athletic events and other school activities. As we integrate our school programs administratively, it might be worthwhile to see if we can, and should, do this in the school's central administration. Should courses in special education be mandated in every administration and supervisor school certificate? What is the administrative organization of a successful inclusion program? Can it be copied by others? These and other like questions deserve our attention.

NEW ROLES AND RESPONSIBILITIES

Parents

Parents provide critical information about family issues and cultural concerns (Laadt-Bruno, Lilley & Westby; 1993). Parents are beginning to recognize that their support of education is the single most important thing that they can do to ensure the success for their children. Educated parents become empowered parents. Empowered parents advocate on a long-term basis for the needs of their children. Historically, that role has been assigned to parents of children with disabilities. Inclusion expands the philosophy of advocacy to all parents (Tiegerman-Farber, 1998). We are seeing the benefits of an educational system that works more effectively and efficiently when the parent plays a role as decision maker and contributor. Parents can contribute greatly to their child's learning and educational generalization. Parental insights, input and general intuition can provide valuable information that can be used in conjunction with professional educators to help determine educational objectives and goals.

If this is to work effectively and if parents are to become empowered advocates, we must provide advocacy training to parents who understand the needs of their children. Parents will have to be included as members of the inclusion process if schools are going to achieve successful inclusive classrooms. The institution of education must redefine the role of parents within classroom decision making. If inclusion is successful, it can change how parents contribute to the education of their children; how parents and teachers interact. Going one-step further, successful inclusion involves parental empowerment, parental advocacy, and collaboration.

Parents of children with disabilities and parents of general education students have viewed themselves quite differently. The needs of both groups will have to be considered for successful educational decision making. Schools set the policy for inclusive classrooms. However, implementation occurs at the classroom level. Parent-teacher partnerships are the key to the successful development of the inclusive classroom.

If effective collaboration is to occur, the overall philosophy of a school must include the significance of relationships between home and school (Comer, 1995). Schools must formalize parent education programs with working parents in mind. Policies and structure may need to be implemented to encourage and expect meaningful collaboration. At the current time, schools simply permit it to occur. In order for this to happen, parents too, have a responsibility to work toward greater involvement. Some corporations are permitting parents to have flexible work schedules so that they may attend school meetings during the day or visit their child's class. The state legislature in Utah has entertained the idea of mandating similar policies for large companies (Christensen, 1997). Future parental roles will include becoming active agents in promoting such policies so opportunities for involvement in their child's education is assured; and in becoming active peers and not passive clients.

Teachers

There seems to be little doubt that the roles and responsibilities of both general and special education teachers must change if inclusion practices are to be successful. Ideally, general education teachers need to have training about and experience with students with disability at the preservice level. There is some evidence that this is beginning to happen. As part of the new five year general teacher training program at West Virginia University, all students enrolled will experience strands in special education, multiculturalism and technology. Related learning outcomes will be incorporated in all the required common core courses. Infused throughout their program will be field experiences in professional development schools (PDS). Every potential general education teacher from WVU will be required to work with a special student by assisting in developing and implementing that student's Individualized Education Program (IEP). Potential special education teachers will be required to have at least one course in collaboration and consultation based on a multicategorical service model. As such, these future teachers should be knowledgeable and better prepared to work in integrated settings. At the inservice level, it seems advisable that training should be encouraged using a team approach. For example, with the Ravenswood Project (Lombardi et al., 1994), general teachers, special education teachers, and parents all received integrated training relative to new roles and responsibilities. According to Fritz and Miller (1995), each teacher, whether with a general or special education background, must assume the role of a team member with other teachers, therapists, and family members. Within the classroom, they are jointly responsible for developing, implementing and monitoring instructional plans and curricular adaptations and modifications. This may involve a wide range of team teaching practices including co-teaching, parallel teaching and station teaching.

Peer tutoring has been highly successful for many students who have learning and behavior problems. Teachers should be willing to organize their schedules so such support is available as needed. According to McLaughlin and Warren (1992), a unified curriculum should be stressed for all students. Teachers must recognize that differentiation for disabilities comes in instructional methods and materials but not in content. All students have similar needs in terms of knowledge and skills for productive lives. In his book, *Responsible Inclusion for Students with Disabilities,* Lombardi (1994) offers a variety of methods that could change the way classroom teachers present materials. These include using advanced organizers, preteaching vocabulary words, providing repetition of instruction, previewing major concepts, making time adjustments, and providing corrective feedback. Computer based instruction can allow students with disabilities to be more independent in the classroom. Special education teachers may find their roles changing to even a greater extent than general teachers. They will need to serve as change agents, advocates and trainers to a greater extent than in the past. Their greater assets will be their knowledge of effective learning principles and good communication skills. Their direct teaching responsibilities, with some exceptions for unique and profound problems, will be in resource rooms supporting both students with disabilities and the general teachers who are providing education.

Psychologists

Madeline Will (1988) states that "while it would be difficult to discern the contribution this initiative has made to a revolution in school psychology, it is important to recognize again the goals of this 'shared responsibility' and the role of the school psychologist in this initiative" (p. 476). In order to meet the needs of today's school, the role of school psychologists is seen as the crux of all of the changes and they are increasingly being pushed into the most challenging school situations as front-line workers. Broad changes in roles that school psychologists play can be seen in: (1) increased collaboration; (2) a shift away from psychometrics and labeling; (3) focus of success for all students; and (4) expanded involvement/broader role. "School psychology in the 21st century should be about creating and enhancing capacities in agencies, institutions, families, and individuals" (Yessledyke et al., 1997, p. 12).

The need for increased collaboration has developed because the difficulties of many of today's children transcend the capacity of schools. This has forced schools to develop partnerships with parents and community agencies leading to important roles for school psychologists with an emphasis on interprofessional collaboration.

A recent study of school psychologists by Woodrum (1998) found that all respondents agreed that school psychologists can help schools develop challenging but achievable cognitive and academic goals for all students. Furthermore, they felt that school psychologists should spend a proportion of their time delivering a broader range of indirect services, such as teacher consultation and social skills interventions. One respondent replied that "indirect services should be helping to design curriculum and individualizing instruction for all children. School psychology is not only for special education, pupil service and counseling but should also primarily be for its impact on curriculum and instruction in regular education."

One question from the checklist generated written responses that implied that the potential is there for school psychologists to help schools develop challenging but achievable cognitive and academic goals for all students. The responses indicated that if this was to happen there would need to be a systemic change. The responses further indicated that limited or responsible inclusion can work well in rural areas and that school psychologists can be a voice for moderation in advocating for an increase in inclusive education options to meet the needs of all students. The school psychologists have included working with volunteers, regular teachers trained in inclusion, limiting the number of special needs children in a regular classroom, having access to a special education teacher, and good co-planning time as prerequisites for success.

Yesseldyke et al. (1997) also found that school psychologists will play an important role in advocating for reductions in all forms of demission-expulsions, suspensions, and "drop outs"–and for increasing inclusive education options to meet the needs of all students especially in light of those students most commonly disenfranchised from the school system.

It simply does not make sense to respond to the increase in diversity in our schools by creating more narrowly defined categorical programs. Consequently, the psychometric functions needed to test and label will decrease in importance and school psychologists will have more opportunity to exercise a more useful form of school psychology in the schools. School psychology can take the lead to improve assessment, problem solving and intervention practices as they move toward more diverse assessment of student learning.

As we enter the 21st Century, school psychologists are positioned to deliver psychology not only in schools but in the broader, emerging school-family-community framework. Among successes in the field, we find school psychologists who help in designing alternative schools, evaluating charter schools, assisting in creating effective school-community linkages, collaborating with the medical community to develop effective programming for students with medical problems, or participating in a long-rage strategic planning effort at a district or building level. Of primary importance to the future growth and development of the field, is the need to form partnerships with all others who serve children in a integrated manner. School psychology as a discipline must actively participate in the design ad implementation of solutions needed as we head into the next century. This includes not only the child, but also the family, school, district, community, and profession (Yesseldyke et al., 1997). There is a specific role for school psychologists to serve as a liaison between parents and teachers which is particularly appropriate since parents clearly wish consultations with school psychologists about their children's learning, behavior, and development. School psychologists view this role as being feasible (Christensen, 1977).

Administrators

According to Chance and Grady (1990), school administrators must have a vision of what their school can be and the goals that it can achieve. Such a vision, as it relates to inclusion, is described by Pete Gameros (1995). His study noted that visionary school principals accept the challenge to create an inclusive environment, accept ownership of all students, and promote the policy that students with disabilities are the responsibility of all school personnel. This vision is shared with school personnel, parents and community leaders. An expanded role administrators must assume is that of problem solver, particularly for finding ways special and general education teachers can collaborate. This may include creative scheduling and finding time for teachers to plan together. Other concerns may relate to building modifications, effective transportation, and updated inservice training for all school personnel. A major new challenge for school administrators will be to justify the effectiveness of the inclusion program, not just for students with disabilities, but for all the students at that school. They may need to ask potential new personnel about their belief of inclusion before hiring.

Although every inclusion program will look different to some degree at each school, there are certain guidelines available that should help the administrator meet his new role and responsibilities. Beninghof and Singer (1995) have authored a wonderful book which provides specific support on inclusion for school administrators. They wrote this after attending one of the nation's largest professional association conference for educators. With only one out of 500 workshops devoted to inclusion, they listened for three days to some of the brightest and creative educators from around the nation. They concluded that in order for inclusion to be successful, it must be viewed as an integral part of each aspect of education. The general chapter topics from the book address leadership, planning process, assessment, curriculum and instruction, student supports, family and community, business management, and personnel consideration.

Many administrators are very much committed to inclusion. Lombardi (1997, Appendix A) provides a checklist which can be used to give a general measurement for consideration.

CONCLUSION

Although the literature continues to chronicle that which is wrong with schools, it does need to be recognized that the United States has done something that no other nation has even attempted. It provides universal enrollment of all children in schools while seeking the dual goals of excellence and equity in education. The U.S. embraces this concept for all children regardless of creed, national origin, race, or disability. "Schools increasingly enroll all children, and the 'all' is becoming increasingly diverse" (Yesseldyke et al., 1997, p. 2).

It is impossible to imagine all of the potential problems that can and will arise as we develop inclusive schools. We now know that attitudes will have to be changed, and the key stakeholders must become committed to the concept of inclusive schooling. We must believe that inclusion offers the opportunity to change the process of child learning and allows for parents, teachers, school psychologists, and administrators to study program effectiveness and to alter those program components in order to benefit all children.

Inclusion should not be viewed as a district, school or classroom. Many believe that inclusion is actually social justice. If this is true, and social justice is the key issue, then educational reform must include all children and all schools. One can hope that the momentum that we currently are seeing will continue to build. Over the next few years there will be a continued refinement of the understanding of the change process and how best to bring meaningful reform to the majority of American schools. Inclusion will continue to be the most used word as we enter the new century.

REFERENCES

Arick, J.R. & Krug, D.A. (1993). Special education administrators in the United States: Perceptions of policy and personnel issues. *The Journal of Special Education 27 (3)*, 348-364.

Ballard, J., Ramierz, B.A., & Weintraub, F.J. (1982). *Special Education in American: It's legal and governmental foundations.* Reston, VA: Council for Exceptional Children.

Beninghof, A.M. & Singer, A.L.T. (1995). *Ideas for inclusion: The school administrator's guide.* ERIC: 386888, 147 pages.

Bracey, G.W. (1997). What happened to America's public schools? Not what you may think. *American Heritage,* November, 38-52.

Carr, M.N. (1993). A mother's thoughts on inclusion. *Journal of Learning Disabilities, 26(9),* 590-592.

Chance, E.W. & Grady, M.L. (1990). Creating and implementing a vision for the school. *NASSP Bulletin,* 74(529) November: 12-18.

Christenson, S.L., Hurley, C.N., Sheriden, S.M., & Fenstermacher, K. (1997). Parents' and School Psychologists' Perspectives on Parent Involvement Activities. *School Psychology Review (26)*1, 111-130.

Christenson, S.L. (1995). Best practices in supporting home-school collaboration. In A. Thomas & J. Grimes (Eds.), Best Practices in School Psychology-III (pp. 253-267). Washington, DC: National Association of School Psychologists.

Comer, J.P. (1995). School power: Implications of an intervention project. New York: Free Press.

Conrad, P.A. & Dill, C.F. (1984). Secondary teachers' perceptions of their professional role regarding implications of Public Law 94-142. *ERIC* ED245439, 23 pages.

Davies, D. (1993). Benefits and barriers to parent involvement: From Portugal to Boston to Liverpool. In N.F. Chavkin (Ed.), Families and schools in a pluralistic society (pp. 205-216). Albany: State University of New York Press.

Dwyer, K.P. & Gorin, S. (1996). A National Perspective of School Psychology in the Context of School Reform. *School Psychology Review (24)4,* 507-511.

Elam, S.M. & Rose, L.C. (1995). The 27th Annual Phi Delta Kappa Gallup Poll on the Public's Attitudes Toward the Public Schools. *Phi Delta Kappan 77(1),* 41-56.

Elliott, D. & McKenney, M. (1998). Four inclusion models that work. *Teaching Exceptional Children, 30(4),* 54-59.

Epstein, J.L. (1986). Parents reactions to teacher practices of parent involvement. *The Elementary School Journal*, 86, 277-294.

Epstein, J.L. (1995). School/family/community partnerships: Caring for children we share. *Phi Delta Kappan*, 76(9), 701-712.

Ferguson, D.L. (1995). The real challenge of inclusion: Confessions of a "Rabid Inclusionist." *Phi Delta Kappan 77(4)*, 281-287.

Fritz, M.F. & Miller, M. (1995). Challenges of the inclusive classroom: Roles and responsibilities. *Contemporary Education 66(4):* 211-214.

Gameros, P. (1995). The visionary principal and inclusion of students with disabilities. *NASSP Bulletin 79*(568), 15-17.

Geenen, K. (1995) Barriers, sources of support and relevant skills for school psychologists' active participation in Goals 2000. Unpublished master's thesis, University of Minnesota, Minneapolis, MN.

Henderson, A.T., & Berla, N. (1994). A new generation of evidence: The family is critical to student achievement. Washington, DC: National Committee for Citizens in Education.

Kagan, S.L., & Schraft, C.M. (1982). When parents and schools come together: Differential outcomes of parent involvement in urban schools. Boston, MA: Institute For Responsive Education (ERIC Document Reproduction Service No. ED 281-951).

Kellaghan, T., Sloane, K., Alvarez, B., & Bloom, B.S. (1993). The home environment and school learning. San Francisco: Jossey-Bass.

Laadt-Bruno, G., Lilley, P., & Westby, C. (1993). Collaborative approach to developmental care continuity with infants born at risk and their families. *Topics in Language Disorders*, 14(1), 15-28.

Lombardi, T.P. (1994). *Responsible Inclusion of Students with Disabilities* Fastback 373. Bloomington, IN: Phi Delta Kappa Educational Foundation.

Lombardi, T.P. (1997). Inclusion of children with disabilities. In D.R. Walling (Ed.), *Hot Buttons: Unraveling 10 Controversial Issues in Education.* (pp. 191-215). Bloomington, IN: Phi Delta Kappa Educational Foundation.

Lombardi, T.P., Nuzzo, D.L., Kennedy, K.D. & Foshay, J. (1994) Perceptions of parents, teachers and students regarding an integrated education inclusion program. *The High School Journal*, 77(4), 315-321.

Meacham, M.L. & Peckham, P.D. (1978). School psychologists at three-quarters century: Congruence between training, practice, preferred role and competence. *Journal of School Psychology (16)*, 195-206.

McLaughlin, M.J. & Warren, S.H. (1992). *Issues and options in restructuring schools and special education programs.* University of Maryland at College Park and Wastat, Inc. National Educational Goals Panel: (1994). *National educational goals report:* Washington, DC: U.S. Government Printing Office.

Paul, J.L., Rosselli, H. & Evans, D. (1995). *Integrating school restructuring and special education reform.* Forth Worth, TX: Harcourt Brace & Company.

Roach, V. (1995). Supporting inclusion: Beyond the rhetoric. *Phi Delta Kappan*, 77(4), 295-299.

Scheerenberger, R.C. (1983). *A history of mental retardation.* Baltimore: Brookes.

Stoler, R.D. (1992). Perceptions of regular teachers towards inclusion of all handicapped students in their classrooms. *Clearing House, 66(*1), 60-62.

Scruggs, T.E. & Mastropieri, M.A. (1996). Teacher perceptions of mainstreaming/inclusion, 1958-1995: A research synthesis. *Exceptional Children 63(1),* 59-74.

Smith, A. (1997). Systematic education reform and school inclusion. A view from a Washington office window. *Education and Treatment of Children, 20*(1). 7-20.

Smith, D.D. & Luckasson, R. (1995). *Special education: Teaching in an age of challenge,* Needham, MA: Allyn and Bacon. U.S. Department of Education. National Commission on Excellence in Education. (1983). *A nation at risk.* Washington, DC: U.S. Government Printing Office.

U.S. Department of Education. (1991). *America 2000: An education strategy.* Washington, DC: U.S. Government Printing Office.

U.S. Department of Education. (1996). Eighteenth annual report to Congress on the implementation of the Individuals with Disabilities Education Act. Washington, DC: U.S. Government Printing Office.

Vidovich, D. & Lombardi, T.P. (1998). Parents', teachers' and administrators perceptions of the process of inclusion. *Education Research Quarterly 21*(3), 41-52.

Villa, R.A, Thousand, J.S., Meyers, H. & Nevin, A. (1996). Teacher and administrator perceptions of heterogeneous education. *Exceptional Children 63*(1), 29-45.

Webb, N. (1994). Special education: With a new court decision backing them, advocates see inclusion as a question of values. *The Harvard Educational Letter, 10*(4): 1-3.

Will, M. (1988). Educating students with learning problems and the changing role of the school psychologist. *School Psychology Review, 17*(3), 476-478.

Yesseldyke, J. & Geenen, K. (1996). Integrating the Special Education and Compensatory Education Systems into the School Reform Process: A National Perspective. *School Psychology Review, 25*(4), 418-430.

Yesseldyke, J., Dawson, P., Lehr, C., Reschly, D., Reynolds, M., & Telzrow, C. (1997) *School Psychology: A Blueprint for Training and Practice II.* Bethesda, MD, National Association of School Psychologists.

APPENDIX A

Checklists for Administrator, Teacher and Parent

The more "yes" answers, the more positive toward responsible inclusion.

Administrator Checklist

1. Does your school mission statement embody the belief that all students can learn?
2. Would the students with disabilities at your school attend this school if they were not disabled?
3. Do you encourage general teachers to accept students with disabilities in their classes?
4. Do you allow time and flexible scheduling so that special and general teachers can consult and collaborate?
5. Do you recommend students with disabilities for placement based on individual needs, rather than categorical labels?
6. Do you promote social integration of students with and without disabilities through school dances, clubs, athletic events and other activities?
7. Do you promote physical integration of students with and without disabilities in home-room assignments, lunch schedules, locker locations, and other placements?
8. Do you expect students' with disabilities who have IEPs to be as successful in reaching their goals as other students?
9. Are related services, such as speech and physical therapy, brought to the student in his home school and program, instead of taking the student to the service?
10. Do you encourage parents of students with disabilities to become active members in school organizations such as the PTA?

Teacher Checklist

1. Are you willing to have age-appropriate students with disabilities in your class?
2. Do you modify your curriculum, instructional methods, and materials to meet the diverse needs of your students?
3. Are you open to suggestions and modifications in your teaching and classroom management?
4. Are you willing to share your teaching responsibilities with other professionals?
5. Do you expect disabled students to be as successful in meeting their own goals as nondisabled students are in meeting theirs?
6. Do you call on students with disabilities much as you call on other students in your class?
7. Do you use heterogeneous grouping?
8. Do you use peer tutoring?
9. Do you use adaptive technology and customized software?
10. Have you attended training sessions about responsible inclusion?

Parent Checklist

1. Does your disabled child attend the same school he or she would have attended if not disabled?
2. Do you take your disabled child to the same social functions you would attend if he or she did not have a disability?
3. Are your rules at home the same for your disabled child as for your other children? (If you have only one child, do you set the same rules that you would establish if the child did not have a disability?)
4. Is your disabled child given specific chores and home responsibilities?
5. Do you encourage your disabled child to participate in social and recreational events with nondisabled peers?
6. If your child is capable of doing so, do you encourage him or her to participate in the development of goals and objectives for his or her IEP?
7. Do you discipline your child without special regard to the disability?
8. Will you allow or provide independent living arrangements for your disabled child as he or she matures?
9. Have you attended meetings at which the education of children with your child's type of disability was discussed?
10. Are you willing to serve on a home-school team to encourage appropriate placement of children with disabilities in responsible inclusion programs?

APPENDIX B

Inclusion Checklists for School Psychologists

Please answer the following questions. Space under each question has been left for comments.

1. School psychologists can help schools develop challenging but achievable cognitive and academic goals for all students?

2. School psychologists should spend a proportion of their time delivering a broader range of indirect services, such as teacher consultation and social skills interventions?

3. School psychologists are committed to making a positive difference with all children and youth not just those students with disabilities?

4. School psychologists have a role to play in advocating for an increase in inclusive education options to meet the needs of all students?

5. Children with disabilities should attend the same school that she or he would attend if they were not disabled?

6. Is it important for school psychologists to participate in collaborative teams of regular and special educators?

7. Do you believe that inclusion is an option for most children with mild disabilities?

8. Do school psychologists have the competencies and skills necessary for collaboration?

9. Have you had training concerning responsible inclusion?

10. Does a best practices model of school psychological services subscribe to "inclusive schools?"

An Evolutionary Process
with an Uncertain Future:
Commentary on Inclusion Practices
with Special Needs Students

Thomas K. Fagan

University of Memphis

SUMMARY. Inclusion is discussed as a long-term evolutionary development since the era of compulsory schooling. Special education is seen as a late comer in a generally broader societal movement. Themes in this volume on inclusion and conclusions relevant to the future are provided. *[Article copies available for a fee from The Haworth Document Delivery Service: 1-800-342-9678. E-mail address: getinfo@haworthpressinc.com <Website: http://www.haworthpressinc.com>]*

KEYWORDS. Inclusion, school psychology, special education, individualized education

The historical study of school psychology and special education has led me to three broad conclusions that apply to the current debate on inclusion: (1) service origins, innovations, or reforms never occur with

Address correspondence to: Dr. Thomas K. Fagan, Department of Psychology, University of Memphis, Memphis, TN 38152-6400 (E-mail: tom-fagan@mail.psyc.memphis.edu).

[Haworth co-indexing entry note]: "An Evolutionary Process with an Uncertain Future: Commentary on Inclusion Practices with Special Needs Students." Fagan, Thomas K. Co-published simultaneously in *Special Services in the Schools* (The Haworth Press, Inc.) Vol. 15, No. 1/2, 1999, pp. 193-202; and: *Inclusion Practices with Special Needs Students: Theory, Research, and Application* (ed: Steven I. Pfeiffer, and Linda A. Reddy) The Haworth Press, 1999, pp. 193-202. Single or multiple copies of this article are available for a fee from The Haworth Document Delivery Service [1-800-342-9678, 9:00 a.m. - 5:00 p.m. (EST). E-mail address: getinfo@haworthpressinc.com].

universal agreement, (2) when understood in their historical context, such change is better appreciated as a well-intended effort at improvement (i.e., it seemed like the thing to do at the time), and (3) such change never occurs uniformly across settings. Articles in this volume acknowledge several historical aspects of inclusion (Little & Little, 1999; Lombardi & Woodrum, 1999; Reddy, 1999) which in part reflect my conclusions. The inclusion movement spans more than 100 years of education in the United States. It begins with efforts to achieve nationwide compulsory schooling and it's broadening to include persons who were often excluded including women, ethnic minorities, Native Americans, and children with mental, emotional, or physical defects that did not fit readily into the classroom (Children's Defense Fund, 1974). These groups have been differentially accommodated by our educational system over the past century, and we have often altered the ways in which we have included them. In this perspective, inclusion is not a reform movement, but rather an evolutionary process of widening the doors to our schools.

HISTORICAL PERSPECTIVE

Special educational facilities in school districts date to the 1890s and spread rapidly to urban school districts in states that achieved compulsory education. Advocates for special education argued that compulsory schooling laws extended to handicapped children and required special diagnostic and educational services (Wallin, 1914). It was in the context of compulsory schooling that routine contemporary practices such as medical inspections for school entrance originated. It was not long before psychological examinations emerged to better identify children for a limited range of available special education services. The scope of diagnostic and special services available early in the century appears in Van Sickle, Witmer, and Ayres (1911), and Wallin (1914), and the early quantitative growth of special education services is described by Dunn (1973).

Recent efforts at inclusion are the result of a complex series of changes in the overall landscape of special education. That early services were typically segregated can in part be explained by our limited understanding of children's conditions, the possibilities of their being contagious, the absence of medical treatments and medications, and the lack of instructional research and applications. The American countryside is dotted with facilities that were originally for children and adults with tuberculosis, often placed there from urban locales. Born in 1943, I recall times when children had contagious diseases that were not easily remedied (e.g., measles, mumps) and that school attendance was disallowed by public health authorities who would place a warning sign on the front of your home that read "Quarantined." Removal or segregation was the order of the day, and was considered the safest option for others and a best treatment option for the individual; corresponding to this, segregated services were often applied to educational decision making. Too often differential diagnosis meant, "please diagnose this person and place him or her somewhere different." Medical advances reduced the need for highly segregated facilities for many childhood conditions.

Changes in mental health technology have also occurred. Deinstitutionalization was fostered by advancements in psychotherapy and psychopharmacology. Despite school and domestic violence, child abuse, and risk factors, children today grow up with better general health and life expectancy than when special education originated in this country (Demos, 1986; Hiner & Hawes, 1985). In a relatively safe society for children, one where there are less contagious conditions and where remedies are available, inclusion is a more acceptable and achievable option.

Racial integration with busing, deinstitutionalization with community mental health centers, and managed care with predominantly outpatient services are inclusion movements that have preceded school inclusion for children with a disability. By comparison, special education is a late comer in society's overall movement toward inclusion. Nevertheless, the century-long changes were achieved without universal agreement and as this volume demonstrates, special education is no exception. Special education and school psychology services have progressed on the basis of what practitioners believed to be in the best interests of children and society at that time based on available knowledge and technology. Public and professional attitudes toward change are important but not sufficient to effect change in the absence of knowledge and technological advancements. There were always concerns expressed about segregated and integrated special education services. Decisions to train, credential, and hire school psychologists were a struggle in many settings (and still are). I prefer to understand these histories by considering what were the modal practices in an era, while recognizing that several other lifeforms of practice existed to a lesser extent. For example, the early history of special education was more segregated than today but options were available. The early practice of school psychology included consultation services but the mode was psychoeducational assessment for eligibility.

That school psychologists are closely tied to the inclusion debate is an obvious fact of its history which reveals a parallel growth of school psychology with special education (Fagan & Wise, 1994). In the special education service delivery models that evolved, school psychologists were an integral part of the process, usually as "gate keepers" for diagnostic classification, and more recently as multidisciplinary team members under federal and state regulations that replaced the former single-psychologist service model. The practice of school psychology would have evolved differently, if at all, had the new technology of tests (especially the Binet Scales) not been discovered or so widely accepted by educators (Sarason, 1975). In the absence of testing technology it is even doubtful that special education would have evolved in its current form. There continues to be concern that modal special education services continue to be segregated (Cook & Semmel, 1999; Schulte, Osborne, & Erchul, 1998), and modal school psychologist services continue to be psychoeducational assessment (Reschly & Wilson, 1995). Practices are changing but we are far from modal changes in most settings. The instructional and classroom management methods, and the team, district, and parent strategies discussed in this volume are attempts to demonstrate the feasibility of inclusion using now available methods and technologies (Gravois, Rosenfield, & Vail, 1999; Pfeiffer & Cundari, 1999; Thousand & Villa, 1999).

As acknowledged by virtually every article in this volume, the special education inclusion movement has not been attended by universal agreement on the applicability of these technologies, nor other aspects of the concept. Special educational services have historically been on a continuum from highly segregated services (e.g., institutionalization) to highly integrated services (e.g., regular classroom). There has been a gradual shift toward the more integrated side of the continuum. The broad, century-long shift reflects a change in ideology of decision-making on the basis of what seems to be in the best interests of the majority, to what seems to be in the best interests of the individual. This is a major shift and is reflected in the legal decisions discussed in Little and Little (1999). The shift is also reflected in making placement decisions based more on what could be done to maximize functioning in the regular class setting than looking at segregated options first.

SPECIAL VOLUME THEMES

The articles in this volume convey several themes that summarize the status and issues related to inclusion. Foremost among them is the lack of a generally accepted definition of the term itself. Inclusion has several meanings depending on the disabilities, settings, percent of time in placement, legal-ethical considerations, and educational philosophy one has adopted. For the future, however, there is need of greater consistency in defining the concept. To assist this, it would help to develop a single set of diagnostic criteria to reduce the differences in IDEA, DSM-4, Section 504, ADA, etc. State level differences in application would continue but at least there would be a set of national guidelines with high consensus. Then, when discussing inclusion in broad categorical terms (e.g., Coleman, Webber, & Algozzine, 1999; Cook & Semmel, 1999), there would be greater consistency in the child characteristics being considered. This would also allow inclusion advocates to better judge which students they are considering when they push for inclusion.

Another theme pervading this volume is the primacy of the individual in the concept of the individual educational plan (IEP). As noted herein, there is no written requirement for partial or full inclusion in the IDEA or its predecessors. A continuum of services and service options based on individual child needs seems to be the most popular interpretation. Additionally, inclusion is more than a location (see e.g., Tucker, 1989). It is a service decision based on the judgment of complex variables that result in an IEP that attempts to normalize *one* child's education and community involvement to the maximum extent considered possible, feasible, and reasonable. Though the authors in this volume seem reluctant to say it, several seem to consider as illegal, unethical, or at least unreasonable any practice that forces all children into regular classroom settings, all of their time, irrespective of their disabilities. I concur and I believe that such an extreme position on inclusion is as mistaken as placing every child at the other end of the service continuum. It is also unclear how the inclusion movement will blend into the broader general education reform movement to increase academic standards. If the school curriculum is going to get tougher and graduation demands more stringent, how will returning special education students adapt to an academic environment that is more difficult than that from which they were previously removed? An inclusive environment that improves social acceptance of the disabled at the expense of their gaining knowledge and skills in that environment is unacceptable.

Another theme is the need to accept the fact we must take action in the context of incomplete or inconclusive research. We have been through this before in discussions of mainstreaming. The point needs to be made that the absence of successful outcome data for one approach is an insufficient basis for advocating the success of another. I am reminded of the notion that differing positions are often taken by advocates who believe it when they see it, and by others who see it when they believe it. Much of public education is driven by changing attitudes and political forces. If educational practices were driven by research findings, the schools would be considerably different; and if driven by consistent and conclusive findings, the schools would be bogged down by inaction. The information in this volume is both research-based and authoritative opinion on what should be considered as best practices. There are few significance tests presented to demonstrate the consistent success of the advice and checklists for responsible practice; and many could logically be applied to the implementation of any educational program. Incomplete and inconsistent findings are a fact of life we must live with and signal the importance of professional and parental judgment in the process of planning for individual children. Nevertheless, the importance of professional experience and judgment should not be discounted. In addition to the advice presented, I recommend a review of the mainstreaming literature of the 1970s including Kaufman, Gottlieb, Agard, and Kukic's (1975) considerations for blending service responsibilities, times, and locations, and Turnbull, Strickland, and Hammer's (1978) reference to the IEP as perhaps the impossible education program. The best practices manual of the Illinois School Psychologists Association (1994) is also helpful. We need to support and keep abreast of research efforts on inclusion and special education services generally.

Another aspect of this debate is that legal decisions, and subsequently service expectations, vary from one court to another (Little & Little, 1999), and no doubt from state to state, district to district, and classroom to classroom. It is common to find inclusion practices in selected buildings in the same district where segregated services are still the norm. The practice of school psychology is also characterized by variation and there may be more variation within a state than across states. For the foreseeable future, inclusion will be a growth process but not a radical takeover of the schools. Returning all children to regular settings would raise regular education's enrollment by several million, adding to already crowded and understaffed conditions in many buildings. On the practical side, what would communities do with the school staff and facilities of existing programs that are not considered inclusive?

Responsible inclusive practices in assessment and placement are only as secure as the individuals involved. The reality of teacher, administrator, IC-Team member turnover, and family mobility, means we are forever in a process of becoming but never arriving. The survey data on attitudes and practices (e.g., Lombardi & Woodrum, 1999) are interesting but the subject groups involved are changing continuously. Even if school district turnover was minimized, a new group of children identified with disability and their parents enter the same system every year. The inservice program described in Gravois et al. (1999) is not a solution to a problem but a method of alleviating problems on an ongoing basis. The program is reminiscent of an earlier University of Maryland program for teachers on child study (Prescott, 1957). Turnover and the need for redevelopment are persistent issues in regular and special education. No program can overcome them. A related need mentioned in this volume is how to keep educators and psychologists abreast of new information and methods. The IC-Team and other inservice practices may help. Unfortunately, too many teachers and even school psychologists find it difficult to get time to keep up through reading, workshops, conventions, telecommunications, and other avenues. Many teachers do not even have opportunities to discuss their methods with other teachers in the same building. This will not be easily remedied but I believe schools would profit from systematic continuing education of their entire professional staff.

OVERALL CONCLUSION

Whatever the future for inclusion may be, special education services will continue to evolve in various ways across settings, and the continuum of services will be applied in numerous ways. Will we have a future of full inclusion for all as the current most ardent advocates define it? I doubt it. It is neither feasible nor reasonable. However, we could have something close to full inclusion for children with milder, higher incidence disabilities, and those children in other disability categories who for some reason can be managed inclusively. Nevertheless, inclusion is gaining in popularity, and it is neither a fad nor a lousy idea whose political moment has arrived. It is a continuing outgrowth of earlier special education services, the practice of mainstreaming, and the Regular Education Initiative. If it is perceived to become too radical in implementation, backlash will undercut its growth and perhaps work against the important contributions inclusion has to offer. Recent analyses of school reform are instructive on the failures of bandwagon movements (Cuban, 1993; Sarason, 1990). In whatever evolves, team efforts will supersede individual efforts and collaborative planning among psychologists, teachers, administrators, parents, and others will be required to provide an optimal educational program for individual children. School psychologists already have the skills to assist in this process. School systems will need to consider not only a continuum of special education services, but a more comprehensive continuum of services that encompass the most capable and the least capable students, and that include substantial remedial and other services to maintain as many students in the regular educational program as possible. Recent developments in school-based comprehensive clinics, and prereferral intervention models encourage this (Pfeiffer & Reddy, 1998; Nastasi, 1998). Finally, Beery's (1972) advice on mainstreaming is just as applicable to inclusion, to wit, we need to regularize special education while specializing regular education.

REFERENCES

Beery, K. (1972). *Models for mainstreaming.* San Rafael, CA: Dimensions Publishing.
Children's Defense Fund (1974). *Children out of school in America.* Cambridge, MA: Author.
Coleman, M. C., Webber, J., & Algozzine, B. (1999). Inclusion and students with emotional/behavioral disorders. In S. I. Pfeiffer & L. A. Reddy (Eds.), *Inclusion Practices with Special Needs Students: Theory, Research, and Application* (pp. 25-47) New York: The Haworth Press, Inc.
Cook, B. G., & Semmel, M. I. (1999). Inclusion and students with mental retardation:

Theoretical perspectives and implications. In S. I. Pfeiffer & L. A. Reddy (Eds.), *Inclusion Practices with Special Needs Students: Theory, Research, and Application* (pp. 49-71) New York: The Haworth Press, Inc.

Cuban, L. (1993). *How teachers taught: Constancy and change in American classrooms.* New York: Teachers College Press.

Demos, J. (1986). *Past, present, and personal: The family and the life course in American history.* New York: Oxford University Press.

Dunn, L. M. (1973). An overview. In L. M. Dunn (Ed.), *Exceptional children in the schools: Special education in transition* (pp. 1-62). New York: Holt, Rinehart & Winston.

Fagan, T. K., & Wise, P. S. (1994). *School psychology: Past, present, and future.* New York: Longman.

Gravois, T. A., Rosenfield, S., & Vail, L. (1999). Achieving effective and inclusive school settings: A guide for professional development. In S. I. Pfeiffer & L. A. Reddy (Eds.), *Inclusion Practices with Special Needs Students: Theory, Research, and Application* (pp. 145-170) New York: The Haworth Press, Inc.

Hiner, N. R., & Hawes, J. M. (1985). *Growing up in America: Children in historical perspective.* Urbana, IL: University of Illinois Press.

Illinois School Psychologists Association (1994). *Manual for best practices on inclusion.* Bloomingdale, IL: Author. (Contact ISPA, P.O. Box 847, Bloomingdale, IL 60108-0847)

Kaufman, M. J., Gottlieb, J., Agard, J. A., & Kukic, M. B. (1975). Mainstreaming: Toward an explication of the concept. *Focus on Exceptional Children.* 7(3), 1-12.

Little, S. G., & Little, K. A. (1999). Legal and ethical issues of inclusion. In S. I. Pfeiffer & L. A. Reddy (Eds.), *Inclusion Practices with Special Needs Students: Theory, Research, and Application* (pp. 125-143) New York: The Haworth Press, Inc.

Lombardi, T. P., & Woodrum, D. (1999). Inclusion: A worthy challenge for parents, teachers, psychologists, and administrators. In S. I. Pfeiffer & L. A. Reddy (Eds.), *Inclusion Practices with Special Needs Students: Theory, Research, and Application* (pp. 171-192) New York: The Haworth Press, Inc.

Nastasi, B. K. (Guest Editor). (1998). Mini-series: Mental Health Programming in Schools and Communities. *School Psychology Review, 27*(2). 165-289.

Pfeiffer, S. I., & Cundari, L. (1999). Interagency collaboration: Recurring obstacles and some possible solutions. In S. I. Pfeiffer & L. A. Reddy (Eds.), *Inclusion Practices with Special Needs Students: Theory, Research, and Application* (pp. 109-123) New York: The Haworth Press, Inc.

Pfeiffer, S. I., & Reddy, L. A. (1998). School-based mental health programs in the United States: Present status and a blueprint for the future. *School Psychology Review, 27*, 84-96.

Prescott, D. A. (1957). *The child in the educative process.* New York: McGraw-Hill.

Reddy, L. A. (1999). Inclusion of disabled children and school reform: A historical perspective. In S. I. Pfeiffer & L. A. Reddy (Eds.), *Inclusion Practices with Special Needs Students: Theory, Research, and Application* (pp. 3-24) New York: The Haworth Press, Inc.

Reschly, D. J., & Wilson, M. S. (1995). School psychology practitioners and faculty:

1986 to 1991-92, trends in demographics, roles, satisfaction, and system reform. *School Psychology Review, 24,* 62-80.

Sarason, S. (1975). The unfortunate fate of Alfred Binet and school psychology. *Teachers College Record, 77,* 579-592.

Sarason, S. B. (1990). *The predictable failure of educational reform: Can we change course before it's too late?* San Francisco, CA: Jossey-Bass.

Schulter, A. C., Osborne, S. S., & Erchul, W. P. (1998). Effective special education: A United States dilemma. *School Psychology Review, 27,* 66-76.

Thousand, J. S., & Villa, R. A. (1999). Inclusion: Welcoming, valuing, and supporting the diverse learning needs of all students in shared general education environments. In S. I. Pfeiffer & L. A. Reddy (Eds.), *Inclusion Practices with Special Needs Students: Theory, Research, and Application* (pp. 73-108) New York: The Haworth Press, Inc.

Tucker, J. (1989). Less required energy: A response to Danielson and Bellamy. *Exceptional Children, 55,* 456-458.

Turnbull, A. P., Strickland, B., & Hammer, S. E. (1978). The individualized education program-part 2: Translating law into practice. *Journal of Learning Disabilities, 11,* 18-23.

Van Sickle, J. H., Witmer, L., & Ayres, L. P. (1911). *Provision for exceptional children in the public schools* (U.S. Bureau of Education Bulletin, No. 14). Washington, DC: Government Printing Office.

Wallin, J. E. W. (1914). *The mental health of the school child.* New Haven, CT: Yale University Press.

Index

203